17.95

The Making of Anti-sexist Men

The Making of Anti-sexist Men presents the life histories of eight men who have responded positively to feminism and the challenges brought by changes in gender identity and activity since the start of new-wave feminism in the late 1960s.

The interview data are presented in two ways. The author takes a cross-sectional analysis of the sample, bringing out themes distinguishing these men's experiences from those of male chauvinists. He reflects generally on how anti-sexist men are 'made': for instance, lack of identification with 'traditional' father figures, strong mothers, personal association with strong women. Then the eight interviewees tell their life stories in their own words in a way that will appeal to non-specialist readers. The book contributes directly to our understanding of the life experiences of anti-sexist men, will encourage all those opposed to sexism and help reduce the isolation of those who have gone against society's dominant expectations.

The Making of Anti-sexist Men will appeal to all those interested in changing oppressive gender attitudes and social structures, members of anti-sexist men's groups, feminists, lesbians, gay men and undergraduates in gender studies and sociology.

Harry Christian is Lecturer at the Department of Sociology and Social Anthropology, Keele University.

Male orders

Edited by Victor J. Seidler

Goldsmiths' College, University of London

MALE ORDERS attempts to understand male forms of identity, practice and association in the modern world. The series explores how dominant forms of masculinity have helped shape prevailing forms of knowledge, culture and experience. Acknowledging the challenges of feminism and gay liberation, the series attempts a broad and critical exploration of men's lives as well as engaging constructively with malestream definitions of modernity and post-modernity.

Also in this series

Recreating Sexual Politics
Men, Feminism and Politics
Victor J. Seidler

The Achilles Heel Reader
Men, Sexual Politics and Socialism
Edited by Victor J. Seidler

Men, Sex and Relationships
Writings from *Achilles Heel*
Edited by Victor J. Seidler

Men's Silences
Predicaments in Masculinity
Jonathan Rutherford

Unreasonable Men
Masculinity and Social Theory
Victor J. Seidler

Fathers and Daughters
Sue Sharpe

Dislocating Masculinities
Comparative Ethnographies
Edited by Andrea Cornwall and Nancy Lindisfarne

The Making of Anti-sexist Men

Harry Christian

ROUTLEDGE
London and New York

First published 1994
by Routledge
11 New Fetter Lane, London EC4P 4EE

Simultaneously published in the USA and Canada
by Routledge
29 West 35th Street, New York, NY 10001

Typeset in Times by LaserScript, Mitcham, Surrey
Printed and bound in Great Britain by
Mackays of Chatham PLC, Chatham, Kent

British Library Cataloguing in Publication Data
A catalogue record for this book is available from the British Library

Library of Congress Cataloging in Publication Data
Christian, Harry.
The making of anti-sexist men/Harry Christian.
p. cm. – (Male orders)
Includes bibliographical references and index.
ISBN 0–415–09761–4: $45.00. – ISBN 0–415–09762–2 (pbk.): $14.95
1. Men – Psychology – Case studies. 2. Men – Attitudes – Case studies. 3. Sexism – Case studies. 4. Feminism – Case studies.
I. Title. II. Series
HQ1090.C49 1994
305.3 – dc20 93-39857
CIP

ISBN 0–415–09761–4 (hbk)
ISBN 0–415–09762–2 (pbk)

Contents

Acknowledgements

I thank the men who agreed to be interviewed for this study. They entrusted me with their life stories and very personal thoughts and feelings. I also thank friends and colleagues for their encouragement and valuable comments at various stages of this research. In particular to Janet Thomas, Mike Savage and Hiranthi Jayaweera of Keele University; Marion Jones of the North Staffordshire College of Nursing; and Pat Green of Wolverhampton University. Also to Janet Christian and Simeon Colton. I am grateful for Vic Seidler's helpful and encouraging comments and advice. None of these is responsible for the book's shortcomings.

Part I

Overview

Chapter 1

Introduction

What are anti-sexist men? Do they really exist? In order to identify the subject matter of this book a distinction is needed between the terms 'anti-sexist' and 'non-sexist.' To be 'anti-sexist' means having an active stance opposed to sexism, whereas the term 'non-sexist' indicates an ideal way of relating to women, to which anti-sexist men aspire, not necessarily fully achieved. The research presented in this book aimed to study anti-sexist men, who undoubtedly exist, rather than possibly non-existent beings who are completely non-sexist.

The term 'anti-sexist' could also imply public political involvement, but since, as feminists have shown us, the personal is political too, I believe the term can also be validly applied to men who are not active in anti-sexist men's groups but who are trying to live in a non-sexist way in their relations with women on a personal level. My use of the term anti-sexist in this book includes both these senses.

In the past twenty-five years, women, by their changing outlooks and by their social and political advances, have increasingly put pressure on men to relate to them on equal terms. Simultaneously, demographic, economic and social factors have become less favourable to men in maintaining their traditional dominance over women. Changes in economic and social conditions have substantially altered many men's experiences and expectations of life and traditional ideas of masculinity have been seriously called into question in the late twentieth century.

Even women not involved in the feminist movement have been influenced by it in that they have become less prepared to accept subordinate and dependent status in relations with men. The traditional division of labour between the sexes – men going out to work as the sole or main family breadwinners and women staying at home restricted to being housewives and childcarers – has been widely eroded.

Women were 47.5 per cent of the UK labour force by 1990 and nearly 60 per cent of workers in service industries. Counting only full-time workers, more than 35 per cent were women by 1990 and over 45 per cent of workers in the expanding service sector (Department of Employment, UK 1990). By 1990 almost three-quarters of women aged 20 to 54 were in some form of paid employment (Office of Public Censuses and Surveys, UK 1992: 72, table 4.5). Many boys growing up today experience women earning their own incomes, succeeding in education, pursuing higher-status careers and taking independent personal decisions (see Appendix).

As American writer Kathleen Gerson noted, 'A changing structure of gender relations has eroded the structural supports for female domesticity and uncontested male dominance, it has also changed the role men play in women's lives' (Gerson 1987: 126).

Most men are probably still trying to ignore the changes among women. Some actively oppose them, individually in their everyday lives, or even in backward-looking anti-feminist organisations. This book, however, concentrates on men who are attempting to respond positively to the challenge of feminism. It is a contribution to studying the effects on men of these changes among women and in society, and in particular it focuses on a particular type of male response, that of pro-feminist or anti-sexist men, and others of like mind attempting to live non-sexist lives.

In his recent book, American sociologist Michael Kimmel provides a definition worth quoting here. 'By profeminist men we mean active supporters of women's claims against male violence and for equal opportunity, political participation, sexual autonomy, family reforms and equal education'(Kimmel and Messner 1992: vii).

The main focus of the book is on life histories of a sample of such men, obtained by qualitative interviews. The interviewing was preceded by my own participation in anti-sexist men's groups. My purpose in doing this research was two-fold: to contribute to a fuller sociological understanding of such men's subjective reconstructions of life experiences which have been conducive to their developing this kind of outlook; and also, by helping to break down the sense of isolation commonly felt by those who try to go against the grain of society, to provide encouragement to men of this kind (among whom I include myself) who are opposed to sexist oppression. The men whose life stories are presented in this book are probably an untypical minority, but I hope they may be exploring a road which more men may increasingly travel in future.

The book is also intended to contribute to an extremely neglected area of literature, that of empirical sociological studies of such men. Recent American books in this area have provided some material on pro-feminist men (e.g. Brod 1987; Kimmel 1987; Kaufman 1987; Kimmel and Messner 1992), and several British books have analysed sexism and masculinity but these have all been theoretical or methodological in emphasis (Brittan and Maynard 1984; Seidler 1989, 1991; Brittan 1989; Hearn 1987, 1992; Hearn and Morgan 1990; Segal 1990; Morgan 1992; Rutherford 1992).

As Harry Brod, one of America's pioneering scholars of men's studies, has noted, 'What is . . . needed are analyses that show how men both form and are formed by their conditions' (Brod 1987: 13). Referring to contributors to his own collection he says,

> One also finds a determination to listen to the voices of men themselves. . . . In inverse fashion to the struggle in women's studies to establish the *objectivity* of women's experiences and thereby validate the legitimacy of women's experiences *as women*, much of men's studies struggles to establish the *subjectivity* of men's experiences and thereby validate the legitimacy of men's experiences *as men*.
>
> (ibid: 5–6)

There seems to be an almost complete lack of empirical sociological studies of this kind on British anti-sexist men. One or two recent books have made partial contributions to the provision of empirical data on variations in masculine experience – an autobiographical account (Jackson 1990) and a useful historical collection (Roper and Tosh 1991). Andrew Tolson's pioneer study (Tolson 1977) also contained some empirical material. Popular books on men and masculinity using interview data (e.g. Ford 1985) do not undertake academic interrogation of the evidence. There is also little focus specifically on anti-sexist men. This book therefore begins to fill a yawning gap in the literature. I hope it will inspire further qualitative research of a similar kind.

I wish to emphasise that though on one level my purpose in writing this book is to fulfil research and publication expectations in an academic career, on a personal level it is written as an expression of my own anti-sexist convictions. Further, while I am pro-feminist I am also a man, and I therefore acknowledge that I am obviously more sympathetic to the kind of feminists who can conceive of the possibility of seeing anti-sexist men as genuine allies in a common cause. No doubt separatist feminists who see all men as undifferentiated enemies will remain unconvinced of my sincerity. There is nothing I can do about that. My aim nevertheless is not to encourage divisions among feminists but to help broaden the alliance of all those opposed to gender oppression in all its forms by increasing understanding of the outlooks and life experiences of members of anti-sexist men's groups.

The book is therefore also a contribution to the study of gender oppression and concentrates on one aspect of attempts to eliminate it, focusing on the experiences of that minority of members of the dominant sex/gender group who believe in the principle of eventually eliminating male domination and the oppression of women. As Brod has stated,

> Politically men's studies is rooted in the pro-feminist men's movement, analogously to women's studies' rootedess in feminism . . . men's studies should be unabashedly explicit about its roots in the search for progressive profeminist change in male roles . . . men's studies should . . . wear its activism as a badge of honor rather than shame.
>
> (Brod 1987: 45, 49)

And what Shiffman, another American writer says also applies in Britain,

> Struggles for women's equality in the United States have included male activists from the very start. . . . But these profeminist men have always been a small minority of the male population. It is only since the most recent wave of the women's movement that men have struggled independently, both in support of women's rights and for alternative forms of masculinity, in such a way as to constitute a social movement.
>
> (Shiffman 1987: 295)

THEORETICAL ISSUES

I take a thoroughly sociological view that gender is socially constructed and is therefore not determined by biological sex. This means that understanding the actions and experiences of either sex involves recognising that all human beings are fully human rather than naturally masculine or naturally feminine. Nor are they usefully seen as varied mixtures of two pre-given fixed essences. Both sexes are potentially capable of the full range of human abilities and emotions but each sex is socially restricted to part of their common human potentials. It is not biology but the experience of society which restricts each sex to those characteristics and activities defined as feminine or masculine within any one society or era. No innate and universal gender qualities automatically accompany physical sex differences. Biological functions directly related to reproduction are the only ones which naturally differentiate the sexes.

On this assumption it is perfectly feasible for gender to change while biological sex remains the same. Feminine and masculine roles and identities can be redefined and lived differently, and ultimately both sexes could reclaim their full human potential by eliminating gender distinctions. Without femininity and masculinity there could be fully human males and females. Sexist attitudes and actions are currently an integral part of the dominant masculinity, but if masculinities are socially constructed by and for each generation of males growing up, rather than genetically inherited, then masculinities can change and sexism can in principle be eradicated.

Most of the interviewees in the qualitative case studies presented in this book were chosen because they had been members of anti-sexist men's groups, or they had been recommended as like-minded by members or former members of such groups. They were selected because the intention was to interview men who had taken a clear stand against traditional masculinity by aligning themselves with efforts to achieve sex equality and/or by attempting to change their own lives in ways which rejected established sexist assumptions.

What therefore is 'traditional masculinity' from this point of view? At this point I want to stress that the term 'traditional' is not used here to mean an ancient role model but refers to the stereotypical twentieth-century male-chauvinist outlook and activities resulting from the kinds of gender socialisation conventionally seen as appropriate to males in Western industrial societies since at least late Victorian times. It corresponds to what the Australian sociologist Robert Connell has called 'hegemonic masculinity' (Connell 1987: 183–8).

As Brod says, 'The concept of hegemonic masculinity incorporates into the sociology of masculinity a dynamic sense of the construction of gender and relations of power within each gender' (Brod 1987: 20). I find Connell's concept particularly helpful in socially identifying and locating the type of masculinity from which the interviewees studied in this book differ. It is worth looking more closely at what he says about this concept.

'Hegemonic masculinity', he says, 'is always constructed in relation to various subordinated masculinities as well as in relation to women. The interplay between different forms of masculinity is an important part of how the patriarchal social order works' (Connell 1987: 183). He uses the term 'hegemony', as in Gramsci's (1981) analyses of class relations, 'as a social ascendancy achieved in a play of social forces that extends beyond contests of brute power into the organisation of private life and cultural processes'. It is 'embedded in religious doctrine and practice, mass media content, wage structures, the design of housing, welfare/taxation policies and so forth' but, 'it does not mean . . . the obliteration of alternatives. . . . Other patterns and groups are subordinated rather than eliminated' (ibid).

Connell states that 'hegemonic masculinity' is different from a generalised 'male sex role'. As a cultural ideal it 'need not correspond at all closely to the actual personalities of the majority of men' (ibid: 184). 'The public face of hegemonic masculinity is not necessarily what powerful men are, but what sustains their power and what large numbers of men are motivated to support.' The main reason for this support 'is that most men benefit from the subordination of women, and hegemonic masculinity is the cultural expression of this ascendancy' (ibid: 185).

He goes on to state that since hegemonic masculinity is constructed in relation to subordinated masculinities as well as in relation to women 'these other masculinities need not be as clearly defined, indeed achieving hegemony may consist precisely in preventing alternatives gaining cultural definition and recognition as alternatives, confining them to ghettoes, to privacy, to unconsciousness' (ibid: 186).

This study contributes to empirical exploration of varying forms of non-hegemonic masculinity and towards their 'definition and recognition as alternatives'. The best known alternative forms are gay ones but this study does not focus primarily on gay men. Instead it focuses mainly on a form of identity displayed by men who are mostly non-gay but who nevertheless reject and oppose the dominant form of masculinity in its oppression both of women and of non-dominant types of male identity. Nevertheless, though my focus was mainly on heterosexual men I included in my sample a small number of gay or bisexual men who were also members of men's anti-sexist groups, since these were of considerable interest for comparative purposes.

Connell's discussion makes clear that there can be various kinds of alternative or non-hegemonic masculinities, quite apart from variations due to class, ethnicity, generation and other influences. As American scholar Michael Kimmel writes,

> New models for men have not replaced older ones, but have grown alongside them, creating dynamic tension . . . we live in an era of transition in the definition of masculinity – what it means to be a real man – not, as some might fantasize, in which one mode comes to

> replace another mode, but in which two parallel traditions emerge, and from the tension of opposition between them a new synthesis might, perhaps, be born.
>
> (Kimmel 1987: 9)

METHODOLOGICAL ISSUES

My research objectives were to examine the changing social experiences that may affect masculine gender identity by studying men who had shown clear signs of non-conventional gender identity, paying attention to individuals' lifecourses seen as dynamic dialectical processes.

I chose a qualitative life-histories approach because of its appropriateness both to my research objectives and to my standpoint on sexual politics. Plummer aptly describes 'the humanistic method in social science' as a

> style of investigating and understanding human experiences which simply advocates getting close to concrete individual men and women, accurately picking up the way they express their understandings of the world around them, and, perhaps, providing an analysis of such expressions.
>
> (Plummer 1983: 1)

I am aware, however, that there is more to a life history than simply a verbatim tape-recorded account. One has to remember that it is a selective retrospective reassessment of an individual's memories.

> In sociology life histories as autobiographies have typically been treated as unproblematically referential of the material realities of the lives so 'described' while elsewhere . . . autobiography has been conceptualised as the textual (graphing) construction of a self (auto) that actually does not exist in life (bio) in the unitary and coherent form invoked through the conventions of the genre.
>
> (Stanley and Morgan 1993: 1)

My intention is not to treat 'autobiography as unproblematic' but to illuminate the interdependence of 'single lives and social structures', recognising that this involves 'questioning and indeed rejecting conventional sharp distinctions between structure and action and relatedly, individual and collective, as presenting an over-dichotomised view of social life' (ibid: 2).

The history of the project started when I joined a men's group in

Stoke-on-Trent in 1986. I enjoyed being in the group and benefited from meeting men with similar outlooks to my own. I took part primarily as a participant but from the start I was aware that it was interesting sociologically and that as a sociologist I might some time use the experience for research purposes. The same was true of my participation as a saxophone and clarinet player on the jazz scene in the English Midlands in 1982–6, which led to an academic publication (Christian 1988), and my participation in a campaign opposing closure of rural schools in 1980–2.

I also briefly participated in another men's group in the mid-1980s but it was not until 1988 that I started research on anti-sexist men and began interviewing men I had met in these groups. For a time the research was halted by other commitments but I returned to it late in 1991 and completed a second, larger round of interviews during 1992.

In explaining why I chose the men in my sample as appropriate subjects for this research it is easier to say what they are not like. To gain a clearer idea of the dominant masculinity which these men saw themselves as opposing or departing from I found it useful to formulate some typical male chauvinist attitudes which support hegemonic masculinity. No doubt many other points could be added but at the risk of being somewhat stereotypical I suggest the following as taken for granted assumptions:

1 Men and women are inherently different, and 'real' men are superior to women and to any men who do not conform to the conventional dominant masculine standards.
2 Any activity or behaviour typically associated with women is demeaning for men to perform.
3 Men should not feel, or at least not express, most of the range of human emotions except anger and lust, and sensitive and vulnerable emotions must be suppressed.
4 The ability or desire to dominate others and to succeed in competitive situations is essential to a man's self-identity.
5 Toughness and hardness are of high value.
6 The breadwinner role is central to men's lives, whether they live on wages, profits or rents, and breadwinners should be men.
7 Male company is preferable to female company except when having sex; and having sex is the only acceptable masculine way of getting on close terms with women.
8 Sex is as much to do with exerting power as to do with pleasure, so real men's sexuality is a means of demonstrating domination or superiority over women, or of competing with other men.

9 In extreme situations men may have to kill other men or be killed by them, and it is cowardly and therefore unmanly to decline do so if necessary.

Membership of men's anti-sexist groups is hardly conventional masculine behaviour but there are other ways of being non-traditional. Two other non-traditional images of men have come into public awareness in recent years, these are 'New Men' and 'Wild Men'. I want to make it clear that these should not be confused with the men in this study.

The 'New Man' image, widely propagated in mass media and advertising in the 1980s, is of a narcissistic man portrayed as macho with a 'soft centre', a man who takes an active part in childcare, at least when the cameras are about. Hardly an ally for feminists! As Rowena Chapman has written, 'whilst the new man may well have provided some useful role models for those redefining their masculinity . . . [this] is an ideal that even the most liberated men would never lay claim to' (Chapman 1988: 226–8).

In spite of numerous mass media references to the 'New Man' in recent years, the concept remains dubious. Evidence from British sociological studies on men's participation in domestic work and childcare, for example, by Lydia Morris, in an era of high male unemployment and increasing female employment, suggests that most men are not changing much away from old images of masculinity and sexist attitudes and in fact these may be being reinforced (Morris 1990). I do not dissent from the overall conclusions of those studies, though Jane Wheelock's work does suggest some change has occurred (Wheelock 1990). Graeme Russell's Australian study of shared-caregiving fathers is also of great interest on this point (Russell 1983).

Among employed men, the increasing demands of employers in the 1980s made it even more difficult for men to change long-established masculine activity patterns during these years.

Another image that has come into some prominence recently derives from the writings of American mythologist and poet Robert Bly (Bly 1991) who has encouraged groups of men to go off camping in the wilds to release their feelings and undergo imitations of old tribal rituals aimed at initiation into manhood. While Bly disclaims hostility to feminism his movement places no emphasis on helping in the struggle against women's oppression and seems to be part of a series of inward-looking 'men's liberation' activities which may perhaps be of benefit to some men but are hardly likely to benefit women, and may even be part of the anti-feminist backlash. As Dave, one of my interviewees, commented, 'There's been some absurd reactions in the men's movement, that American thing inspired by Bly, it seems to be turning personal politics on its head and in effect blaming women for the fact that men aren't masculine enough!'

The anti-sexist men studied in this book should not be equated with 'New Men' or 'Wild Men'. They are members of a minority, who not only think seriously about gender issues as applied to men but also make efforts to relate to women in non-oppressive ways and try to be their allies in the struggle against gender oppression. This minority of 'anti-sexist' or would-be non-sexist men are of interest as distinctive participants in the social history of the recent and current era.

The subjects of this study, therefore, are men who either consciously or implicitly reject 'hegemonic masculinity' by attempting to live non-sexist lifestyles, and who believe in equality of the sexes. They are men who see themselves either as allies of feminists or at any rate as allies of women – whether accepted as such or not – in their fight against male domination.

My sampling aim was to locate members of a distinctive minority in the male population who I believed were significant in relation to theoretical concepts of differing types of masculine identity. Choosing my interviewees meant selecting men who differed from most, if not all, of the listed male-chauvinist attitudes. I did not assume they must differ from all of them since, for instance, a man might feel a duty to perform the breadwinner role or find it difficult to express tender emotions, but still favour sex equality. These characteristics need not be associated with oppressive attitudes and actions, so I still regarded such men as sufficiently non-traditional for my purpose.

Indicators used to select the kinds of interviewees to contact were:

1 Men who were or had been members of anti-sexist men's groups.
2 Men recommended as like-minded by members of anti-sexist men's groups.
3 Men known to have been involved in activities supportive of women's events, e.g. running crèches, baby sitting, supporting feminist demonstrations.
4 Men who had chosen to take on caring and nurturing family roles out of conviction rather than through force of circumstances.

My procedure was therefore theoretical sampling, making use of the snowball technique in which initial interviewees are invited to recommend others of a similar kind. As Rose (1982: 311) states, 'snowball sampling can be very useful for studying populations which are deviant or clandestine, where a sampling frame is impossible to obtain'.

These men could not be identified on any available list usable as a sampling frame and so sampling decisions were made as part of the research process. The achieved sample was a collection of men who formed part of a 'working universe' of anti-sexist men living within my research area during a particular period of time and who were identified partly through my own participant observation and partly through interviewees themselves.

Throughout the process of interviewing I always had a further list of about ten other men I could follow up, recommended by ones already interviewed and this was still true when I halted the snowball sampling as I already had far more good life histories than I could use in this book.

Though snowball sampling was the most appropriate method for my purpose the uncertainty of its representativeness must be accepted. Consequently the study must be seen as exploratory, the findings tentative, and I make no claim that the results apply, except by inference, to areas other than that in which the study was done.

The main fieldwork method I used in the study was intensive qualitative life-history interviewing. Recent feminist writings on methodology in the social sciences are highly relevant to my approach in doing this research and to the ways I present my material. For instance, Liz Stanley writes,

> By constructing 'what is known' at a conceptual and categorical level, even if reference is made to 'research findings', then how these are known to be such is rendered invisible. . . . The result is alienated knowledge, a product apparently complete, bearing no apparent trace of the conditions of its production and the social relations that gave rise to this.
>
> (Stanley 1990: 11)

For this reason I present the bulk of my data in Part II in the form of uninterrupted life histories in the interviewees' own words. Admittedly they have had to be condensed through shortage of space but I have attempted to retain all important areas covered. Apart from condensation and some tidying up for the sake of readability, the life histories are given here in a form close to the original tape-recorded accounts both in content and wording.

Stanley goes on to say,

> The most pertinent dimensions of an 'unalienated knowledge' . . . are where: – the researcher/theorist is grounded as an actual person in a concrete setting; – understanding and theorising are located and

> treated as material activities and not as unanalysable metaphysical 'transcendent' ones different in kind from those of 'mere people'; and – the 'act of knowing' is examined as the crucial determiner of 'what is known'.
>
> (ibid: 12)

For these reasons I wish to make it clear that as a sociologist I have a strong preference for interpretive theoretical perspectives and qualitative research methods. I also write from the standpoint of a white English middle-aged heterosexual employed professional originally from a working-class background, and from the viewpoint of a long-term political commitment to opposing sexism, racism, classism and heterosexism. In this book I deliberately use 'I' to 'own' what I'm doing. By making clear my own social and intellectual position I identify myself openly to my readers, as I did to my interviewees, as a member of the social category being studied. I have revealed my purposes as being political as well as academic and I also try to make my data-collecting methods and methodological assumptions clear in order as far as possible to avoid 'alienated knowledge'. As Stanley says, (ibid: 13) 'One of the preconditions for "good research" is that it should account for the conditions of its own production.'

All the interviews were carried out and transcribed by myself. I was already known to some of the interviewees as having anti-sexist principles. Other men I had not previously met were approached by saying that they had been suggested by an earlier interviewee who was known to both of us. I explained that I wanted to find out what life experiences had led to the subject's having anti-sexist views as an adult and that I would not reveal names or any detail they did not wish to have revealed.

All the men who agreed to be interviewed were friendly and helpful, remarkably frank and co-operative and generous in giving their time. A surprising number of the interviewees ended sessions by saying things like, 'I enjoyed that, when are you coming again?' or 'That was really therapeutic', and I too found the experience enjoyable and looked forward with enthusiasm to the next one. On many occasions I ended an interview with a man I had not known well previously, or had not met before, with the feeling that 'I would really like this man as a friend'.

The interviews took a form which was partly like a friendly chat but also partly like a counselling session in which the attention is focused on one person. The equipment used was a small battery-operated cassette tape recorder with a lapel microphone and a checklist of topics to remind me of what I wanted us to cover. I seldom had to refer to the checklist except near the end of the final session. I brought to the interviewing situation previous experience of research interviewing, five years experience as a newspaper reporter many years ago and recent experience in co-counselling. I had no qualms about revealing aspects of my own life when asked and I occasionally volunteered information about myself if it seemed appropriate, but the subjects mostly seemed content for the focus to be on themselves. All the interviews took place in venues chosen by the interviewees, most commonly their own homes, but four were in their places of work, one was in my office, another in my car parked in a country lane, and another was on a park bench with enthusiastic bell ringing in the background.

I regard this interviewing as closely parallel to the feminist interviewing of women discussed by Ann Oakley, 'the goal of finding out about people through interviewing is best achieved when the relationship of interviewer and interviewee is non-hierarchical and when the interviewer is prepared to invest his or her own personal identity in the relationship' (Oakley 1981: 41). As she says, 'A different role . . . seemed especially important in . . . in-depth interviewing. Without feeling that the interview process offered some personal satisfaction to them, interviewees would not be prepared to continue after the first interview. The interviewee's definition of the interview is important' (ibid: 49).

I also agree wholeheartedly with her call for 'mystification of the researcher and the researched as objective instruments of data production' to be 'replaced by the recognition that personal involvement is more than dangerous bias – it is the condition under which people come to know each other and to admit others into their lives' (ibid: 57).

It must be admitted, however, that there are problems with life-history research. It clearly does not produce cases which can be claimed to be representative. I simply do not know whether my sample is typical of anti-sexist men elsewhere and at other times. My findings do at least raise important questions which should stimulate further research. Reliability is also almost impossible to assess with this kind of research, but it is unlikely that if the study had been carried out by someone else the evidence would have been precisely the same. The interviewees knew I had participated in men's groups in that area, and in some cases remembered the way I had participated. This clearly influenced, and I have no doubt enhanced, the co-operation I received. The validity of my evidence is likely to be high for the same reason that reliabiliity is low.

My sample necessarily had to be small since the interview style was the intensive life-history type with two or three visits per subject and I was concentrating on obtaining rich qualitative data in a way unstructured other than by a checklist. My purposes were exploratory analytical description and a contribution towards grounded theory construction rather than positivistic theory-testing. It was not therefore appropriate for this study to include life histories of a control group of men who did not have anti-sexist views.

Altogether 72 interview sessions were completed with 30 subjects. By coincidence 13 were from manual working backgrounds, 13 from non-manual, and 4 were ambiguous. Only 3 were currently in manual work, though 11 had experienced it in the past, including 5 from non-manual backgrounds. When interviewed, 4 men were not employed and several others had been unemployed, 2 were in temporary part-time jobs and one was a full-time art student. Three were housepersons and primary child-carers, 4 had experienced being lone fathers and 2 still were. By self-definition 26 men were heterosexual, 2 bisexual and 2 gay.

CONCLUSION

Despite reservations about drawing inferences from statistics, I was impressed by the consistent picture I found in them of women increasingly making their way as independent persons (see Appendix), and it is only to be expected that, whether they hold feminist ideals or not, they will be less and less prepared to tolerate men's treatment of them which does not accept them as equals.

It is likely that fewer and fewer women will want the kind of men whose only advantage is being a steady breadwinner. To be acceptable to the new women men will have to be sensitive and genuinely sharing partners with nurturing abilities and in touch with their own vulnerable feelings. This does not mean becoming effeminate. It means men reclaiming that part of the common human heritage which their upbringing has taken from them.

Men make a variety of responses to change among women but if they are to be acceptable partners to the new women, pressure will be increasingly on them to shed old images of masculinity which involve unthinking assumptions of superiority, crude displays of toughness, and incompetence in relating and in expressing their more sensitive or vulnerable feelings. Instead they will need to develop a less-restricted form of manliness, expressed in lifestyles which include a readiness to value, in themselves and in women, characteristics usually dismissed as feminine, as well as being able to take a pride in being men in ways which do not oppress women.

What kinds of men are trying to make this change and how far are they succeeding in doing it? What kinds of life experiences are conducive to their making such a change and what kinds hinder them? What are the problems men face, or feel they face, when they do attempt to change and try to live non-sexist lifestyles? These are some of the questions which the life-history data presented in this study are intended to help answer.

It needs re-emphasising that I do not claim the men in this study are a representative cross-section of the male population. On the contrary, they were deliberately chosen knowing them to be untypical, and studied in the belief that they are significant because they are facing up to issues concerning masculine-gendered activities and how these need to be changed in modern conditions. In other words, the men were selected on the grounds that they had shown evidence of rejecting the dominant (hegemonic) type of masculinity which oppresses women and also many men.

In the rest of this book I present data in two contrasting forms. In the next chapter I present an analysis of interview content in terms of cross-cutting categories suggested to me by the fieldwork experience and which I believe are relevant to theory building in this area. In the substantial following section a selection of men tell their life stories. Finally, the book's concluding theoretical discussion seeks to explore the study's implications, including men's participation in feminist struggles against male dominance in contemporary society and for equality of the sexes.

Chapter 2

Analysis of life histories

I argued at the end of Chapter 1 that for men to be accepted as partners by the women who are changing their outlooks and lifestyles, they will have to abandon images of masculinity which involve assumptions of superiority and displays of toughness – typically leading to incompetence in relationships and in expressing sensitive feelings – and be able to take a pride in kinds of manliness which do not oppress women.

The evidence set out in this chapter illustrates experiences of men trying to do just that. The data are from my life-history interviews with a sample of men in a particular locality. From the thirty men interviewed, eight life histories have been selected and are presented in detail in Part II of the book. The present chapter, however, presents a qualitative cross-sectional analysis of all the interviews by examining selected aspects which were common to the lives of all or some of the men. Each life history is essentially a case history rather than an element in a generalising social survey, so this chapter can of course do no more than provide possible indications as to what may be the experiences and opinions of other anti-sexist men. Nevertheless interesting common themes emerge which I hope will inspire further research into the lives of men of this kind.

The main aim in the interviews was to trace life experiences conducive to anti-sexist attitudes among men, under the following headings:

I What was there in the early life history (particularly gender socialisation) of the interviewee which assisted his developing, or enabled him to maintain, an anti-sexist outlook and activities as an adult?

II What was there about his adult life experience of gender relations which led him to, or reinforced an already existing tendency to, anti-sexist opinions and actions?

III What evidence is there that his anti-sexist opinions are reflected in his current actions and lifestyle as an adult?

The checklist used in the interviewing was as follows:

1 What was the social character of the interviewee's family background, parents' upbringing, personalities and occupations?
2 Did he model himself primarily on his father or mother and what did he think were the effects on his personality?
3 How did he relate to his siblings and with what effects?
4 How did he relate to pre-school friends (both sexes or mainly one?) and with what effects?
5 What were the gender influences at each level of education?
6 What were his relationships with his peers at each educational level and what were their effects?
7 What were his gender-relevant experiences outside formal education?
8 Has he experienced close relationships with women? If so, how did these influence him?
9 What were his employment experiences and their gender-related effects?
10 Has he had experience of the women's movement or of feminist thinking?
11 If appropriate, how did he get involved in anti-sexist men's groups; what was his experience of these and what were the effects on him?
12 What are his current household arrangements, participation in domestic work and, if appropriate, childcare?
13 What are his current views on the most desirable relationship between a man and a woman?
14 What are his current views on marriage?
15 What are his current views on his own gender identity?
16 What are his views on the breadwinner role?
17 Does he feel he is in touch with his more sensitive emotions?

GENERAL FEATURES OF THE SAMPLE

The sample of thirty men ranged in age between 21 and 54. Exactly half were in their early forties and twelve were in their thirties. Nine-tenths were therefore between 30 and 45. Two were in their twenties and one was over 50. There were only four locally born men. Nearly all had moved into the study area from other parts of Britain and one had grown up in Central Africa. All were white, twenty-three had non-manual occupations, three had manual occupations and four were not employed. As previously stated, thirteen came from manual home backgrounds, thirteen from non-manual and four from ambiguous backgrounds. Half the sample called themselves working class.

Twenty-six men said they were heterosexual, two gay and two bisexual. Three-quarters were married or in stable relationships with women. Only four had never lived with a woman, two gay men, one bisexual and a young single man. Exactly half of the sample had lived independently of their parents prior to experiencing feminist influence, most of these (twelve) had lived away from home as students. Eight men were divorced, half of them currently living alone but maintaining an involved access to their children. Two-thirds of the sample were fathers, three were adoptive or foster fathers and two were step-fathers. Four men had experienced being lone fathers and two still were at the time of the interviews. Three men had one child, eleven had two children, four had three and two had four.

The main overall finding from these interviews was that most of the men interviewed, twenty-three out of thirty, had experienced a combination of two interacting and reinforcing influences in their lives:

(a) early life experiences with some unconventional features which departed from traditional gender expectations; and
(b) an adult experience of feminist influence, most frequently in the form of a close relationship or friendship with at least one woman who was actively feminist.

I will now consider these influences in more detail before I illustrate in their own words, some of the main characteristics of these men in terms of their social activities and opinions.

Twenty-four of the men interviewed had experienced (a) and twenty-eight had experienced (b). Twenty out of the twenty-six heterosexual interviewees had experienced close relationships with at least one feminist.

Let us look at the first point in more detail: most of the anti-sexist men studied had some feature of their early life experience which was conducive to their developing an anti-sexist outlook in adult life. There was, however, a wide variety of different conducive experiences. Features of their early life experience which seemed most relevant as predisposing influences were one or more of the following:

1 non-identification with traditional fathers; or
2 identification with nurturing fathers;
3 experience of strong mothers, usually involved in paid work;

4 parents who did not conform to conventional gender domestic roles;
5 the influence of elder sister(s) or elder brother(s);
6 childhood friendships with girls, or with both sexes in situations where gender was de-emphasised.

It is unlikely that adult men will develop an anti-sexist outlook or be converted from a conventional sexist one without having some aspect of their early life experience which has prepared them for this. Many other influences could be relevant but the ones listed clearly appeared in the lifecourses of men in my sample and seem likely to be important.

What appear to be significant findings were that all but four of the men said they did not identify fully with their fathers, and that the four who said they did do so all had unconventional nurturing fathers. In other words, for most of the men, their fathers did not serve as significant role models, except perhaps negative ones, in acquiring their own gender identities, and those that did identify with their fathers had a non-traditional role model available to them. Fourteen of the men said they identified more with their mothers while sixteen reported either a mixed parental identification or said they did not identify with either parent. Of the men who said they identified more with their mothers, all but three were heterosexual adults. A small number of interviewees also emphasised their rejection of the example of a more traditional elder brother or identification with non-traditional elder sisters.

The point about non-identification with fathers has to be qualified, of course, by the fact that the *de facto* absentee father is a widespread phenomenon in a world where men are expected to be dedicated breadwinners and therefore partial or complete non-identification with fathers may be very common. Many boys either have to try to identify with an image of their fathers acquired in their absence or else find alternative male figures to serve as role models, often stereotyped, symbolically traditional ones supplied by the mass media. The following sections illustrate themes from my analysis of interviews.

LACK OF IDENTIFICATION WITH CONVENTIONAL FATHERS

This was very common among these interviewees but was expressed in a wide variety of ways, for example (pseudonyms used throughout):

Dave: I certainly don't identify with my Dad in his political views or anything else . . . I don't think I ever consciously modelled myself on him. I was rebellious. I wasn't having anything to do with it from quite early on.

Steve: I don't know much about him . . . my Mum blocked me . . . She made sure I didn't have a relationship with him . . . it didn't bother me because she'd done a good job of telling me what a bastard he was and how he wasn't worth spending time with . . . I didn't have any contact with him . . . I had a sort of feeling of him not understanding me.

Martin: [W]hen he died . . . I was 5 . . . I don't give my Dad much thought . . . I've always seen its benefits . . . Maybe I'd have turned out more sporty and assertive in a forceful way . . . maybe I wouldn't want to be that way. When he died it was three days before I was told and I hadn't asked. I don't feel I was close to him . . . the toys he bought were typical boys' toys . . . he was pretty traditional about men's and women's roles.

Richard: I didn't really know my Dad. He left us when I was 2. Then he committed suicide when I was 7 and it's not been spoken about much.

IDENTIFICATION WITH NURTURING FATHERS

Some interviewees, however, had nurturing fathers and it is notable that these were the only anti-sexist men who did identify with their fathers.

Simon: I had a good relationship with my father. I've got fond memories . . . he was a caring man. He did a lot with us . . . always taking us out to places and showing us how to do things . . . I never thought if he was unconventional in that setting . . . He was just my Dad and he was normal . . . looking back on it, I suppose he was unusual . . . doing cooking and housework . . . I don't know if he was involved when we were very young . . . changed nappies and so on . . . I wouldn't be surprised. It would be in character. I identified with him a lot . . . I always felt comfortable that this man was my father.

Nigel: He was a loving father . . . I used to go for walks with him. We used to have lots of chats. I looked up to him as a fountain of all knowledge . . . I was never as close to my mother . . . playing with him was important – always cerebral games, elaborate stories – not soldiers, bang, bang. He used to tell brilliant stories. I remember one incident . . . that doesn't fit the usual masculine mould. He was very anti- my having a cap-gun . . . I definitely identified with my father.

Terry: My Dad was always the quiet person in the family, rarely raised his voice . . . he was great to have around. He was good fun and would put time aside for the children . . . I have happy memories of him when I was a child . . . he was a nurturing and caring father . . . I take after my Dad . . . As I've had children I see strong similarities . . . I modelled myself on him.

INFLUENCE OF STRONG MOTHERS

Additional influences are required, apart from non-identification with conventional fathers or identification with nurturing fathers to produce an anti-sexist outlook. More than half the sample, for example, said they had parents who did not conform to traditional gender roles. The kinds of non-conformity though, varied considerably.

Most men whose parents were non-traditional said that their mothers were in regular paid employment at some stage during their childhood – a phenomenon less widespread in most areas up to the early 1970s than has been the case recently. Some said their fathers were regularly involved in domestic work and childcare. Three other men's fathers died young so the subjects had been brought up by working mothers, some with elder sisters.

In the context of unconventional parental gender roles it was mothers rather than fathers who had a more decisive influence – few men had nurturing fathers but half said they had strong mothers.

Alan for instance told me: My mother was a strong character . . . my wife, as soon as she met her, thought her assertive and sociable . . . She was always involved with her own group of friends. She was practical . . . she knew all about chisels and mallets and so on. If something went wrong with the hoover . . . my mother could do it . . . the image of a woman who just dealt with washing and ironing and so on, wasn't there. She was good all her life at practical things.

Martin: So my mother was the hard-working one. She had to, after my father died. She had . . . an independent streak . . . made her own way. The idea of a woman working and making ends meet, she got that from her mother . . . She was definitely the main influence on me because the household I grew up in was my mother and sisters . . . she was a strong personality . . . it was important as a model of a woman who could be strong and support herself.

Simon: On both sides mine was a working-class background. My mother was employed too . . . She used to go off on a moped . . . she had her own income . . . it was obviously important to her to work. I remember her appearing to enjoy telling people about her job . . . It gave her some identity other than housewife . . . it gave me the experience that women can be working women.

Jamie: My father's mother was a suffragette so there's that background in the family that men and women were equal. My father agreed with her views . . . this was an important expression of view, that they were equal even though their roles were so different . . . it was expected that my mother would drive a car and she was very capable and competent.

John: My mother was a forceful person, a strong woman . . . before she got married she negotiated a deal with my father about her being an autonomous person and deciding what she wanted to do . . . she was not a downtrodden woman, she stood up for herself . . . She expected the boys to do housework as much as the girls.

A strong tendency towards egalitarian household arrangements appeared in some cases, for instance:

Alan: My parents had . . . an unusual way of dealing with us and with themselves . . . they had two sons and so there were three men in the household and only one woman, it was assumed we all ought to co-operate . . . you cleared the table when you'd had your food . . . the sons either dried up or made the tea. Who washed up was not necessarily my mother . . . you changed your beds with one of the adults . . . Other people . . . had mothers who did everything for them and fathers who did nothing. Our family didn't seem to be like that.

BROTHERS AND SISTERS

In some cases brothers and sisters were important influences as examples to follow, or to reject, or as younger children to care for:

Anthony: I had three big sisters who I absolutely adored . . . they were more immediately influentual than my mother or my father or my brother . . . My sisters were the most important element in my life. I consciously followed their lead, I was completely like the fourth sister of the family . . . they represented absolutely all the qualities that you could ever want to be . . . They were all very strong women in their different ways.

Richard: I had an older male model available in my elder brother. He was thoroughly vile to me! He was 4 years old when I arrived . . . He's very different from me . . . more tough and macho . . . He used to bully me . . . He was the model but I just rejected it altogether. He showed me how a male could be and I decided that was not what I wanted. With my father not being there I had the choice of either being like my Mum or being like him. But I don't think I'm like either of them. I had to find my own way.

Terry: I took responsibility for my younger sisters but it didn't ever feel a burden . . . having younger sisters influenced me . . . My eldest sister three years younger . . . was always classed as a tomboy and we were close . . . We played together a lot . . . I was 15 when the youngest was born . . . I looked after her, changed nappies and fed her and quite enjoyed it . . . I used to make things for my sisters, for their dolls and stuff like that . . . it must have been a very feminine atmosphere but I wasn't aware of it. I never thought I was missing anything.

John: A lot fell on me as the eldest . . . I was expected to do a lot and I felt responsible for my younger brothers and sisters. I changed nappies and washed and bathed my brothers and sisters and enjoyed it. It didn't seem at all strange . . . I didn't know anything different.

CHILDHOOD FRIENDSHIPS

A high proportion of the sample, nearly half, said they had at some stage had childhood friendships which were unconventional in traditional gender terms – for example, early playmates were mostly girls, and in some cases the childhood friends' gender roles were not remembered as sharply differentiated.

For instance:

Nigel: My two best friends were girls when I was between 4 and 7. It was totally irrelevant that they were girls. Later I was close to one particular girl. I remember being upset when she said we shouldn't be friends any more. People were making fun of her, especially her brothers. I was about 7 or 8 then. I didn't think it strange being friends with girls. I enjoyed a lot of the things they enjoyed.

Roy: There were early friendships before school . . . boys and girls. In such a small village everybody seemed to be friends with everybody else . . . It was just accepted . . . Just a big gang of kids. There wasn't a big division between boys' games and girls' games . . . a lot of the girls were tomboys . . . just joined in everything. We used to play a lot of football and cricket and they joined in . . . there were typical girls' games that the boys joined in . . . I don't know if you'd have found it in other villages.

Anthony: The girl who lived two doors away . . . was my dearest friend but I never saw her at school . . . I'd met her before we started school . . . she was being a bit hived off because she was a girl . . . not being taught the same things . . . She was absolutely my main friend . . . We were perfectly in accord. We had formed this friendship before we could walk or talk.

SCHOOL EXPERIENCES

For some of the men, school experiences had an important influence on their gender outlook, either enjoying being with girls in mixed schools or having adverse experiences as a result of the macho behaviour of other boys or male teachers. For instance:

Roy: My best friend was a girl . . . We were only friends in school . . . it was my first, sort of, sexual experience . . . just exploring each other . . . We must have been about 6 or 7. I didn't have any sisters so this must have been quite important . . . It was a good experience. I felt happy about it.

Also Roy: I have a vivid memory of this characteristic PE master, bully type, pushing me into the pool . . . it was October or something and it was freezing cold and me standing there shivering on the side, and this horrible – Mr Mann his name was – pushing me into the pool, telling me to get in there. He was a real macho type.

Nigel: I made friends with her because she was the only person who'd talk to me. The boys didn't because I wasn't very hot in the games line . . . I got picked on by the boys because I wasn't good at team games and I was always a bit of a loner.

Steve: I didn't want to be running around getting into fights and posing . . . They made fun of me for being with the girls . . . I went a lot further when I moved on to an all-boys' school . . . suddenly a whole section of the people I'd communicated with had gone, the ones I'd felt easiest with. It was quite a shock to find myself in an all-boys' school. I had problems with a lot of bullying . . . there was always somebody . . . slightly more picked on than me . . . But I was always one step away . . . Occasionally you'd get something thrown at you rather than punched. There was a lot of ganging up. They objected that I wasn't . . . a rugby-playing cadet-force member . . . I could see a clear model of what I didn't want to be.

Simon: The games master made fun of ones he thought were a bit sissy. He was a cruel bugger he was! . . . I wasn't one of the stereotyped weaker type of boy that tends to get picked on. I was a real in-betweener, I wasn't one of those that got picked on and I wasn't one of those that did the picking. I just kept my head down.

All these accounts were by heterosexual men, but gay and bisexual men had similar experiences:

John: I don't remember any difficulty knowing how I was supposed to be as a young lad. From looking at other lads at school it seemed they were how I was supposed to be and I could see that I wasn't like that . . . I never felt one of the boys . . . rough games and . . . rushing around and fighting . . . were definitely not me. I felt closer to the girls but I didn't have any special friends who were girls.

Then at senior school: It was an all-boys' school and it was absolute hell . . . so violent . . . I used to get beaten almost every day or threatened and in terror . . . They picked on me and called me a sissy so I got abused and beaten up for that . . . The games master particularly picked on me. You were supposed to have . . . skills as a boy, being able to kick or throw or catch . . . I didn't have those skills . . . I got bad mouthed or hit . . . He showed me up in front of the other boys . . . and criticised in a nasty way.

The other gay man's school experiences reinforced his already emerging sexuality:

Anthony: Because my sisters were good at mathematics and things like that I thought it was all right to be good at them, though I did subsequently identify them as male subjects and mentally refused to do them . . . I thought all these things were completely masculine and I didn't want anything to do with them at all. I consciously rejected masculinity . . . I was obsessively attracted to the arts side.

One bisexual man, Mark, told me: I was always shy . . . and one of the ones at school who would get picked on . . . being smaller and fatter . . . not good at sport and wearing glasses. All the classic things really.

And the other, Ted: I got picked on . . . I was never any good at football. I was always one of the last to be picked for the team. There were no gangs . . . but people who'd pick a fight . . . There wasn't usually fisticuffs but . . . lots of threats and name-calling and pushing.

HIGHER OR ADULT EDUCATION

A minority of the men interviewed had been to full-time higher- or adult-education institutions but for some who had, it had been a powerful influence in their anti-sexist development:

Bob: I applied to Ruskin College and ended up there on a two-year trade-union scholarship . . . I came up against feminism well articulated and argued . . . the women there . . . put arguments against male-chauvinist trade unionists . . . I felt my skull was going to blow open with the intensity of the discussions and debates . . . There was an active group of women at Ruskin and active women's groups in the town who were putting feminist arguments . . . It was all coming in very fast against a background of twenty-five years . . . as a white male from a working-class background.

Nigel: I enjoyed the social life at the Poly. I got in with a lot of the sociology crowd . . . There were quite a number of feminists . . . We had deep and meaningful conversations when we went out rambling or over coffee until three o'clock in the morning. In the course of conversations with friends I think I developed a more rational attitude towards women.

Jamie: when I first went to Coleg Harlech in 1976 . . . they had about 6 or 8 women out of 50 or 60 students. That was dreadful . . . When I went back two years later there was a whole different kind of woman about . . . and more women . . . most of them were feminists . . . I was very interested and aware of it myself . . . There were some women there who I thought of as being great friends. They were people I was very glad to meet.

Tim: At London University I did a course on gender heavily weighted to analyse male bias in social anthropology . . . issues . . . I swallowed extremely easily . . . The groundwork had been done at home. My personality accepted all these ideas . . . things I was doing that weren't acceptable I could make changes to. I didn't have to . . . make a wholesale shift of personality or in the way I treated individuals . . . I read as many feminist books as I could get . . . going to the first lectures I thought, this was for me . . . My background made me receptive. I swallowed the ideas of feminism hook, line and sinker and argued with other men at college about these issues.

GENDER RELEVANT EXPERIENCES OF WORK/ EMPLOYMENT

Several of the interviewees described employment experiences that had influenced them from a gender point of view. For example:

Keith: In most potbanks there were more women . . . than men and doing the same jobs . . . Women would come and help you . . . There's a long tradition of working women in the Potteries. That was an important influence . . . men workers seemed to think 'Tough, that's your problem, you sink or swim' . . . Handling pottery before it's glazed your fingers . . . blister quickly . . . the skin is rubbed off by the end of the day and they bleed. There were tricks about how to avoid that. Women would come and help . . . That gave me a favourable impression of women.

And later, Keith as a trade union shop steward: A majority of the workers I represented were women . . . They were more interested in improved conditions than the men. Each year we tried to improve holidays and working hours. If people had families we tried to get time to drop their kids off at school and that sort of thing . . . women came to union meetings because we fitted them in during the lunch time . . . It was important to have them when women could come . . . I wasn't initially conscious of this . . . it was in order to hold the union together but it proved beneficial all round. Then I felt it was right, between the sexes . . . I felt strongly there should be . . . space for women to be active in the union if it was going to be representative . . . Most branch meetings take place at inconvenient times for women.

Terry had worked in a wholefood co-operative: Working there I got involved with . . . men who'd experienced men's groups and women who were feminists . . . in a working environment that was trying to break sexual stereotypes as well . . . There were jobs men did because they were the skills they'd learned and jobs women did . . . when we divided the work we looked at breaking the stereotypes.

Bob: There were a minority of women journalists . . . They tended to be sent out to cover things that involved cookery, fashion, etc. Heavy crime or . . . industrial disputes were left to the men but that started to fracture on the basis of staffing. There wouldn't be anybody else in the office and so women would go out and do a good job on a major disaster or a big murder. Working alongside women like that was an education . . . Women didn't have to be writing about . . . 'women's issues' all the time. They could . . . cover any news story that a man could cover and do it as well if not better in terms of getting information, not getting flustered, writing, and all the things that male middle-class journalists think – you can't let a women loose on this story or she might get upset or intimidated. There was an erosion of prejudices and preconceptions.

THE INFLUENCE OF FEMINISM AND OF PARTICULAR FEMINISTS

If we look at the second major influence in more detail, that of feminism, nearly all the men who had become motivated to join an anti-sexist men's group said their earlier experiences had been reinforced and further developed by the influence of feminism – more specifically and significantly, in most cases by a close relationship with a particular woman who had a feminist outlook, whether or not she was an active member of a feminist group.

It seems to be a very significant finding that all the men except one bisexual said they had been influenced in some way by feminism, and all but six of these said the influence had come from one or more specific women with whom they had had close relationships. The other bisexual man also reported the important influence of a feminist partner. Heterosexual men who did not attribute their views to particular women cited a combination of involvement in organisations where feminists were active participants; exposure to feminist literature; and the men's own prior commitment to egalitarian values which they had then applied to gender relations.

For example, one of these, Arnold: I don't think any one woman influenced me . . . As a boy my earliest playmates were girls. My partner isn't a feminist . . . My support for feminism grew out of my interest in left politics . . . Joining a men's group was a late development.

Another, Dave, told me: I'm sure women friends helped me develop my views on relationships between men and women . . . women I mixed with were all in women's groups . . . Their ideas rubbed off. It's hard to say how much came from other sources and how much was the result of discussion with women friends. There wasn't one particular woman who influenced me.

A third, Steve, told me: For me it was feminism in general, not meeting Sue that did it . . . I was starting to try to follow feminist ideas before I met her, through my own feelings about what was right and then through the group of friends that got together in Maidstone.

Martin: I'd never had a derogatory view of women anyway and I mixed with women who were interested in feminism . . . opposing attempts by the anti-abortion people to get rid of the legislation . . . I thought it was a woman's right to choose. I'd already reached those views from women friends who wanted the legislation there . . . I'd want access to that if I was a woman.

But overwhelmingly for most of these men it was the influence of particular women that had made the difference:

Alan: Sarah had had a job she'd enjoyed and . . . given it up for a baby, and the baby was not an enjoyment . . . that seemed to tie up quite a lot with the emerging feminist ideas, about why were women always giving up things . . . She went to women's conferences and workshops . . . She knew about the local alternative bookshop . . . where you could get the literature.

Simon: The appeal of feminism was that it seemed . . . to fit in with what I already felt but I'd never verbalised . . . but I'd tried to do it in my everyday . . . living practices. Kitty taught me a lot about feminism and I agreed with what she was saying . . . I already had the beliefs within me . . . they went right back a long way . . . beliefs I still held when I joined the first men's group when I was about 30.

Paul: Moira began getting involved in the women's movement . . . I could see the inherent rightness in it. I recognised . . . the benefits of women's liberation for men . . . it validated the sort of man I was . . . not fitting the stereotype. It enabled me to see myself more positively, rather than somebody who didn't quite fit . . . Moira has obviously been an important influence on me . . . It didn't produce a fundamental U-turn but it was certainly part of a crystallisation of ideas for me.

Terry: Tina was very involved in feminist groups . . . She brought back her new ideas . . . and we looked at them within our relationship . . . I endorsed her ideas . . . I changed because of what she was wanting to experience . . . but having been brought up with four sisters and a Mum that's very strong, I always had a great respect for women.

Nigel: Angela has been a important influence on me. It's fair enough knowing people who have feminist ideas . . . it's quite different actually living with somebody and if she doesn't like your attitude, challenging . . . all the time . . . I've changed since I've known her.

But one interviewee who had not been in a men's group but was a househusband in a role-reversal situation and was looking after two young children, was less certain of the influence of his partner.

Vince: It's possible I've been influenced by feminism. Sue is quite a feminist. She's involved with women's groups . . . Feminist influence might get my hair up on end if it wasn't delivered properly . . . I'd think 'Somebody's standing on a soapbox shouting.' If it's not being hammered down your throat it's more acceptable.

The two bisexual men had contrasting experiences, one had been influenced by a woman partner, the other not:

Ted: I've definitely been influenced by feminism but I think it was all through Helen. Any other channels of feminist influence were pointed out by her . . . She was an important influence on my life. She'd been a feminist for quite a while before I met her. It didn't put me off.

But Mark, by contrast, told me: I suppose I've been exposed to feminist ideas a bit. I think Cathy, my lodger, would call herself a feminist . . . But I haven't really been exposed to much strong feminism . . . It hasn't been that important for me.

While supportive towards feminism, several of the men nevertheless commented negatively on contacts with radical anti-men feminists:

Paul: I and . . . other men in the group did quite a lot in terms of running crèches and just helping . . . setting up their first refuge, but I found it quite a difficult phase. In addition to it striking a lot of chords I actually found it isolating as well . . . part of the women's movement was a strand which saw men as the enemy, full stop . . . that was difficult to take. I remember getting sucked into lots of arguments defending men. That felt awkward.

Dave: I'm very sceptical of the American feminist view which looks at sex differences and relations in the same way as boss and worker relations . . . So you have the absurd result where men are seen as the oppressors in every situation – and the tone of it I find very difficult.

Simon: There were situations where as a man I used to feel threatened . . . some of her feminist friends . . . used to argue on a personal level which I obviously found threatening. I can remember on occasions I got very unhappy about that, but that was the beginning of my political awareness.

Steve: I myself have been oppressed by other men but also by my mother, but that was a thing you weren't allowed to talk about in those kinds of politics. Within a women's group situation it would be hard to raise . . . To criticise women for oppressing men is dodgy ground! It's hard enough for men to accept.

Peter: I've been prepared to . . . take my share with the children and the house, Linda's friends who are feminists, anti-men even, don't frown upon me . . . But . . . there was an incident the other day . . . I went to deliver some food . . . at a meeting of very assertive women, and the woman who answered the door . . . was very aggressive. I didn't say anything . . . I was only delivering stuff. But it can go too far the other way. I can't help being a man. You can't condemn me because I'm a man, but you could condemn my attitude if . . . equally I could condemn [their attitudes] if they went too far.

JOINING MEN'S GROUPS

On the question of how they came to join an anti-sexist men's group, the men mentioned a variety of influences, usually several in combination, but one frequently mentioned was getting involved in discussions with men whose partners were active in a local feminist group.

For instance:

Paul: During that time several men came together. Quite a few of them were men with relationships with women in the women's group . . . That was important . . . questions were raised about respective roles and it provided a space for the men to air those questions and see what they meant for them.

And Roy: It was while I was at teacher's training college that I first got involved in a men's group. Joan and I discussed this and we agreed on my joining. Neither of us saw it as an anti-feminist group. On the contrary, the idea was to support the women's group and to sort out our own problems as men without depending on women.

Simon: The first thing Kitty did when we moved here was to join the women's group. A lot of the women's group had male partners and it was through meeting them that I eventually joined a men's group.

But for some men, joining a men's group was more an attempt to deal with their own emotional problems about their partner's involvement in feminism.

For example, Derek: The men's group came out of the fact their relationships had grounded . . . and they wanted somebody to talk to about it . . . The men weren't the sort who come home and expect their dinner on the table and then go down the pub . . . They were all men who were willing to get involved in housework and childcare . . . it didn't help their relationships . . . It was a really churning up phase . . . I was really going through the mill. It was a coming together of personalities that had suffered.

And Alan: I joined the men's group because I got desperate again. I didn't know what other men felt because you couldn't talk to other men about it. I didn't know what other men thought about lots of things.

Another frequently mentioned influence was a local alternative bookshop and the link it provided with the wider men's movement:

Mark: I picked up a copy of *Men's Anti-sexist Newsletter* in a bookshop and there was a list of contacts . . . Nigel was listed in this area . . . so I went round . . . to have a chat and then I think he spoke to Martin in the bookshop about the idea of starting up a men's group, so I went along to help it start up.

Nigel: I was partly responsible for getting the men's group going in the first place. I came across a copy of the *Men's Anti-sexist Newsletter* in a radical bookshop and I sent a subscription . . . I put my name down as a contact. I met Mark and then I was talking to Martin that runs the bookshop and it just spiralled from there.

Ted: I'm not sure how I got to know about the men's group. I think Helen had seen something in the bookshop. She was in a women's group that met there at the time . . . We moved in the same sort of circles as people in the men's group. I'd met one or two of them before, just being in the bookshop . . . I'd seen men's anti-sexist magazines there.

Alan: I'd heard about it mainly because I was looking for literature on men's experience of the feminist movement, and there isn't much . . . So I went to the alternative bookshop . . . that's where Martin told me there was a men's group starting – and come along.

Such a response would be more likely to be forthcoming from men who had a prior commitment to other social groups in which feminists were also involved. Organisations mentioned included the Campaign for Nuclear Disarmament (CND), a local peace group, Friends of the Earth and Co-counselling. Sometimes a men's group was formed as a result of a public meeting called by a women's group to discuss some gender issue, such as male violence:

Steve: I started to go to a men's group when I was 18. I was still at school. There was quite a strong women's group at the time in

Maidstone . . . they held a mixed meeting on male violence . . . we thought it would be good to do something else with the men involved . . . we took a core of people who were there . . . and partners of women involved in CND or friends of theirs. It came more out of the women's group than out of what men were doing.

Most men would not respond to feminist influence in this way so it is interesting to ask what kinds of characteristics these anti-sexist men had that appealed to heterosexual feminists.

Martin: I think she liked me because I wasn't pushing her . . . She liked the fact that I was male and not pushy, not a traditional man. That attracted her . . . we have a tolerance built into both our characters . . . So it becomes easier to take each other's ideas on board.

Steve: She liked the fact that I wasn't macho and that I was quiet. She was wary of men. The fact that we'd met through *Spare Rib* made her feel I was safe.

Paul: What appealed to her . . . was that I was straightforward . . . I hadn't got established rigid views . . . I was fairly open . . . Ideas from early on about men and women . . . had not been reinforced through adolescence . . . it was easy to cover my timidity . . . by not being macho or acting in the traditional way. Some men might have covered it up by being macho but I didn't.

Since the influence of individual relationships with feminist partners was such a widespread experience of these men who joined anti-sexist men's groups it is perhaps not surprising that only a small minority of men's group members were gay men. They had to find other routes to membership but even these involved feminists:

John: About 1978 . . . I first got involved in an anti-sexist men's group . . . I'm not quite sure how I got into that, maybe there was some advert in a local paper . . . I worked with a member of the men's group in the same office. He was married to a woman who was a prime mover in the women's group. There weren't any other gay men in the men's group . . . I certainly sympathised with the issue of women's oppression by this time.

And Anthony: I felt let down personally . . . and not supported by the gay group. That was one reason I got involved in the men's group. I came across them through the feminists because we'd always mutually joined each other's groups. There was no separatist movement . . . feminists, because the debate was the same debate, joined the gay group. They just came along and talked about sexual politics. The other men in the men's group were husbands or lovers or ex-lovers or would-be lovers of women in the women's group.

FIRST EXPERIENCES OF MEN'S GROUPS

A common response to initial experiences of anti-sexist men's groups was feeling wary about all-male groups but then relief at finding the other men did not fit the macho stereotype. Sometimes the relief took some time to be reached because of other differences, for example, class:

Terry: For a while I resisted it. It seemed totally alien to me, sitting talking about your feelings. I thought 'You must be joking' . . . I didn't want anything to do with it . . . I came away from my first meeting thinking I'd never go again . . . I thought – these people stringing together all these big long sentences with long words . . . they're a different class to me . . . I'll never be able to speak to these people . . . I certainly can't tell them how I feel. I'd never mixed with anyone like that.

Martin: When the men's group started to meet here above the shop I didn't think it would be for me. My impression was that it would be like an encounter group and I'd feel threatened . . . But . . . I got drawn in . . . people I knew thought it was a great idea so I went to the first meeting. I felt safe because I knew people there . . . It felt really weird at first but I enjoyed it. It was good to meet men with similar views to mine.

Alan: When the men's group started . . . I was very apprehensive, but it brought home to me . . . that . . . what you think other men don't think about, they actually do but they won't admit it. I suppose it goes against men's typical upbringing . . . The men in the men's group are . . . more vocal . . . being in the men's group helped me a lot.

Ted: I resented the men's group at first but . . . it grew on me and made me realise you didn't have to be the sort of man who'd stand at the bar and drink sixteen pints a night and say how wonderful the local football team were . . . I felt a lot closer to the men in the men's group than to other men. They seemed more genuine. They weren't really putting on an act . . . and I felt I didn't have to put on an act.

Later experience in men's groups involved new ideas and feelings, mutual support in rejecting macho attitudes, a different and preferred awareness of self, plus fluctuations in membership and activity:

Jamie: There was an aspect of people contributing little or nothing but soaking a lot in . . . I probably got a lot more out of it than I realised . . . greater sensitivity for where I was as a man . . . in the old days men knew what it was to be a man . . . the way women have been changing in recent years is making some men question how they should behave.

Paul: About half-a-dozen of us got together fairly regularly – not in a structured way . . . it was a matter of trying to explore ways of getting together without formal structures anyway. It got going by word of mouth. They were men whose paths crossed at meetings, parties and so on and the issues came up and we decided to get together. A couple of them I worked with . . . It seemed difficult to get a large enough group of men together to keep it going for a sustained length of time.

Ted: It didn't make me anti-sexist. I was already, but it reinforced it . . . It was a congenial crowd of blokes but after a while there was a new infux of members and then it didn't seem right. There were some there who I didn't feel at ease with. Perhaps because they were new and hadn't . . . grown with us . . . I just felt awkward with some of them.

Steve: The men's group was an important step for me. I remember feeling relief when I saw a poster up at college and even more relieved when I found it wasn't a student group but an ordinary people group! It felt like a lifeline to me . . . It helped me realise I didn't have to conform to the ideal of a macho man. There were other people trying to be the way I wanted to be and having the same problems . . . like-minded men who shared the same experiences, breaking down the isolation, seeing there were alternatives. It wasn't easy to live how we wanted because there are few out there to support us in doing it.

Nigel: I wanted to get it going for political reasons, taking action against stereotypes I don't like . . . feeling that men could be allies of the women's movement, though I didn't want that to be patronising . . . I wanted to meet men . . . of a similar outlook, and . . . talk about things you couldn't normally talk about.

Derek: There was a lot of discussion about the way boys are brought up . . . the male hierarchy they didn't want to be part of . . . male figures in people's lives we felt a reaction against . . . the patriarchal thing. Everybody felt vulnerable. There was great emphasis on allowing ourselves to feel vulnerable or sensitive . . . a standard idea in men's groups, open yourself up . . . there was a supportive attitude towards [women] . . . puzzlement over how to carry it out . . . some thought it important to work on ourselves . . . They were worried about the way they reacted to women . . . I don't recall any argument about whether to support women or not. It was taken for granted.

Some of the men got involved in the wider men's movement, subscribing to anti-sexist magazines and attending national conferences. They found magazines helpful but their reactions to the conferences were negative:

Terry: I went to men's conferences but I found all those difficult . . . They were generally more educated, I found the words they used difficult to grasp and their stance difficult to understand – theorising about things. I used to score because I said things which were so obviously grassroots stuff that it stopped them in their tracks.

Paul: I read *Achilles Heel* and the *Men's Anti-sexist Newsletter* which I heard about through the men's group . . . They . . . helped validate what I was doing . . . it was important enough to warrant a newsletter . . . and there were men elsewhere doing similar things. I thought of myself as part of a men's movement . . . men's liberation . . . from the conditioning . . . the macho stereotype . . . not showing your feelings . . . There were . . . anti-sexist men's conferences . . . I ended up feeling I didn't fit in with any of the groups . . . There was a wide variety of men there with different expectations and at different levels of awareness . . . some of the earlier work in the men's movement was . . . feeling guilty about being a man . . . at the conferences probably.

INFLUENCING OTHER MEN

It could be said that men's groups are just inward-looking and are unlikely to influence other men, but some of these men did see the example they set to other men as an important part of their political outlook:

Paul: I remember finding it an exciting time . . . having long arguments in work . . . I took the opportunity to bring it up on lots of occasions and enjoyed challenging the stereotypes . . . I was quite outgoing and assertive about it. I organised my job so that I could take my daughter to nursery school . . . and pick her up at lunchtimes . . . It was more difficult for Moira so I was happy to do it . . . I was open about it in work . . . I provided a good role model for some men in the office. It sounds big-headed but . . . perhaps there were some men in the office who were influenced.

Peter: Our babysitting circle altered a lot of men's attitudes towards looking after children. It's a thing I'm proud of. Because everybody accepted me as doing it, other blokes started to do it, so now nobody's surprised if a man or woman comes along . . . Every man now in the group is prepared to come out and sit. I don't think any of them would say 'You look after the kids, I'm going out with my mates.'

Steve: I'm not just expressing my redefined sense of being a man through my artistic work but also helping to influence other people. It's important . . . for other men to see that they don't have to behave in the stereotypical way. It's a demonstration to both sexes and myself.

ATTITUDES TO THE BREADWINNER ROLE

Half the men had negative or mixed views on being breadwinners. Some were housepersons and active fathers not currently in paid employment.

Jamie: I don't have a great feeling about the breadwinner role . . . work should be fulfiling and if that's employment outside the home that's great, but if it's being a single parent that's a perfectly acceptable alternative to me. It's not centrally important to me to be the one who earns the money. I've not had a consistent career.

Derek: Careers have always been difficult for me . . . I had a lot of worries about it . . . it was always a problem focusing on one thing. I don't remember thinking much about the breadwinner role and I never have done. The relationship started to define my feelings about what I didn't want to be which was the breadwinner and the typical husband.

Keith: I don't have any positive feeling about being a breadwinner. None at all. In my relationship with Ann, I'm not the breadwinner, she earns all the money. I don't feel a main influence there at all. Being a breadwinner isn't important to my sense of self worth.

Ted: I hate the breadwinner role . . . when Helen was out of work a long time it felt I'd got the world on my shoulders. I'd lie awake worrying how we were going to pay bills . . . being a breadwinner was a burden.

But as against this some of the men most firmly anti-sexist and most consistently non-sexist in their lifestyles still regarded the breadwinner role as important to their personal identities.

For instance, Alan: I still regarded my breadwinner role as essential . . . I'd heard of innumerable men who'd changed their jobs and suddenly found there wasn't a job there at all . . . however nice it was hold all these other attitudes, I was still responsible for maintaining the status quo in a monetary sense . . . in my mind money is important because everything I've done works that way. Monetary aspects come into life all the time.

Peter: It is important that I'm in work. That's a central thing for men. I've inherited that . . . if I'm not in work then I think I'm not fulfiling my duty . . . I wouldn't mind being a househusband for a while. We've spoken about this . . . but I still see myself as a major breadwinner.

Paul: With the arrival of our first child, my breadwinner role became important. I didn't consciously feel it as a responsibility . . . it took us time to adjust to it financially because we'd had two salaries before . . . I saw it as a natural thing to do . . . it was what men did . . . I didn't feel that I had to go out to work to earn the money to keep us together. I'd have been working anyway and I was doing the job I'd been trained to do.

And the younger men looking ahead to their role:

Steve: In a way I copped out of my responsibility, I thought, men are supposed to be breadwinners so I'm not going to be a breadwinner. But it's as much a responsibility as ever for me . . . as much as it is Sue's . . .

After a few years I intend to give up work and be with the children . . . Sue can work for a while. We can take it in turns. I imagine myself as a househusband and active father and a breadwinner alternately.

Nigel: We want two kids a cat and a mortgage! It doesn't come cheap. It means plugging ourselves into the system unfortunately. I feel awful about the treadmill. We're going to have a joint breadwinner role. When the children come I'll have to win all the bread I suppose. If she wants to go back to work I'm happy to leave work to look after the kids. We want it interchangeable. I don't mind being a househusband and stay-at-home father.

ATTITUDES TO HOUSEWORK

Strikingly, most of the men interviewed said they took an active part in housework. I am aware this has to be treated with caution in view of the findings of surveys which show that when couples are interviewed on this question there is a disagreement between men and women about the extent of men's participation. It tends to be assumed that the women's view is correct. Nevertheless this is how these men saw their involvement in home life and in most cases it was a matter of principle as well as, in some cases, a matter of long-ingrained habit. It should be noted that surveys have sampled a cross-section of couples in the population, including a substantial majority of conventional sexist men, whereas the men in my sample, as stated, were deliberately chosen as anti-sexist men.

Alan: I have always been involved in housework and childcare because from my earliest days housework was something you just did. All along I was involved, feeding kids and changing nappies was nothing unusual.

Mark: I feel OK about housework . . . I don't mind doing anything. I iron and clean and wash up . . . I don't feel some jobs aren't manly . . . Cathy once did some ironing for me and I was amazed . . . I felt it was extraordinary that somebody should iron my shirts for me and I was really grateful.

Vince: I enjoy domestic work. I don't do much dusting. Sue's not bothered about that either . . . I wash clothes. None of us is fond of ironing so it's a case of ironing what you need before you go out. It probably takes me longer but I do it. I do all the cooking . . . I was an egg, chips and peas man before. Washing up is part of my job now, I don't enjoy it but I don't mind.

Martin: At home the housework is not carefully worked out. That's part of our flexible perspective . . . I do ironing, washing and cleaning but so does she. We are both equally involved and we are both messy! . . . it tends to be me that tidies up first, but if I get stroppy about it she'll start clearing up as well . . . it works out fairly equally . . . I think she definitely feels the same.

Nigel: I do more than my share of housework because mine is a part-time job and my partner's is full-time. That may change soon. I certainly do more than my share of dishes! I love cooking but I don't like washing dishes. But my partner is always ill when they have to be washed! I don't like cleaning up and taking the rubbish out but I do all that . . . I intend to be involved in childcare too . . . I won't be able to get out of it! I'm keen on being involved with everything . . . mundane things as well as nice things.

Dave: We've a rota for housework. We had to establish that, to my shame. I'm not the most organised of people and dust for me isn't a great issue but my partner's asthmatic so I had to get my act together . . . I wash up and hoover and change the beds . . . She hates shopping so I do it and most of the cooking too. I've never ironed anything of mine and she doesn't iron her clothes. I can't think of any jobs I'm not prepared to do.

ATTITUDES TO MASCULINITY

Most of the men did not regard masculinity as important to them. Typical was Arnold who said: I seldom think about it. I don't have to prove I'm a man. I'm not effeminate. I'm a man anyway so everything I do is manly, whatever other people think.

Vince, a househusband, said: I'm not rattled by the idea that what I'm doing isn't seen as masculine. I don't feel feminine . . . I don't feel awkward at the crèche . . . In my role now I've got more in common with women.

Martin: I obviously don't fit the macho image, nor do I fit any gay model, I just see myself as being sensitive. I value my sensitive side. I never doubt it, or see it as a bad value. It's a benefit, not an unmanly attribute . . . It's part of my personality as a human being . . . I can't be a surrogate woman. It would be wrong for me to try to be that.

Nigel: I didn't fit into male groups. I didn't know the social ways of interacting . . . you've got to know a lot of things about cars and motorbikes and football and things. I didn't feel conversant with the typical male conversation subjects. I'd no idea what team I supported.

But by contrast, Tim told me: I think about masculinity nearly all the time . . . my whole existence is dominated by issues of masculinity. I structure my lifestyle . . . so that I don't dominate the woman I love . . .

I'm trying to counter it all the time . . . in my work too . . . it's an issue when I play sport . . . I also put it into a global perspective when I see men going to war . . . masculinity has been bad for a lot of people.

ATTITUDES TO RELATIONSHIPS AND MARRIAGE

On the most desirable kind of relationship between a man and a woman, half the men favoured reformed egalitarian marriage. The other half favoured equal partnerships without marriage, either living independently or together. As Arnold put it: A non-possessive open partnership, not marriage, living close but independently or semi-independently.

Paul told me: Marriage . . . tends to push people into traditional roles. I don't know if we'd get married if we had our time again . . . I understand why some feminists see marriage as oppressive. People get stuck in their traditional roles but couples can arrange things to suit themselves in spite of expectations.

Roy: I don't think there is any point in marriage . . . an ideal relationship between a man and a woman would be if they had separate flats in the same house so they could maintain their independence while sharing communal areas. Sex would then be something that happened by consent between independent people . . . there'd be no assumed obligation in it.

Ted: I wouldn't get married again . . . I don't like the attitude that the woman is the man's property. I'd rather not have that. It happens the other way round too. Marriage isn't an equal relationship, it's constraining. An ideal relationship would be friendship but I don't think it's easy because of other people's attitudes. I remember being friends with various women and it's been spoilt by other people.

These were all men who had experienced marriage but unmarried interviewees, though voicing doubts, were inclined to try modifying it:

Nigel: I went through a phase of not wanting to be married but I came round to it for practical reasons. My partner says it's for any children. I don't buy that one, I think it's our socialisation. I honestly don't think our relationship will be any different. It will be easier to maintain our relationship, in the network of friendships we're in. I don't think they'll see it as different.

Steve: My views on marriage are changing. I spent a long time despising anybody who was married. I ruled it out completely. I don't need that legal thing to stay with Sue. A lot of marriages are a cop-out, with that bit of paper people don't bother working at it. I'll see how I feel later on.

Dave: Marriage means absolutely nothing to me. I'll probably marry my present partner for tax reasons and because she feels pressure at work. I know some feminists think marriage is oppressive to women but our marriage wouldn't be . . . I can't imagine it making any difference to our relationship. We're committed to each other, being married or not makes no difference.

But by contrast Martin had a principled objection to marriage: We're trying to put our ideals into practice . . . we'd never consider getting married. It's part of our politics . . . There's no point in viewing things this way . . . if you're going to fit in with the archetypal example of male domination. We see marriage as oppressive to women. The legal equipment is there waiting. It's designed as an affirmation of male ownership.

RELATIONS WITH CHILDREN AND ATTITUDES TO CHILDCARE

For all the men with children, fatherhood was an important commitment:

Paul: It had great impact on me, becoming a father . . . I remember getting up in the night and changing nappies . . . I got emotionally involved . . . If I hadn't had a full-time job I'd have spent more time with them. I'd have liked that . . . I've always tried to encourage them to do what's right for them . . . not discourage them just because that's not what girls or boys do.

Jamie: Her health was in doubt so I took over as a single parent. I'd like to have custody. Being a father's the most important thing to me at the moment. I gave up my job two years ago. I was advised I'd have a better chance of getting custody. I have my daughters here for long periods of time. It's not a problem being a lone father. It's hard work but fulfilling. I like being an involved father. I get a lot of satisfaction from it. I've grown to be part of their lives.

Dave: I didn't have any drive to be a father but I'm glad about it now. It's important to me. I wasn't bothered about her being a girl rather than a boy, that made no difference. Her mother never wanted us to be together as a family so I adjusted to it. When she was tiny I changed nappies, bathed and fed her. It seems such a miracle they're there in the first place you can't imagine they'll stay alive.

Tim: I'd like to see universal paternity leave, which I didn't get when my children were being born. That was extremely upsetting for me. I went through the official channels and through the union . . . I was granted three days 'compassionate' leave when my first daughter was born . . . the same when we had the second – three days is what you get! To have no agreed situation across the country is barbaric.

And in anticipation, Steve: I intend to have a family. I see myself being very involved. Being a parent is one of the biggest growing experiences I could ever have. I've chosen 50 per cent responsibility in having a family so 50 per cent of the time it's up to me.

BEING IN TOUCH WITH SENSITIVE FEELINGS

A notable characteristic of many of the interviewees was an awareness of sensitive feelings, a belief that it was good to be in touch with these and that this helped them have better relationships:

Paul: Nowadays I feel more confident about myself as a man . . . I think of myself as a different kind of man . . . I feel conscious of my feelings and comfortable about letting them out in appropriate circumstances . . . most men suppress feelings that make them look vulnerable . . . it's important . . . to have the opportunity to let them out . . . being in touch my with feelings helped me form close relationships.

Arnold: For a long time . . . I had to keep most feelings bottled up to cope with work, but I've changed a lot in the last ten years and there's no doubt it makes for deeper and more satisfying relationships. It's pathetic that men aren't allowed to show sensitive feelings, my father even apologised for shedding tears at my mother's funeral, and they'd known each other over fifty years!

Steve: It's a typical experience of men, most emotions are suppressed but it came from my mother in my case . . . when I no longer needed that defence mechanism it was part of my behaviour as a man . . . that's not a natural way to behave . . . not being true to myself . . . Anger or happiness sometimes are appropriate feelings. Being in touch with how I'm feeling . . . is different from the traditional man. It's my ideal to be aware of what's going on within me and . . . what other people are needing.

Bob: There are gains for men in this . . . you can start to develop . . . the caring side that you're not supposed to show and skills you're not supposed to be able to develop. You can get much closer to your children, more emotionally involved with them . . . I'm now more in touch with my feelings . . . I can relax and enjoy things, going out with the kids to the park, cooking with them, seeing them develop and talking with them rather than at them . . . I've benefited a lot from it. I hope to continue that way.

IN CONCLUSION

If we assume these findings are not entirely idiosyncratic and may indicate something about other anti-sexist men they could be seen as encouraging for feminists who are not radically anti-men or for women in general who want intimate relationships with men on equal terms. Evidence from these interviews suggests that feminist ideas have had a definite influence on at least some men, and more particularly, it demonstrates that individual women can have a personal political influence in relationships with individual men. The personal really is political!

At the same time these findings also suggest that there must be fertile ground for such influence – the average male-chauvinist macho-man will not respond. Early life experiences which prepare men for relating to women on more equal terms are necessary for favourable responses to ensue.

In the medium term the recent changes women have been making in their lives could produce a larger pool of men in the coming generation who might be amenable to the influence of feminists, or of anti-sexist men. As stated earlier, boys growing up in future will be more familiar with women earning their own incomes, being successful in education, moving into higher-status occupations and taking personal decisions independently of men.

As Paul commented: Young men growing up now have access to a greater variety of experiences and . . . emotions. At least they have more opportunity now . . . the growth of the women's movement and all that flowed from it – that was happening in the seventies wasn't it? That was a formative time for me.

Part II

Life histories

Introduction to Part II

This part is largely devoted to letting anti-sexist men speak for themselves. Each life history forms a coherent whole and is the personal story of an individual man in his own words. Each provides a unique combination of narrative and reflection on personal life experiences.

The men were mostly interviewed in a particularly locality, namely Staffordshire in the English West Midlands region. Most of them, however, were not local in origin but came from many parts of the United Kingdom. Interviewing was in two phases, 1988–9 and 1991–2; following the first set of interviews a substantial proportion of the interviewees departed to other parts of Britain and one went to Australia.

Nevertheless at the time of the interviews and in the years preceding them these men formed part of loosely interconnected social networks of men involved in anti-sexist men's groups or other activities which were unconventional from the point of view of masculinity as generally understood in Britain in the 1980s and early 1990s. The men's groups referred to met in different periods between about 1976 and 1990.

It follows that some of the men, but not all, know other men represented here and though I have tried to conceal identities as far as possible it is inevitable that some individuals will recognise each other's accounts. The material presented here was therefore checked back with the men concerned and they agreed to let their stories be told in this way. Men, women and children referred to in the life histories were all given pseudonyms and some details are expressed in non-specific terms so as to maximise confidentiality. Apart from condensation and tidying up for the sake of readability, the life histories are given here in a form close to the original tape-recorded accounts both in content and wording.

Part II is divided into chapters in which life histories are grouped together to illustrate similar features. It is often assumed that anti-sexist men are mainly from non-manual backgrounds so it is worth reiterating that about half my sample did not confirm that assumption. Many other connections and groupings could have been made (see my conclusion to Part II) but since the preceding chapter involved chopping up accounts to illustrate analytical categories I regard it as important that in this part, which forms the heart of the book, the life histories should be retained as coherent wholes.

Chapter 3

Non-manual home backgrounds

Affluent non-manual home backgrounds were not typical in the sample I obtained. There was no deliberate attempt on my part to achieve this, since my sole criterion was that the men interviewed be anti-sexist in outlook, as defined earlier. It may be a reflection of the fact that the area in which the study was done – Staffordshire – is not a particularly affluent part of England. Two men from non-manual backgrounds (Steve and John) were from large Catholic families where resources were spread thinly.

Both the men who tell their stories in this chapter came from the south-east of England and moved further north as young adults. Steve deliberately chose to move a safe distance from his parents and out of what he saw as the complacent and unfriendly south. Their experiences of feminism and men's groups were quite different. For Alan, a mature professional man, married with three children, and committed to the breadwinner role, the influence of feminism disrupted a comfortable conventional lifestyle and he joined a men's group to try to understand what was happening to him. Whereas Steve, a young unmarried art student, eagerly absorbed feminist/anti-sexist ideas along with environmental and anti-war ideals as part of his revolt against his upbringing and macho experiences at school. Alan was profoundly affected by a feminist partner but Steve was already 'converted' before meeting his. (See also John and Vince.)

ALAN

I'm 42 and I'm an accountant. I'm married with three children. I was born in south London and I've a brother four years older. My father was from a similar background, established middle class. My mother was from a skilled manual background; her father was a self-employed cabinet-maker. I went to the local primary school in south London, then to grammar school.

My parents met in London and married at the beginning of the war. They worked hard to get where they were. I remember being told they were saving to buy a house and wanted us to help. I didn't have much relationship with my father till later but I didn't realise the effect. I don't recall being identified with him. He travelled 12 miles into work by train, went to the same position and sat with the same people for twenty years. We occasionally went in with him but it was pretty rare.

My Dad was keen on rugby football in his youth, and he used to sit and listen to sport on Saturday afternoons. Saturday mornings he went shopping in kilt and sporran. He belonged to a Scottish clan and had a dress suit, kilt, socks, sporran, and I wore them on Saturday mornings too. I never felt embarrassed about it. A kilt is heavy and below the knee and I thought it quite reasonable to wear it. It didn't seem to cause remarks from school friends. I chose to wear it and I did up to the age of 11. It was a proper quilted jacket and high socks with the tabs – full Scots warrior gear, so it wasn't effeminate . . . but this was in the south of England!

My mother was a strong character. I didn't realise at the time but my wife, as soon as she met her, thought her assertive and sociable. She was always involved with her own group of friends. She was practical, she knew all about chisels and mallets from her father. My brother and I always knew about mortice-and-tenon joints and so on, because we grew up with it and the tools were around the house. Because my brother and I became practical, my father withdrew, he was literary. Although he was quite practical in his own way, he was a bit swamped. He wasn't called on to do traditional masculine things. If something went wrong with the hoover my mother could do it. The image of a woman who just dealt with washing and ironing and so on, wasn't there. She was good all her life at practical things.

When I was small I don't think she was employed, but when I was in secondary school she was. At one time she worked for a Covent Garden fruit broker. She went in early and come back about four. I remember meeting her sometimes from the train. I must have been about 9. She did temporary jobs before that. People say leaving your children is terrible but I must have been left, at half-term she used to give me the money and say, 'You can come to London today.' I'd go on my own, not with my brother. I'd go into London, walk from Victoria Station across Whitehall to Covent Garden, just a little lad, wandering around. What little I know of London I learned like that. I'd go to her office and come back with her.

My parents had what seems to other people an unusual way of dealing with us and themselves as well. I wasn't told it was a conscious decision but because they had two sons and so there were three men in the household and only one woman, it was assumed we should all co-operate. It was understood, you cleared the table when you'd had your food and from a young age it was common practice, the sons either dried up or made the tea. Who washed up was not necessarily my mother. Changing the beds was a communal effort, you changed your bed with one of the adults. It was a Saturday-morning ritual. They were unusual about sharing out the work. Other people I've found out had mothers who did everything for them and fathers who did nothing. Our family didn't seem to be like that.

We were told 'You'll hoover the lounge and you'll dust that', and we did, and why not? I was brought up that when you have a bath you always wipe the bath round afterwards. Other lads I know have never done it in their lives, don't know what to do. Because the whole family did things like that we just did it. We took it for granted as a reasonable demand.

How they set the routine up I don't know, but when I came along I automatically followed it. We always had school dinners, no argument about sandwiches, school dinner was what you had. We had a termly season ticket and you jolly well had it! You didn't argue. There was pocket-money but there was no going round to the chip shop or anything like that. It never entered my head. There was no restriction on what we did but it all seemed clear. They didn't have a particular theory.

I didn't have many early childhood friends. There was only one I had much dealings with. We went to grammar school together. I never had great friends that other people talk about. There was a mixture of kids, a few girls further up the street, but there weren't any girls I got friendly with. Everybody was in their own families, their own little castles.

I went to Crusaders on Sunday afternoons. It's a church-related organisation but independent of the churches. They had camps in various parts of the country. We went to the Isle of Wight for two weeks when I was 14. I must have joined when I was 8 or 9. They were all boys. Infants' school was mixed but all the secondary schools in the area were single-sex schools and virtually all the organisations were single-sex. I became a choir boy and the choir was mixed but that had no effect. There was one girl I liked but every other organisation I was involved in was only boys.

It wasn't out of choice. There was never anything that worried me about girls. I had a girl cousin of a similar age who was in another youth club in the area and sometimes I went there when I got a bit older. I knew her and her mates but if you went to youth club you went with your mates who didn't mix much with girls. I find it odd that my children seem aware of relationships as soon as they get to about 10 whereas at 14 or 15 we were still messing about with the lads. I didn't think about it and talking about it with my wife, she didn't have much exposure to boys either. I don't recall any involvement with a girl at all.

I used to go to birthday parties and I remember two or three girls whose parties I went to till I was about 8 or 9. Up to 11 school was mixed and even when we were doing the ll-plus exam I don't recall any splitting apart because they were girls. They were all part of a gang but there was a lot of implicit sexual differential because girls didn't play cricket or football, they did netball and hockey.

We moved house when I was 11. It was all organised, they knew I was moving school so it was a good time to move house. We moved in the summer holidays so my brother and I went back to school from a different place. It was the same moving to Birmingham later. The week after I finished my exams, we moved. Things never fell apart. It was mainly my mother, but my father was like that too.

I don't remember any corporal punishment. I remember being told off. It never flustered my mother. Other children questioned things but if my parents said 'I don't think it's right that you should be up after eight', I'd accept it. I'm talking about up to the age of 11. It wasn't until I was 12 that we had television and that destroyed a lot of our routine . . . I became addicted to television.

We were treated as responsible from an early age. I remember when we were about 13 or 14, we'd cycle across to Croydon, seven or eight miles away, without any restrictions and then across to Farnborough to visit a friend. It was the days before a lot of traffic but it was a long way, you had to go all the way round London then across out west. My friend came to us too. We didn't use much public transport except to go to the Motor Show. We used to go to that and a group of us used to go off by train to London – nobody bothered. Now as a couple we wouldn't allow our son to do it but I never had any bad experiences or problems so I never worried about it.

Other times at half term I remember being on my own . . . from 12 onwards. My brother might be out because at 16 onwards he was bombing around and he went to college at 18. I remember half term when my mother was working, I made my own dinner. I got fish from the fishmonger and went home and cooked it. I find it odd the way my wife's parents treated her. They wouldn't let her do this and they wouldn't let her do that. When I was a lad I used to cycle to the library in the dark on Monday evenings to look at the magazines and I cycled to the swimming baths in the dark. I don't remember anybody at school or the police, saying be careful.

I didn't think it strange to change to a single-sex school at 11. I didn't see any alternative. Everybody did it. I don't remember regretting they were single-sex schools. I do now, but not at the time. I was in the post-war birth-rate 'bulge' and there were a vast amount of children around. At grammar school there was some picking on boys that didn't fit the masculine image, not good at games and so on. I was never sporty but I mixed with quite a few who were similar, some were good at sport, some weren't. There didn't seem to be much antagonism or picking on us. I don't remember it, so it obviously wasn't a problem for me.

It was the first days of mass television. After I went to grammar school my parents got one. We were deemed a bit late. A regular thing on television then was wrestling, so the school was full of wrestling on the playing field. I could do a hammerlock as well as any bloke. I don't recall people being deemed bullies. I think I was lucky I followed my brother. When I went there and was in the first and second forms I'd got my big brother at the school. That helped, especially when he was a deputy prefect, but I don't recall ever having to use it.

I recall at a school camp in Scotland some people from a Glasgow school were there as well. We were mixed in with them and there was some picking on there. One day somebody really got me annoyed and I lost control. I went berserk but that was unusual. Macho bullying did occur but most of us kept a group going as a defence. The bullies would be manoeuvred out and become the solitary ones.

The routine on sports was, winter term rugby, spring term hockey, summer term cricket, no exceptions. When the ground was unsuitable for rugby we went on a cross country run. One afternoon a year there was an athletics event. Everybody had to go. We had a PT lesson which in the winter term was in the gym and in the summer term it was athletics, wandering around in shorts and nothing else – and it could be cold! They were ruthless, PT was done just in shorts, no half measures. There were lots of teams and you had to be in one. I was normally in the fourth team. I never liked games. My father was a dedicted rugby supporter but I didn't take after him in the least. I didn't mind hockey but never got involved. Cricket – the bowler used to bowl so the batsman could have a good crack at it over the boundary so you 'lost the ball' for half an hour!

I did cross-country running of my own choice. It was not a team game. I'm not a team person, never have been. Individual sports appealed to me. I've been able to swim since about 5 or 6 but I've never been a powerful swimmer. I wasn't enthusastic enough to be in school teams. My brother swam for the county but I enjoyed the activity rather than being competitive. I didn't have the commitment to training.

I never had much problem with maths and most of the sciences, but in English, I was in Set Four – which was the dregs! Some subjects were seen as more important. Maths and English were deemed of double value, then came French and other languages, the sciences, geography, history; and half-value were music, art, woodwork, metalwork, PT. But it wasn't whether they were seen as manly or not. The headmaster's aim was university entrance. You were expected to go for that. On a careers day my father put me down for accountancy as a career, which didn't require a degree then. This was accepted because it was a profession but when it came to doing A levels the pressure was on to go to university.

The emphasis was on the sciences and yet at the girls' school sciences weren't given the same recognition. There were some joint activities with a girls' school, the school dance, but only in the fifth and sixth forms. None of the others were invited. You had to be 15 or 16. In school plays, little boys couldn't play Lady Macbeth very well so there was an exchange of suitable individuals but those were ones that were good at acting. In house plays, younger boys with unbroken voices played female parts. The schools weren't near each other and there wasn't much interaction, no mixed sports. Athletics competitions, rugby and other things were between boys' schools. It was all very segregated.

Some boys started having girl friends, went out with their friends' sisters, that sort of thing, but lots of us didn't. It didn't seem the right time or you couldn't do much about it anyway. I didn't want a girl friend. It changed as we got older, certainly in the sixth form but it was something I wasn't used to, I lived a male-orientated existence.

I was fascinated by my brother's girl friends. His education was different. He wanted to do art and I'm absolutely staggered at what the school allowed. The headmaster made arrangements with a school of art for him to go there. That was completely mixed and much more free and easy, so he developed a lot of girl friends there and brought them home. I remember Angela, she was a real corker! I was at that naive age. He brought her home because he wanted to sketch and I thought, Mum and Dad are letting him take her upstairs to sketch! They didn't bat an eyelid. She modelled for him, she just sat there and he drew, but for me it was all rather – whew!

It made me want to have girl friends but I didn't have the nerve to do anything about it. I got to know a few and went out with some of them but they were never anything more than friends. I'd have liked to get serious but they never became like that. We used to go out as a group.

When I was 15 my leg was broken playing football and I got carted off to hospital and spent a month there. I was moved into an adult ward and was with two lads a couple of years older than me. The lad I was next to was always chatting up the nurses. They were only about 18 and they played back. It was interesting. I just treated them as people, but this sexual thing . . . I don't know if I lost something or if it never developed, but I never could work out how to chat a girl up.

Because my father was at work a lot, I used to go with my mother to the Women's Institute and all sorts of things. I met women much older than I was and never felt lost chatting with them. So I had a lot of involvement with older women and didn't feel embarrassed, but I didn't have confidence with younger women. Flirty behaviour was not my scene. I didn't understand the patter and never developed it or understood it either. I got involved with friends and their girl friends but I never took a girl home to my parents. Not that they'd have said anything, they'd have been quite happy.

I got involved with doing up motorbikes and going to scrambles. My parents had friends who had sons with motorbikes. I was friends with them and spent ages on bikes but I never had a macho image. Picking up a girl and going off on a motorbike would never have occurred to me. I didn't have the confidence. So I was labelled a wimp but I did things a lot of macho lads would like to do. With my elder brother we took dangerous corners at 95, not to prove a point, it was something I liked.

Near my A levels, my father was offered a job in Birmingham so as soon as I finished exams we moved. That took away my contacts. They were all waiting for their exam results. I'd been offered a place at Manchester University but didn't get the grades. So I went back to my original idea of accountancy. I got a job in Birmingham to do articles and went in with a group of other young men. There were girls in the offices but at the time there were no female articled clerks and no female audit seniors, just secretaries who were all a bit older than me. I went in at 18. On audits I met a lot of 16-, 17-, 18-year-old girls who I liked, but somehow in my upbringing I missed something. I never quite worked out what it was.

For a long time I didn't have any friends. I had my correspondence course for exams and I did well. In twenty months I took my Intermediate, went sailing through without any problem. But I started thinking, 'I'm not doing anything with my life.' I spent Saturday going off to bike shops on my own and I'd stay in on Saturday night, I didn't want to go to the boozer.

I didn't have any male friends, just work. Obviously there were other lads of about my age there but they lived in different parts of Birmingham. Having moved I didn't know anybody. At the time I was into Bob Dylan, I'd got a mammoth number of his records, it was my scene and my language. They were all very depressing – about people who were down and out, at least his early stuff was.

Then I thought, I've got to go out socialising. I was also interested in jazz and at Digbeth there was a jazz club, so I went there a few times. I was quite well up on jazz and I met people there but I was always an early-to-bed person. Going out on a Saturday night, I'd arrive at about 9 and nobody really comes in till about 10 and then they're drinking like fury till about midnight and I'd got to get home again. It wasn't for me.

Then an 18-Plus Club started nearby and I got involved. The club became the only social life I had and it was useful. I heard about it and thought, I must do that. It may have been an undercurrent of wanting to mix with the opposite sex but I thought, I don't know anybody anyway and I wanted a social outlet. Not wanting to join the rugby club or the cricket club, I was a bit stuck. I wasn't interested in traditional masculine activities, going out drinking and so on. I didn't have a male peer group. The other lads I worked with had their own social life because they'd grown up there. I met a chap at 18-Plus. We were good friends. I still didn't get girl friends, but there were women around and I got to know a lot of them and we used go off to binges at various places. I was about 20. I got on the committee and became treasurer – typically, as an accountant.

It didn't interfere with my aim which was to get my exams. I was not under parental pressure to get them but it was a definite objective. Everybody else in the firm was pressuring me because they were used to people who didn't bother. I was naive enough to take it straight in and not argue. I put a lot of time into it, so by the time I was 22 I'd qualified. I went straight through four-year articles, which was a bit unusual, it was the way big professional offices wanted you to do it because they wanted newly qualified people, and there was a big carrot of money involved.

I started going around with this chap from 18-Plus Club, then I got involved with a girl called Dawn. She was a year older than me and I went around with her quite a bit. I was still naive and I didn't know what to do but she was far more of a girl friend. Through her I had met Sarah. There was a library do and I went with Dawn and a couple of others.

Sarah was there. She'd only recently left school and was working in the library temporarily before going to library college.

She came to the 18-Plus Club and I started up with her pretty quickly. One of her problems was her height. She had problems with little lads and being self-conscious about it. I was a bit taller than she was so that was all right and we seemed to get on pretty well, and at the time I had a bust up with Dawn anyway because she was two-timing me. I just told her to hop it. It's not like me at all but sometimes I really get wound up.

Sarah then went to college and by then I'd met her parents. Her father was happy she'd got involved with an accountant rather than some of the herbs she'd been involved with before. She did two years at college and after that we were into the realms of getting married. I was 24 then and she was 21. So we were young, considering we'd gone through school and further education. It's something we've reflected on since. At the time Sarah was happy about it and I didn't mind either but we realised, a decade later when we had children and all sorts of things, that there was a great amount of our life when we never had much freedom. Although she'd gone to college she was already attached and the four mates she lived with were virtually all tied down and unadventurous. We didn't do much splashing about. Whether we would have done is another matter.

I started to branch out, having got a certain amount of confidence with Dawn, and I went off to other 18-Plus do's. I went to Stourport and met a girl there. It was amazing for me, I paired up with her and took her home. I was as naive as anything but I was coming out of myself. Then I shut myself off and the relationship with Sarah became a convenience.

I used to go to see her at college. Being on audits I was away all the time . . . in Wolverhampton, Dudley, Ludlow, Sutton Coldfield and all over the place. I'd stay in hotels, my parents didn't see much of me. Thursday night was 18-Plus night, other nights I got on with my correspondence course. I stayed with the same firm until 1970.

We got married and bought a flat in Edgbaston. Financially I was very flush, my salary was double the rate for car-assembly workers. We lived there about eighteen months and then moved to North Staffordshire, a bungalow in the country. It was a long way from anybody else. Sarah couldn't get a job for a while and got depressed about it. Then a chance came up to work with the mobile library and suddenly we were full of money again because I was doing well and she was too. We extended the house, she had a car and I had a car, because we went different ways. I got another job, exceedingly well paid, and was provided with a car quickly. Then the question of having children came up. Adrian was born and Sarah pulled out of her job, so she was there in the bungalow with him and it was difficult because there wasn't anybody around. Then we found the house we have now.

Sarah was by then developing friendships – which is why my problems started. Up till then she'd been quite ordinary in the sense of someone who'd been working and then had a family, but she started reacting to the fact that she'd had a job she'd enjoyed and she'd given it up for a baby, and the baby was not an enjoyment. It created more demands as well as the demands of having a bigger house. There was a lot of work. She had a friend called Sue and another called Lynn who encouraged her to have her own views and suddenly that tied up with emerging feminist ideas about why were women always giving up things for home and children when in fact you might not find these very interesting.

One day a week Sarah and Sue wouldn't look after their children. When one had a day off she'd drop off the children to the other. At the time they were both doing Open University [OU] courses, which I was quite OK about, but things started getting complicated. She was wanting more of an identity for herself. When she'd done a couple of years OU and our second child had come, Sue was on her third and Lynn was on her second, they were getting quite adamant about their roles.

I thought, OK she can go on about these things but I'm not going to do anything . . . What really put the boot in was when she went to Open University summer school and, true to tradition, she formed a relationship there. She saw it as her salvation and she expected me to take it. I felt jealous. I couldn't accept breaking the traditional role.

She'd been quite conventional till then, in my eyes not in hers. About two weeks before she went to summer school my mother died very suddenly and it threw me upside down and took me months to get over it. I went to marriage guidance and everything, I couldn't work it out. Eventually it settled in me, but the problem was that I couldn't see the problem – this thing of women's roles, my mother did her own thing, but Sarah's upbringing was completely different. It was definitely her father who said 'We're going to do this now' and everybody scurried around and did it. He was the boss and still thinks he is, though his daughters get at him for it.

That caused my system to get completely uptight and caused me to reflect an awful lot, but there wasn't much I could do about it. I was hanging my life around her, I didn't have much else, and work got very complicated because of the recession. I tried to develop outside interests but her involvement with Sue widened. She went to women's conferences and workshops at Camden, things in the women's movement. She knew the local alternative bookshop because that was where you could get the literature. Being a librarian she'd always known about the Women's Press and that sort of thing. There were arguments about should my role change, should we both work as joint people and should I not have the work ethic? Roles kept being thrown up and down and I couldn't work out anything.

I've always been involved in housework and childcare because from my earliest days housework was something you just did. All along I was involved, feeding kids and changing nappies was nothing unusual. But I wasn't committed to destroying my work ethic. I still regarded my breadwinner role as essential. In a depression situation I'd heard of innumerable men who'd changed their jobs and suddenly found there wasn't a job there at all. However nice it was to hold all these other attitudes, I was still responsible for maintaining the status quo in a monetary sense, in my mind money is important because everything I've done works that way. Monetary aspects come into life all the time.

I used to leave for work and get on with it. I might go a long way round and drop the kids off at Sue's on the way, and I'd pick them up on the way home as my contribution, which was not in any way like any other men I knew. It was way outside what other people thought was normal. People at work found it weird. If I said I'd got to fetch the children, Sarah's working, they'd say, 'Why does she do that, why doesn't stay home?' Then I'd have to persuade the boss I had to have a holiday at a particular time because that was when my wife was going to summer school. The relationship of hers died quickly because the other man involved didn't want the responsibility. He was happy with a week's fling and maybe a few days at other times, but he didn't want her as a responsibility. She was trying to latch on to him as something like an escape.

Sarah and the other two women had been friends for a long time but things started getting odd. I didn't know about it until later but Sarah was told by these two, who were both married and one had three kids and the other had five by then, that they were having a lesbian relationship, which caused immense complications because it meant her being excluded. It caused a great deal of heartache to Sarah who felt dropped in the mire.

Then about 1985 an interest in skiing developed. The kids, the elder three of theirs and the elder two of ours, went skiing with the father and Sarah in Scotland and stayed in a hotel. I was looking after our youngest and Sue had their two little ones. I took time off work so they could do it. I accepted it, I'd known him for years. Well, I don't know whether it was a reaction against Sue or what, but those two started a relationship.

When Sarah came back she said that sexual implications were starting. She was not so much scared as she felt it correct to tell me. Afterwards it came out that she wanted my permission, which caused a hell of a problem! Another bloody blow-up that was! Even more complicated, all sorts of other blames started flying around. Sue got quite nasty, even though Sarah had by then been told about her relationship with Lynn. So I was then told about something Sarah had known for a year!

That really turned my whole system upside down! There I was, a naive bloke who'd only had two girl friends in his whole life for more than an evening out. When she told me about it they were going to a Tai-chi class. They were coming back late and I started accusing them, and I was right. It proved to me that my intuition is right. It took me a long time to find out but that's what's come out of it. I tried marriage guidance again and they said, 'What are you defending yourself from? What is it that you are holding on to?' A lot of it is protecting yourself and you develop ideas in your mind which aren't what the other party feels anyway.

I joined the men's group because I got desperate again. I found it useful. I didn't know what other men felt because you couldn't talk to other men about it. I didn't know what other men thought about lots of things. I heard about the group because I was looking for literature on men's experience of feminism, and there isn't much. So I went to the alternative bookshop and that's where Martin told me there was a men's group starting, and come along. I was apprehensive, but it brought home to me a fact which has calmed me down an awful lot, that what you think other men don't think about, they actually do but they won't admit it.

A lot of it is fright at letting feelings out. Men are more frightened about losing face than they'll ever admit. They don't want to be like Rambo but they daren't admit they have other feelings, it's dangerous territory. It goes against men's typical upbringing and that's where problems develop because they won't talk about it. The men in the men's group are more vocal. Being in the men's group helped me a lot.

STEVE

I'm 21 and I'm an art student. I'm not married but I've been in a permanent partnership for four years with a woman who lives in Sheffield. At present I share a house with another men's group member. I was born and brought up in Kent and came to Stoke as a student after a year as student in Maidstone. I study glass design and I hope to set up my own studio when I leave college.

I'm the youngest of six children, my oldest brother is nineteen years older and my youngest is nine years older. I've one sister, seventeen years older. They weren't important models for me because they'd mostly left when I was a child. My nearest brother was the only one at home when I was there. My mother is Catholic, father is not religious. I don't know much about his background. Both had lower middle-class backgrounds. Father was a headmaster until he retired. His father was a Methodist minister. The only grandparent I knew was my mother's father.

My father was in the army and then went straight into teaching. My mother enjoyed the war years. She was in the Women's Land Army. They married just after the war. They're now in their sixties and still together for some reason. I don't why. I'm not sure they know!

My mother had a strict traditional Catholic upbringing, mainly by her mother because her father was away a lot. He was a civil engineer who travelled all round the world. My mother worked part time. When I was born she worked as a hospital auxilliary. Most of my childhood she worked in the food industry, then in a supermarket. Recently she's been working in a nursing home. From school she joined the Women's Land Army and then got married. The Land Army was an important experience. Her upbringing was sheltered. She went to a convent school. The Land Army was an opening out. There were Italian prisoners of war working on the land. It was the first time she'd met men.

She was more intellectual than my Dad. She knows that. He must have done well to become a headmaster, but he was basically a hard worker. I don't know much about him. Men don't talk to their fathers about personal things and my Mum blocked me doing that. She was possessive. She made sure I didn't have a relationship with him. At the time it didn't bother me because she'd done a good job of telling me what a bastard he was and how he wasn't worth spending time with. She did that from birth to when I started to question it. She brought me up and I had less and less contact with him. She did that to all of us. We all reached an age when we realised he was worth knowing and spent time getting to know him and hating her for it and then getting to somewhere in the middle.

My father had a couple of breakdowns. It was easy to say he was weak and no good. Mum's opinion is that women are superior to men, she has said so. She gave me the impression she was better than him. She says he only became a headmaster because he was hard working, but he was working hard because he wasn't getting what he wanted from the relationship. He turned to work because he wasn't getting emotional support. He's quite a family man but he wasn't allowed to be. He's quite a broken man, he's been so dominated. I'm not sure if he was like that before his breakdowns and before forty-odd years of a relationship that didn't work too well. I've several nephews and he was quite physical with them, and his grandchildren. He'd hug them and sit with them, so he obviously wanted to do that with me, but the way my mother brought me up stopped me doing that. It didn't feel comfortable. I didn't believe men weren't capable of it but I was led to believe men weren't worth showing emotions to.

I regret it because I could have a good relationship with my father now if my mother wasn't around. They still both want your time and you have to divide it up, see one in their space and then the other. There's jealousy between them. I still feel torn but it's getting easier, because I'm more in control. I feel sure enough now to hug my Dad when I see him. It's easier if there's a break and you see somebody again. It's only recently I've managed to start hugging him. I don't feel completely comfortable doing it, but I want to show him I care. My mother made him lonely.

I wouldn't say my mother's a strong person, there's a kind of vulnerable strength. She needed to bring the family towards her. It always felt like a war going on. You had to be one side or the other. Today I choose to be in the middle. They can fight it out for themselves. I didn't want to see much of him because that was how I'd been taught to be. My earliest memories of him were coloured by how I was told he was. I had a feeling of him not understanding me. When I was 3 he took me to the sea. I was scared of the water but he still took me to the sea and that was evidence to me that he didn't understand me.

I was sheltered from my brothers' and sister's views because they'd left home and could talk about it with people their own age. My nearest brother seemed to be my father's favourite. The rest of us looked like my Mum. He looks more like my Dad. They did more things together but I've still got the feeling that he was more supportive of my mother than my Dad, but he did get on with my Dad. Dad introduced him to masculine activities. He tried to do that with me but I blocked it, or my mother did. I remember he used to make jokes like, 'Do you want a doll for Christmas?' Reinforcing male ideas that way. He was traditional in his views on men and women. If he said anything about being male it was a 'normal' view.

My mother was – not independent but separate. If she'd been growing up today she'd probably be a separatist from men but her views were coloured by being a Catholic. She thought women were superior and that if a job was worth doing it was worth being done by a woman. Intellectually superior, tougher. She thinks that if you can't take things you're being male . . . she'd never show any emotion. Even when my grandfather died she refused to cry at the funeral. She considers emotion weak.

It's something that's got increasingly ingrained. If she thought my father wasn't coping she'd make herself cope more. She took on most of running the family herself and she needed to be tough to do that with six children. It must have involved a lot of work and working part time as well from about the time I was born. I don't think my Dad ever wanted her to work but she wanted financial independence. She didn't like taking housekeeping, although at the same time saw it as her right.

My sister was quite a big influence on me. She liked me a lot, we still get on well. She was that much older and she'd gone through being used and pushed around and she could see it happening to me. She was a hippy at that time. She was quite a strong woman like my mother, but she's not afraid to say she can't cope, though she does still take too much on. That's a trait we've been given. I'm trying to learn when to say I've had enough.

My sister is a caring person and takes time with people. I learnt how not to do it from my Mum. My sister takes time with me and it's far more on an equal feeling because I knew, although she was so much older, that she was my sister. There was a generation in between us but you could ignore that. I've always tried to be older than I am. I hated being treated as a kid and my views not being listened to.

My brothers' influence was a bit of a mixture. One brother went into social work and he cares about people. He was a good model for me. I didn't necessarily think of it in gender terms at the time but he was one male who took time with people. So there were a few influences around, like women being strong and capable and assertive and men who had a caring side and were showing it. My nearest brother was the one I spent most time with. He has never got over how Mum treated him. He still seems unassertive and unsure of things.

It was a kind of dominance my Mum had. This sounds like stereotyping but among Catholic women there's a martyr kind of model. She'll do anything for you but she'll make you feel guilty about it without even seeming to. She's doing her 'duty' and giving everything up for you. Sacrifice, like saying 'Look what I'm doing for you.' I've a lot of resentment about it but it's mellowing now. It may not sound like it. I went through some time hating. I was brought up to hate my Dad which switched to feeling sorry for him and hating my mother. Now I feel sorry for them both. They tried their hardest but it happened not to be right for me. One thing I was taught was not to show anger, so it took time to come out. I took on a combination of her qualities of not showing anger, keeping working and not giving in to emotion, but at the same time unassertive as well. My nearest brother took on unassertiveness without the surface manner. He hasn't come out of that. I've still some way to go too.

I didn't have any early friendships because I didn't go to nursery school. We were brought up by my Mum the whole time. I didn't know anybody my own age before I went to school. It was a baby-boom year so my year was full and I was put into the year above because there wasn't any room. So I spent two years in that instead. Again I was with people slightly older. There was less play involved. That's what I wanted. I wouldn't have liked sitting around playing in sandpits.

I had two school friends, a boy and a girl. I spent a lot of time with the girls rather than the boys. It made me feel better. I didn't want to be running around getting into fights and posing. I didn't mix much with the others. I was shy. They made fun of me for being with the girls. It was mild really. I got a lot more of that when I was at secondary school. I was good at the work and that was another reason I got picked on.

I wasn't interested in games but I did play football for my primary school for about a year. I enjoyed that because my nearest brother was also into football. I wanted to be like him but I didn't want to get involved in fights. I didn't want to do anything wrong. It was my Catholic upbringing. I went to a Catholic school from 11 to 13 but primary school was Church of England. I enjoyed school less and less as I got older.

The friend who was a girl, we drifted apart as as we got older and she felt more self-conscious about having a boy as a friend. By the time I left I didn't know her that well. I still felt older than the others and thought about things more. I tended to get pissed off when they were childish. I didn't want anything to do with that. That's also why I thought more about school work than about playing games and fights.

As toys I didn't like Action Men . . . they were dolls – I saw through the packaging. I did some playing with guns but it was just playing. It felt a childish thing to do. I got paint and that sort of thing a lot. I was involved in artistic things even then and I read a lot, probably more than most people my age. The books varied. I enjoyed traditional boys' adventure books and I was into science fiction and science, how it would be in the future. I used to read about space stuff. Quite a lot was learning things. I read about electronics, that's quite a boys' thing, building bricks and Lego as well, construction – Meccano, I really liked that. I never quite understood it but I liked it. That's usually considered a boys' toy. I think I'd have refused to play with something I thought was a girls' toy. I don't know why that was. My mother's influence might have led me to think girls' things were superior.

They'd just phased out the ll-plus exam. I did two years at a mixed Catholic middle school. It increased my tendency to be with the girls rather than the boys. I played football in the playground but the people I talked to were girls. I didn't want to do what I had to do to conform. I felt increasingly isolated. It went a lot further when I moved on to an all-boys' school at 13. I preferred female company. That was the case until I made a conscious decision that it wasn't going to be any more. That was when I was about 15, when I got involved with people who were thinking about sexism and so on. From then on I went on to closer contact with men.

At one stage I wondered about my sexualtiy because you got called it a lot. It's a strange thing, if you are with girls a lot you must be gay! I remember when I was about 14, feeling chuffed because I started finding women attractive – so I couldn't be gay. At that time it felt important that I wasn't that much not male, although there was never any going out with girls involved. A lot of boys seemed to go out with girls from 10 on, but it never occurred to me to do that.

It was a more noticeable change at senior school, an all-boys' school. Suddenly a whole section of people I'd communicated with were gone, the ones I'd felt easiest with. It was a shock to find myself in an all-boys' school – appalling! Also it was a very right-wing school, any emotions were out. There was the Combined Cadet Force [CCF] and rugby . . . like an old traditonal grammar school, anything feminine was frowned on. I had problems with bullying, not feeling I was fitting in and not wanting to be there. I was happy going there at first because my nearest brother had been there and he'd had a good time. I remember it when he was in the sixth form which is more open, and he could do things like sport, so he fitted in.

I ended up taking a lot of time off, partly because I was ill but also I had no reason not to be ill. If I wasn't ill it would mean I'd have to go back to school and what was the use of that? I tore my knee ligaments and that didn't heal for months and months. I wasn't sorry about it. After that I had glandular fever. I never deliberately played truant but my body was protecting me in a way. I was wary of fights and games where I might get hurt. There was always somebody slightly more picked on than me but I was always one step away. There was a constant threat. It was mainly name-calling. Occasionally you'd get something thrown at you rather than punched. There was a lot of ganging up. They objected that I wasn't a traditional male, a rugby-playing CCF member. Increasingly I didn't want to be like that. They seemed . . . basically fascistic . . . wanted to be in the National Front. I could see a clear model of what I didn't want to be. It pushed me further the other way.

I didn't take part in games much. I didn't enjoy them. It was so competitive, I didn't want to be involved . . . the games were very macho-physical. Some teachers were sympathetic because they saw I wasn't fitting in, but some were like boys who'd not grown up. They'd gone to that kind of school and straight into teaching, didn't know anything different. A lot were leaders in the CCF. There was a woman teacher, there weren't many, but she was a history teacher. She taught me in the fourth year and I think she was sympathetic because her politics were similar and she could see . . . when bullying takes place it's out of sight . . . but it's clear when somebody isn't getting on.

The whole atmosphere was not congenial. It started off not right and got worse and worse. One or two I could talk to – never friends – the kind you never quite trust. If it came down to it and somebody started picking on you for your politics – they had the same politics, or they'd make out they did. There were people who couldn't pretend to be macho but had enough in common with the bullies to get by. It's interesting to think about the ones who didn't quite fit, what they did – kept to right-wing politics so they were OK, or in the CCF. They acted tough now and then with a person they knew was less tough than them.

Others camped it up the whole time and got away with it . . . one has since come out as gay. I don't know about the others. They were accepted because they made a joke . . . there was never any suggestion they were gay. It was like bringing the subject up before anyone else could . . . maybe it was the only way they could deal with their sexuality in that environment. I didn't think, 'They're gay and covering it up' because it was so macho, right-wing, what they did, making fun of it.

I wasn't conscious of gender at the time. I got increasingly unhappy at school. It wasn't just that suddenly there weren't any women around. I got more and more isolated. I didn't have contact with women outside school until my fourth year when I started to go out in the evenings. I joined the Campaign for Nuclear Disarmament – people in their thirties with one or two younger who I didn't feel comfortable enough to talk to. It was about a year before I got to know them. Then I went to Friends of the Earth and met people who'd been involved in more things. They were late teens, early twenties, alternative enough to accept me. That made school tougher because there was more contrast – I was aware it didn't have to be like that.

Again I was with people older than me, people my age had nothing to offer me. That's still the case with the men's group. They're all older than me, and at college, in my department there's a lot of mature students but they don't act mature enough for me. I act towards them more on a level but maybe it comes down to personality differences. They don't want to care about lots of things.

What led me to join CND and Friends of the Earth was that my politics supported them and I wanted to make a protest. I came to those views because of my parents' politics – my Mum was a lifelong Liberal. Dad was lifelong Labour until the SDP came along. Originally my politics had been woolly liberal like my Mum's, because she was who I'd identified with, but I wanted stronger change and felt the Liberals wouldn't do anything, just talk about it. I got more anti-political and when I was 16 or 17 I was anarchist. That was an influence of the people I mixed with then.

There never was anybody in my family who was right-wing, other than my grandparents, they were Tory, but they were old style Tory, pre-Thatcher, when the Tories had a social conscience as well. So my influence had been Liberal but my brothers they had all gone through a stage of radical politics in spite of Catholic upbringing. There's only one brother who is not a Labour voter. He's still a Catholic and has kept my Mum's politics.

There was no major move for me from right to left. I'm surprised I didn't react more against my parents' views. The time I'd have started to react I had this clear model of what being right-wing meant . . . all those boys trying to beat me up, and I already had views about not wanting to oppress women. At about 11 I mouthed my mother's views on women's rights which were basically separatist feminist but in a Liberal way. Her view was that women should be able to do what they want but Women's Lib was a bit extreme. You shouldn't shout about it, just get on with it quietly.

My views started to change – why shouldn't you shout about it? She thought women should be allowed to do what they wanted but men weren't capable of doing what women did, there was something sexist about that attitude. When I got involved in CND and Friends of the Earth I began to mix, I suppose, with the sixties generation grown up, who I had sympathy with already, because my brother and sister were that age group and I always felt good about being born in the sixties. I've a hazy picture of it as a time when people were trying hard to get things right even if in a crude way. My sister was a hippy for a while.

I felt sympathetic to the ideas that came out of that era. On women's issues they were pretty appalling, but for me the link was things like CND re-emerging. Being in those groups helped me be an adult which I always wanted to be and in that situation people treated you equally. That was a contrast with school and home as well. My mother never treated me like a child but at the same time you could never do what you could if you were an adult – 'If you pick up a plate to wash it I'll take it off you and push you out.' It was the martyr thing. That was the only time I had physical contact with my Mum, when I tried to do housework and she'd push me away. She was starting to hold me back.

At school I favoured arts subjects, where I could express myself, but the school was geared towards sciences. It was part of the macho thing. So if you were doing arts subjects you weren't treated as seriously. When I was 8 or 9 I enjoyed science. I didn't identify science as being macho and therefore go against it, but boys that got involved in it were that way. In the third year we had a large loud CCF dominant tutor for chemistry who most people liked. He put me off and scared me. I gave it up at the end of that year. I always enjoyed drawing although I wasn't terribly good at it until later. I also enjoyed history. Science I did less and less. Biology linked with nature for me. I enjoyed that but I tended to get macho shits for tutors and that was off-putting, it means you don't ask questions. . . .

For A levels I did art, politics and history. They were good choices. Art I wanted to do anyway and politics . . . one tutor was a local Labour Party candidate. I didn't feel I could say anything in his lessons but I felt safer there because he knew the answers, he could deal with the fascists and put them down quickly. That reassured me. A levels were easier to get on with because I could express myself more. There were fewer rules and I was involved with things outside school. I was thinking more positively rather than trying to live from day to day. I had a section of my life I enjoyed rather than feeling there wasn't any point in doing anything.

In the sixth form I had more confidence in myself because I started to get good at art and that's what I wanted to do anyway. I nearly left at 16 because I'd had enough of school. I only stayed because it was a tradition in our family. I thought, I'll give it a term and if I cope with it I'll carry on. I still had trouble with the macho crowd but things were slightly more personal because you had smaller groups . . . and people started to grow up a bit more – not always fascist but only conservative!

The friendships of a group of people a few years older helped. I was welcomed because of what I believed in rather than being outside because of it. That felt good. It was an area where I could grow. At first it was a relaxation and opening out, then a growing, particularly when I started to go to a men's group when I was 18. I was still at school. There was a strong women's group in Maidstone. They held a mixed meeting on male violence and we thought it would be good to do something else with the men there. We had a core of men who were there and partners of women involved in CND. It came more out of the women's group than out of what men were doing. Feminist ideas were an influence.

Our first meetings were difficult because we felt we needed to get closer to other men and there were unresolved things. We decided we couldn't just be a feminist group, it needed to be about ourselves too, but it was a response to seeing how women were, and thinking why men mistreated them. We sympathised with women's situation and wanted to understand what men were doing. I'd been oppressed by other men but also by my mother but that was a thing you weren't allowed to talk about in those kinds of politics. Within a women's group situation it would be hard to raise – thinking about oppression of men. To criticise women for oppressing men is dodgy ground! It's hard enough for men to accept.

My partner is the only partner I've ever had, I met her at that stage . . . through feminist politics. She'd written to *Spare Rib* saying she'd recently moved to Maidstone and was lonely and wanted to meet other people – she didn't specify other women, she wanted to meet anybody she could share with. She was in a right-wing single-sex school, the other half of my school. A woman friend of ours wrote on behalf of us all saying would you like to meet us? I was occasionally a reader of *Spare Rib* at that time. I came across it through this group of close friends. One of them would buy it and pass it round. It was a woman that bought it but it wasn't presented like, 'This is a woman's thing, keep away.' It was like, 'There's this good article. Do you want to read it?' So we discussed them.

There were four of these friends, two men and two women, who had a close friendship before I came into that group. Because we were all political people we talked about politics. My partner came into that. We started to do more varied things. It's been a strong thing for our relationship. We came together because we wanted someone safe we could talk to and it stood us in good stead. The fact that she was a woman meant we could get closer quicker. My sexuality was heterosexual. I still found it easier to talk to women than to men, I was closer to the women in the group than the men, and when I started going to the men's group after that, it was partly a decision to try to change that.

After A levels I did a foundation course at Maidstone Art College. It was a shock coming back to a mixed education system again. It felt weird for a while. One advantage of going into art was that I didn't need to be academic. You need five O levels but your A-level grades aren't important. That got me out of having to play the game at school. They were after high grades and people going to Oxbridge. I didn't want to play the status game. This was more an expression of myself and it's got more the case and more important, self-expression, it had been put down so long at school. If I expressed myself it wouldn't have been anything people could accept. So it would be double trouble really. I was trying to break out from the oppression I felt at school and from the hangups my parents had left me with – shyness and failure to feel my emotions well.

It's a typical experience of men, most emotions are suppressed but it came from my mother in my case. I picked that up and then school confirmed it as the way for me, in that if I said anything I got bullied, so the best thing to do was not to say much. It was useful defence mechanism, the problem was that when I no longer needed that it was part of my behaviour as a man because if I didn't have the macho side then I had to have this other side, this quiet not being in touch with feelings side. I was aware of sensitive feelings that came out through my art, and deciding to take it up as study, and being interested in nature and caring about things which I was aware men weren't supposed to do, I felt very isolated.

Feeling it didn't have to be that way really began once I met my partner. She was a solid support for me. I still felt isolated despite the men's group who were good safety point for me, and CND and Friends of the Earth, but they only lasted two hours at a time and she was around for me all the time and knew enough about me to say, 'Why do you do that?' I didn't feel threatened by her doing that. I met her when I was still in the sixth form. The first night I was with her I was quiet, I talked so quietly you could hardly hear me. I was shy, continually blushing and scared of people, even in a shop, scared of having to talk to anybody in a shop because I'd got into a high state of this distancing.

She liked the fact that I wasn't macho and that I was quiet. There was the feeling that I was safe. She'd had an unstable childhood, her Dad had left home and she sided with her mother who was becoming strongly feminist at the time. She was wary of men. The fact that we met through *Spare Rib* made her feel I was safe. I felt her to be a strong character, determined. I liked that and we had a shared hurt from our childhood. We had a lot in common and aware that life was not easy and that we were victims of our past. We were doing our best but we didn't have the information to make other choices. I felt I had a safe space to talk. That's been important in our relationship.

One reason I moved to Stoke was that I was fed up with the south because it's so unfriendly. I knew it was friendlier up here. It was the minimum far enough north to get away from my parents. I didn't want to be within visiting distance. I wanted somewhere else I could call my home. We both felt a good move for us would be to get out of the south. I was freeing myself to grow in a different way. I still feel the south is an oppressive part of the country, people's attitudes and how they're brought up to be. It's so insular, everybody wanting to get what they want, never mind anybody else. When I visited Stoke to see the college they were from a different planet! I still find Stoke people the friendliest I've ever met. I'm really glad I came here. I could feel people weren't out to get me.

Students are so superficial, how they live. I'm here to study, to find out about my course and about myself and about another part of the country. They are into doing things which I've not found interesting like going to pubs, getting drunk, smoking drugs, things I feel are barriers between me and finding out about people. My ideal when I'm talking to somebody is to be talking to them without alcohol, in a house rather than a pub. Alcohol is an artificial way of enlivening the conversation. The first year in Stoke I was living in a tower block full of students and still isolated. I wasn't with anybody from my course. I didn't go to student societies. I was commuting to Sheffield to see my partner who was studying there. So I felt my life had another side to it, attached somewhere else.

I had moved to a place where I could be friendlier with people and carried on with my old shyness and out of touch with feelings. The men's group was an important step for me. I remember feeling relief when I saw a poster up at college and even more relieved when I found it wasn't a student group but an ordinary people group! It felt like a lifeline to me. That was in November of my first year, the group had been going six months or so when I joined it. That was a safety point for me, where I could start to think again about why I was the way I was. I'd done an assertiveness course with the men's group in Maidstone, so I could see there was an alternative and had glimpses of being able to live that alternative.

When anybody wants to make a change in their lives they need people around pushing them on and reminding them of what they'd committed themselves to doing. I felt the men's group here definitely helped me that way. During the first year I went to it, it was important to me. It slipped after a while and that increased with going more to Sheffield, but it helped me realise I didn't have to conform to the ideal of a macho man. There were other men trying to be the way I wanted to be and having the same problems I was having in being it – like-minded men who shared the same experiences, breaking down the isolation, seeing there were alternatives. It wasn't easy to live how we wanted because there are few out there to support us in doing it but there was an alternative.

It was liberating to hear people being so in touch with their feelings and it was a way of getting over what had happened in my past. I did some co-counselling with one of the men's group. I learned a lot from that. It made me realise that from about 14 I'd been determined to change the way I'd been. I was aware of being dissatisfied. I started to get contacts outside the men's group and at that point I wanted to start pushing myself more. I found the men's group then held me back a bit because people do things at different speeds and some of the men at the group wanted to grow more slowly. I wanted to push back my barriers. I also started to feel I'd been in men's groups for a couple of years then and I was beginning to say the same things over again and what I needed was to act on it. I felt the men's group in Maidstone had been closer than the Stoke group, partly to do with it being smaller and a more regular membership. The Stoke group was more fluctuating. We did some good social things but I wasn't getting enough new stimulation to behave differently. We did an assertiveness day and I felt that was how I want it to be.

My most recent growing experience has been in something called ISA [Institute of Self Analysis]. It cleared the past for me and I see everything as a learning experience. The men's group helped me. I still had a lot of guilt about being a man, it's always men who do terrible things. That was from my mother. Now I feel it's up to me to stop men behaving that way. The most immediate way I can do that is by behaving in a positive male image myself. I feel far happier being male. I was quite jealous of women that they could give birth, but now I feel we do one thing, they do the other. I look forward to having children. I feel much more at ease and I can feel what I'm capable of being as a man. I'm aware I have certain advantages getting places, but once I'm there I can behave differently and start to change people. I want to change other men too.

One thing about my glass work in studying art is that I've challenged the way men 'should' behave. Glass is traditionally seen as a feminine material to work in, as an art material it's dominated by women. It was a chance for me to use a material which was feminine identified. That's one reason I chose that material. It was a strong consideration, 'Why are all these women choosing it and men aren't? That must be a good reason for me to choose it.' I was aware of that. It's been good for me to express myself in, because the work I do is in touch with that side of me too. I can create far more balanced pieces of work. As an artist this is important. I see other men on the course still trying to be macho but I see male and female as complementary rather than opposites and it's a chance to bring them together and balance them.

I wouldn't be doing this work now if I hadn't had the chance to see things differently. Before, I felt I had to make definite statements but now I can be relaxed about it. My personality flows through my work. I'm not just expressing my redefined sense of being a man through my artistic work but also, I hope, helping to influence other people. That's important. We are screwing up the world at the moment – men particularly. I need a definite outlook for myself, and for women I need it so they see it's not necessary to hate all men, and for other men to see they don't have to behave in the stereotypical way. It's a demonstration to both sexes and myself. This is the right way to be.

It has gone together with developing my relationship with Sue. We've both grown together and share more and more. I've realised I don't have to be a quiet male, I can be angry if I need to be, or excited. I don't have to be on a level because that's not a natural way to behave. It's not being true to myself. If I'm in touch with my emotions then I can choose 'Do I need to be angry in this situation or not?' Being in touch with how I'm feeling every moment and being conscious of what's going on within me is different from the traditional man. It's my ideal to be aware of what's going on within me and to be aware of what other people are needing.

My views on marriage are changing. I spent a long time despising anybody who was married. I ruled it out completely. I don't need that legal thing to stay with Sue. A lot of marriages are a cop-out, with that bit of paper people don't bother working at it. I'll see how I feel later on. I'm moving to Sheffield soon. I've decided I want to be full time with Sue. The last six months we've had a house in Sheffield and I go there whenever I can. I'll always live up north. I like the people and get more done. There's less bullshit to cut through to get on with people.

I intend to have a family. I see myself as being very involved. Being a parent is one of the biggest growing experiences I could ever have . . . I've chosen 50 per cent responsibility in having a family so 50 per cent of the time it's up to me. I want to spend two or three years in a well-paid job, doing anything, to find out what it's like and get enough money to support my family well. In a way I copped out of my responsibility. I thought men are supposed to be breadwinners so I'm not going to be a breadwinner. But it's as much a responsibility as ever for me to be a breadwinner, as much as it is Sue's. I used to veer away from that.

After a few years I intend to give up work and be with the children for a while, and Sue can work for a while. We can take it in turns. I imagine myself as a househusband and active father and a breadwinner alternately. That also relates to my glass work. I can perhaps do some of that when being a househusband for a while. The key for me always is my relationships with people, not my work. My priority list is my family, then my work and then personal growth, though all three are important. I'd never do anything which distances me from Sue or my family.

Chapter 4

Manual home backgrounds

More fully represented in my sample were men from solid working-class home backgrounds (see also Anthony), but unlike the stereotyped portrayal of English working-class upbringing presented in Tolson's book (1977: 40–6), all three men who tell their stories in this chapter had nurturing non-traditional fathers. Simon and Terry were from intact families but Tim, whose life story is I feel in many ways the most moving in the whole book, came from a family where he was the youngest of five sons brought up by a lone father. Both Simon and Terry were significantly influenced by feminist partners, whereas Tim, as he says, 'grew up in a men's group.'

TIM

I'm 30. I've been married seven years and I have two daughters aged 3 and 1. I'm a primary school teacher. I teach 7- and 8-year-olds but my training and experience were in infant teaching. I took the juniors job to get into Derbyshire. As it's at the lower end of juniors there's not much difference. I like young children. I always wanted to work with children somehow. My other ambition was going round the world, that's why I studied anthropology at university. I managed to achieve one of them.

I had two years doing any old job to live and pay for the house while I did some research that never got off the ground. Going into schools and seeing what younger children were like and relationships you can have with children, I decided I wanted young ones.

My Dad is retired. He was a printer from 14 years of age in Manchester. He worked on newspapers occasionally but it was mainly things like cartons and packaging. My mother died when I was 2. I don't remember anything about her other than photographs and things my Dad has told me. All my memories are of a childhood spent without a mother but with the memory of a mother still there. I was brought up on that. It was something I cherished. My mother's father was a bus driver in Manchester.

I'm the youngest of five brothers. I'm not sure whether my brothers wanted her memory kept alive or felt discomfort because they remembered her but because I was so young I don't think I was traumatised by it. It was just part of my childhood. I can't remember what it was like. I remember crying for my Dad not for my Mum. My household was absolutely all-male. There was no female input whatsoever. Occasionally home helps from Social Services came round to cook and clean but they soon went. I only remember once when my maternal grandmother came round to cook a meal when my father broke his leg. She lived in Manchester too.

All my early memories are of Manchester and being cared for by my Dad and my bigger brothers, trouping around with them. It was a male-oriented environment. My experiences and the way they're internalised may be slightly different to how they are in my brothers. My eldest brother was 10 when my mother died, the next 8, the next 7, the next 5 and I was 2.

My mother was a librarian before she was married, but of course I had no experience of a woman in paid work. My Dad's experiences of marriage were in a lot of ways traditional. I've tried to look at the reasons why he was able to take on what he did. He went out to work, he brought home the money, and his wife looked after the kids and fed him amply and feathered his nest, which he enjoyed.

The breadwinner role was important to him. He worked in a male-dominated environment, very macho, he's got tattoos on his arms – but talking to him, he seems to have lived a double life, and still does. Going to work he switched to his work-role and persona, more masculine in the traditional sense, competitive and vulgar and sexist and exploitative and degrading, and jokey camaraderie. He hated it at the same time as loving it, which a lot of men do. From early on I knew it was a release for him from his house and his commitments to his children but I knew that as soon as he was away from work he was running home to do whatever was needed.

He carried on with his job to bring in the money. He took some time off at first but nothing much. He got things organised pretty quickly. He had to get on with it. He could either make the decision not to take it on or to look after his children, or we could live in extreme poverty by him giving up his job. He didn't do that and it was probably the right decision to make, looking at the way one-parent families are financially.

He stopped doing overtime for ages, which meant he worked 8 to 5, and his work was 200 yards from our primary school. A family close to school were after-school child minders when I was very young and my elder brothers took a lot of responsibility for looking after me. Also I was let into nursery school when I was only 2. That was lucky. We were church members and it was a Church of England school. My mother had been a churchgoer and a respected figure. From talking to people in the area, she was well known and liked. It was a great shock to people that a woman could die so young with so many children. She was only 31. Our image came from that, knowing we were motherless. We had a lot of sympathy. I had lots from teachers.

My father chose not to do the traditional thing, find another woman to look after his children. He rejected advances, either through suspicion or memory of his wife. He's an emotional chap with strong ties to individuals, certainly his wife, who he knew for such a short time when I think about it. He was married nearly eleven years and I've been married for nearly seven and I think how short it seems. His relationship with her must have played an important part in his decision, given the way he talks about it. It was a good relationship. I think that's underrated, individual relationships and how they affect people's actions. There was a sense of loyalty, and once the momentum got going, a kind of fortress mentality, him and the kids against the world. He was determined to cope, not just be seen to do it but to do it. He doesn't ask for any recognition and never has done, though I try to give it him.

I was talking to my Dad yesterday and he mentioned that once when his overtime was cut while he was married, my mother had to go to work part time. He looked after the children in the evening. He'd come in from work and she'd go out to temporary part-time work at a store. So he had practical experience of looking after children before she died. It also shows his income was marginal, if he didn't have overtime money they were short. They were dependent on overtime as most working-class families are.

He was an only child and so hadn't looked after younger brothers or sisters. He may have had a good relationship with his mother but he was by no means an expert at childcare and was bad at practical aspects of housework. He learned from scratch. He copied a lot of the things he'd seen his wife do. He'd bake the same cakes, with terrible results, the same meals on the same days, in the same order, to maintain consistency.

The house was a terrible mess, you'd think it was squalor. It was just unskilled. He only did essential stuff and now and again we all had a thrash at it. We all went to the laundry on a Sunday. We had a washing machine when my mother was alive but when it broke it wasn't fixed and we had to go to the laundry. He didn't do any ironing. Clothes were festooned in one big room, you went to get your clothes where they were. Ironing is a thing I don't do now. I can but I hate it. I'll clean the toilet, stick my hand down it or anything, but I don't like ironing. I don't mind anything else. My second-eldest brother is the best ironer. He did it for himself from early on. He just did his own unless someone wanted something for a special occasion. I did it for myself as a teenager when I got into having to look respectable for girls.

There was a division of labour between us. Dad must have organised it. First the oldest one did most and as we grew up the others did more. I did all kinds of things around the house from an early age, even ironing on special occasions, shopping and everything. Because we weren't organised we'd shop every day, there were shops a few yards from school. As my brothers left primary school the ones still there did the shopping. By the time I was 8 or 9 I was doing it on my own. There was never a list. I knew where the stuff was on the shelves. We always did it by memory.

Before my mother died Dad changed nappies and bathed us when he came home. Listening to the kind of woman my mother was I don't think he'd have got away without doing it. He pulled his weight when needed. She was a strong character and influential, outside the family and within.

My father was a very nurturing man at home. I've a memory of a man with two identities. I was aware of his work identity. He'd say what he did at work and that he hated it, although I knew he enjoyed the escape. He took me to see what it was like, I waited outside for him after school. I once waited outside all afternoon when the school closed early – from one o'clock until five. I didn't tell anybody I couldn't be looked after, so I just waited for him.

He didn't tell us in detail about his work. He told us all about the nastier side and that we should stay away from it. He didn't want us to go into printing at all costs. He wasn't happy at work but it gave him distance from the awful reality of being left with five children. He'd served an apprenticeship when he was young. His father was a printer too.

Before his wife died he turned from job to job within printing, always looking for more money. He was not content staying where he was. He always says he hated work but there's an enormous paradox, he hated it for keeping him away from his children but he loved it because he could get away from them. He hated it for the type of place it was but he loved it because a change was as good as a rest. There was a time when he absolutely absorbed himself in work. Talking to people that knew him in the sixties, he was like a Stakhanovite, to clear his brain of the pressures of bringing up children.

On occasions he found it burdensome but a strategy he developed was to get us out of the city at weekends and certainly on a Sunday. We'd come out here to the Peak District and go rock climbing and mountaineering, adventurous things. One of my earliest memories is walking around here, where I live now. It's a kind of soul-base for me here. We did that with rucksacks on our backs in a little troup. It was part of his strategy to get out of the mess we were in. We were different from other people.

I remember my childhood as happy and totally secure, except for the memory of knowing that I'd lost my mother, nothing else. My father was very loving, absolutely. I can remember being slapped but that's a normal part of childcare. For a long time I slept in the same bed as him. I remember crying my head off when I had to go into my own bed and I must have been more than 5. I was very attached to him.

I've modelled myself on his ideas and practices. I could list them. The attitude I have towards relationships is based on his absolute commitment to five children, and I've got the same absolute commitment. I also have the same absolute commitment he had to his wife. My attitude to work and home is similar. I've also taken on board his selflessness. He's totally selfless and I also have few expectations or requirements for myself.

I thought money was tight and that with my Dad not doing overtime we were poor. My brothers say it was bad management, but either way, money was tight. He was a printer and in working-class terms they were the 'labour aristocracy.' He must have been pulling in good money because he was number two on the payroll, which meant he was the second highest blue-collar worker in the printing works – but five children demand a lot of money. I think it was a combination of a lowering of income and bad financial management based on lack of experience.

I'm not putting him down, absolutely not! I forgive him. I feel very loving towards him. I well up when I talk about it. It's so important to me. My relationship with him has been so fundamental in my own personal development and the way I perceive the world. I admire him a lot. His story is amazing, I'll write it down one day. The only reason I haven't is that my priority is my wife and family. I don't want to spend time on words. One day I'll do it, I hope before he dies. It's a story worth telling.

It was a ramshackle and making-do-by-any-means set up, our home life. The only relations around were all relations of my mother. She had three brothers and a sister. They were around but not in any day-to-day caring role, only things like day visits every now and again. Both my father's parents died before he was married so I've no memory of them. In the summer we used to go to my Gran's, my mother's mother. We walked there every day, about 2 miles, in the holidays, and she'd look after us. Dad gave her money for it, for the meals. There were no other relations helping much. It was as though everything was normal. That's how he wanted it.

Maybe he rejected help. An important incident was when Social Services tried to alleviate the situation. They tried to get another family to adopt me because I was the youngest. We visited them but when Dad found out what was going on he rejected it outright and took us home quickly. He wanted to keep the family together. He was aware people thought it wasn't a thing a man could do. He was determined to prove he could. The principle is deep in my mind that these are things men can do and it's nonsense to think otherwise. If you want to do something you have a go.

I don't need to be as determined as that in anything I do because none of my situations necessitates that. His was desperate. He had to prove either to himself or others that he could do it, disprove the idea that men don't look after children. I don't have to prove that, because he did. I don't have to prove men can be infant teachers. I don't have to prove I can do things around the house or change nappies or bath babies. I perceive them as jobs to be done, I share them because that's the way our relationship is. Apart from ironing that's the way I perceive everything. It's as much my role as hers, absolutely.

My brothers were also very important to me, more so when I was young than when I was a teenager. They were protectors in a hostile and sometimes violent world. I never got into many scrapes but my brothers did, and they kept me out of them. They didn't let me go to the youth club where they went. They tried to keep me away from all the bad places, though I managed to get to a few when I was older and they were less involved. One of my eldest brothers had a reputation as a street fighter and we all had a tough reputation, which I didn't participate in.

Our part of Manchester was a tough place, inner city, very working class. It was a 'twilight zone' of bedsitters, students and prostitutes, quite cosmopolitan, West Indians and then increasingly Asians. The area around was council housing. Our house was an owner-occupied semi-detached. A lot of those had been turned into flats but we kept ours as a large family house. It must have been respectable when they moved there in the late fifties but the area had deteriorated, or you could say it got more colourful! It deteriorated to the point where there was regular muggings and rapes and murders and fights and things you get in inner-city areas. So I needed protecting by my brothers and I was guided away from the worst aspects of that kind of life. Being a family of boys, people expected you to be tough but the others lived up to that more than I did.

I played with children in the street and friends at school. I never had a 'best friend' at school, always a group of three or four. My education right through was in mixed schools. My friends at primary school were mainly boys though I did have a girl friend. At secondary school and in my older teens most of my friends and people I went around with were girls.

In an all-male household I'd had no experience of girls at all. I'm not sure how important my girl friend at primary school was. I don't know how long it lasted, it was on and off. We were friendly but it was no more than a kiss on the way home. I don't think we played together. I always played football or cricket with lads in the street or in the park. At school I was in all the teams for everything. I've always played football.

I wasn't aware of gender differences at school. I was totally absorbed in the idea that boys do certain things and girls do other things. The only things I was questioning were what I was doing at home. I did the shopping, the laundry, tidying up, and my father did, but I didn't question the things boys and girls did at school or in sport. I was happy to go along with them at primary school. At secondary school I became more aware of my own experience and that things weren't as they should be.

It may also have been part of my socialist upbringing. Dad was a socialist. He's still a member of the Labour Party. My mother was a member as well. There was something of a utopian in me from an early age, certainly the idea that things should be better for the people than they were and that everybody could be doing everything. I was increasingly aware of my working-class background as I got older. I knew from an early age that we were poorer than everybody else or seemed to be. We had holes in our trousers that weren't mended, there was a lady who sometimes mended holes in our trousers, that was all she did. She was attached to the Little Sisters of the Poor. They had a branch in Manchester.

The primary school was mainly working class, the kids were poor, and I had a perception that we were poorer than the others. My secondary school was socially mixed because it was an unusual comprehensive school specialising in arts and that attracted some middle-class parents. So I was aware of being working class as I grew up and when I went to university.

I was successful at primary school. I was top of the Infants and top of Junior One till they stopped giving prizes. I was vice-captain of the football team. I was always in the athletics and rounders teams and the quiz team. I was a bright spark at primary school and the girls liked me. It was the same at secondary school. I had a good status because I fitted into all the different groups. I could fit into the academic-minded group and I could fit in with the girls and I could fit in with the male things, football and other sports. I had no problems fitting in at all. I went to the same secondary school as three of my brothers. I went on a bus with them. Two of them were there for another two and four years respectively so I was looked after even then. I was lucky being the youngest.

With my background I don't know how I fitted in with the girls. I must have had a complex view of myself coming into my teens. At first I didn't have a good image of myself. I didn't think I was attractive to girls. I set up relationships that were friendships with girls because of the way I was. I'd had no experience at home of relating differently to girls, so I just related to them as friends. It may also have been the type of school I went to that allowed that to happen, there were more girls to mix with.

I didn't have close girl friends. I wasn't confident enough to set up an intimate relationship. Not through lack of desire! I was desperate for it, we all were, but it never happened. Looking back I think I missed opportunities on so many occasions, but I was just being friends with girls. I only felt shy when I could see I could have some kind of sexual relationship, not if it was friendship. I'm still not shy with women.

My Dad didn't give me and my brothers as a group any general advice on what to expect of girls and women, but on many occasions he talked to me and it was clear he was keen that I should respect them and not treat them badly. They weren't to be treated in whatever way you wanted. I'm not sure if there was anti-sexist influence from him because it was still couched in terms like 'birds.' I'm not sure it was even on the agenda that you had to treat them correctly because of any ideals. That's the way he treated his wife. I always had it in my mind not to treat girls badly.

I may have picked up something from my father that my other brothers didn't. Because I was the youngest I spent more time talking to my Dad about these kinds of things. Certainly he said things like 'Treat girls with respect.' I remember him finding a soft porn magazine under my bed and not making an issue of it but saying in private to me later 'You don't need those. When the right girl comes along you don't need those things.' There was no overt anti-sexism but I'm sure he put across ideas of respect.

I grew up in an atmosphere that was devoid of the female touch, and to me, femininity, and women and girls, were alien but also attractive. I got no clear message from my Dad, or anywhere, about what to expect. The relationships with girls I saw my brothers having, seemed quite traditional at the time. I'm not sure I learned anything from their experiences. I didn't go out with my brothers then. I remember them going out to pubs but me at home with my Dad, and when I did start going out at 14 or 15 it was with my friends not with my brothers. My Dad's influence was more important. Later when I was at university I remember arguing with one of my brothers about anti-sexism and the position of women in society as I understood them on the theoretical level.

I was friends with everybody at school. When I first met Sophie – when you start an intimate physical bonding relationship things are said that throw light on you – she said I was everybody's pal. I get on with anybody. It's part of my outlook on life. She found it difficult at first to understand that I had friendships with women without intimate physical relationships. I don't do it now because it's perceived the wrong way.

I was on the arts side at school. I was terrible at maths and sciences or technical subjects, woodwork, metalwork. We did cookery and sewing at school. Girls did sewing more but we did do cookery. I'd always done some cooking anyway, there were six meals to get on the table – though we never set the table, those kinds of things went out of the window. The cookery we did at school was cakes and things we didn't have every day.

My primary school was about a third white, a third Asian and a third Afro-Caribbean. They seemed to get on with each other. I'm not sure racism was that big an issue. I never came across it other than racist remarks. I remember racist jokes and gossip about fights, but nothing major. As a white little boy everything seemed happy. My experiences would probably have been different if I'd been black. I was glad I was wasn't black or Asian. I felt guilty about that later – working towards anti-racism you have to come to terms with your own racist thoughts and analyse them – but the children got on together, as children do.

My secondary school was predominantly white but there was still a mixture because there were Jewish children and Afro-Caribbeans. I remember an atmosphere of anti-racism rather than racism as I was growing up. I was sympathetic to the anti-racist movement. When issues arose like a National Front march through our area there was certainly opposition to it.

I grew up in an atmosphere of anti-racism from my family. My father was anti-racist. It was linked with his socialist ideals and he'd been to their meetings in Manchester in the forties and met Paul Robeson. Robeson sang to him personally, he was into all that. I was not aware of it though, it came over subtly from him and in the kind of literature in the house. There were always serious books about, a general atmosphere of oppositon to oppression conveyed from my father. My brothers have that as well without a doubt. I was brought up in that atmosphere through school. Maybe some were racist, but I wasn't, certainly not.

I played sport twice a week as a teenager as well. They didn't let me join the Cubs or Scouts or youth club. I just went to school and came home, made tea, played in the street or watched television or did my homework. I was never keen on motorbikes. My father put me off them. He'd had them when he was young and thought they were dangerous.

I carried on at school to 18. I enjoyed the sixth form, friendships, girls and boys, going to France on a school trip and that sort of thing, though I never had girl friends. I only got geography at A level. I didn't work hard enough, I was enjoying being a 17- to 18-year-old. Because I failed the others I went to a further-education college in Manchester. One brother failed his A levels twice but, it was always the attitude in our family, it doesn't matter if you fail, try again and get on with it. Dad always had the idea, it must have come from my mother, of bettering ourselves educationally. He had us doing piano lessons and all kinds of things.

At college I had a few girl friends, a few dates, but I had no sexual relationships before I met Sophie, either through shyness or lack of opportunity but I desperately had the desire. I had party-type things where you kiss and cuddle but no more. I was going to parties every other week from about 14 to about 19, with a group of friends from school, both boys and girls, and occasionally got off with a girl if I was lucky.

I had a fantastic year at college. I got the train there every morning because we moved out of Manchester in 1980 after the riots in Moss Side. We were too close for comfort. As I was coming to the age when I'd be leaving home and my Dad would be on his own we came to a family decision. There had to be a consensus for my Dad to do things. I worked hard and thoroughly enjoyed it and the social life. There was a balance between working hard in the daytime and the evenings in the week, playing football on Saturday morning for the college and then going out Friday night and Saturday, and playing football again on Sunday.

I had some nice girl friends that year. Sometimes I wonder if I was too nice. I remember a girl saying 'I didn't realise you were so nice', meaning she'd thought I was going to treat her the same way as the other boys did, like an object presumably. Young women were surprised and were not sure what to make of it. When men they perceive as some kind of a sexual contact are friendly and have more about them than they were expecting, they're taken aback, certainly when men are caring and non-threatening and can talk about the things women talk about. To women most men are threatening, to men most men are threatening! If I'd played my cards right in the sexual card game I could have got more, but I didn't.

I got my A levels and went to Goldsmiths' College, London University. I was 19. The first week was spent chasing girls and drinking, but it only lasted four days because I met Sophie that first week. It was at a sherry party to introduce you to new people, and that was that! I told her my life story, she was the first person I'd told it to. It seemed right, certainly for me and I think for her, and we've never looked back.

It affected my social life at college. I was different to other single men. After the first week I didn't sleep in my own room for three years. We lived together in a single room unofficially. I paid for my own room and did all my work there. It was fantastic. I could work hard then go into a soft and loving phase. That's reminiscent of my Dad, working hard and competing, doing what he'd got to do and then going back to the family.

I had to work hard to get to the standard of the others, especially in the first year but my marks were OK. I didn't like geography much but I loved anthropology. I stumbled on it as a subsid. subject. The next year I changed to joint anthropology and geography because they weren't doing single-honours anthropology.

I had a good friend I went everywhere with in lecture times. He was 6 foot 4 so I looked like his little lapdog. If I wasn't with him I was with Sophie. I've never been alone apart from the first four nights at college. After that I was always with somebody. I've no desire to be alone.

My social life at Goldsmiths' was mainly Sophie, we did everything together apart from football. I'd go from my room to her room and from college to hall of residence. I still live that way. I switch into a different mode, the transition is driving home. It's not just in my head, it's physical. When I go to play football I switch into a different mode. I don't feel schizophrenic about it, the transitions are reasonably smooth.

The anthropology department was two-thirds women lecturers whose research and the course content were weighted towards women's issues. They were feminists. They were very influential. The second or the third year I did 'Sex and Gender in Anthropology' which was analysing male bias in social anthropology and looking at patriarchy and those kinds of things, which I swallowed extremely easily. The groundwork had been done at home.

I felt uncomfortable at times in situations where male oppression of women was being highlighted, but I was happy to sit through and give my ideas and learn about the dynamics of oppression at all levels, at the macro level and at the personal level. My personality accepted these ideas and I reassessed my own lifestyle, and the things I was doing that weren't acceptable I'd make changes to. I didn't have to make a wholesale shift of personality or in the way I treated individuals.

It also fitted into the men's movement that was developing in the early eighties around the magazine *Achilles Heel* with Vic Seidler and others. One of my tutors introduced me to him because my final dissertation was on lone fatherhood. He discussed it with me and put me in touch with papers and books. I went to several meetings. There were certainly seminars I went to that were a men's group by another name. I think they were the *Achilles Heel* Collective but I didn't know any of them personally other than Vic. There was that chap from Australia who wrote papers I got copies of – Connell. He was very good, down to earth. But I never became really involved in that group.

It was an active phase of the men's movement in Britain, catalytic. Men who were coming round to anti-sexist thinking turned to those early issues of *Achilles Heel* and I got on the mailing list. I had a full set of them. On and off I read other things I picked up in bookshops, the *Anti-sexist Men's Newsletter*. I saw a few issues, but I never subscribed.

I didn't see much of Vic Seidler but I remember him clearly. He became almost an unofficial tutor who I could talk to about my research, with the idea that I'd be doing something further in the future. I felt I had a link to the men's movement, it keeps your ideals going, I knew there were other men thinking along the same lines. I read something Vic wrote and liked his style of writing – about everything that you do at personal level has to be related to the big issues and those issues have to be related to your personal background, otherwise it's just words on paper.

The ideas came from feminism. I read as many feminist books as I could get within the structure of the 'Sex and Gender' course. I read more feminist anthropology than sociology, but I read all the Ann

Oakley and the general ones. I was really interested in that course, absolutely. On first hearing the content and going to the first lectures I thought, this is for me. The fact that it was from a feminist angle was OK. I used to tell people I was a feminist because I accepted feminist ideas. Obviously I wasn't, as a man. What I meant was that I was sympathetic to the ideas, and I was happy to hold my hand up and say, 'Yes I need to look at the way I am.' My background had made me receptive.

My wife isn't particularly interested in feminism. I don't think she was as a student. I was more vocal. There was a learning process. I put across the ideas I'd heard and read about and we'd talk about them, but obviously I learned a lot from her about women if not about feminism, because she was the first woman I'd been close to. She was strong and delicate and multi-faceted at the same time. That appealed to me. Sometimes she thought I was over the top because I swallowed the ideas of feminism, hook, line and sinker and argued with other men at college about these issues.

My best friend at college was doing the same course units and was also very much into it. He later became more interested in issues of race and has now finished a doctorate on black identity. We threw ideas at each other and we both swallowed feminist ideas. He was from a working-class background too but more traditional in that he had a conventional family. He was very sporty, athletic, similar to me, able to fit into the sporting life and other situations you have to be in as a man, seen as a strong man, but he was also receptive to issues of anti-sexism and anti-racism. We influenced each other a lot. We still get together sometimes.

Our working-class background was important when we started college. We were ducks out of water the first few weeks and clung on to each other. It made me aware of my working-class background and I felt comfortable having somebody from the same background, and also Sophie. She was from a middle-class background but her father was working class in origin. They were the main influences. I still carried on playing football on Saturdays on and off. I played for the college in the second year.

It worked out well for me at university. I got a good degree and we got married less than a year after we graduated. I'm still good friends with my mate. I stayed in London for a year and I registered for an MA but my anthropology background wasn't suited to the kind of sociological research I wanted to do, so I did a course on research methods, but I hated it. I wanted to do research on lone fatherhood and needed to know more at the theoretical level to get to grips with it.

I got a job for a few months as a residential social worker. I needed to work to live in London but I didn't like the course and didn't like the social work so I stopped both after two or three months and worked in a warehouse in Harrow in an all-male environment. I started writing down things based on the reading I'd done about men in work and on ideas I'd formulated on my father's experiences. I tried to make use of the situation and put ideas down. That lasted about nine months.

We got married that year and lived in Harrow next to the school. It was uncomfortable going to work in the mornings and coming back all dusty, walking past all those posh Harrovians, but I did it. It was a strange surreal experience for a few months. It made me very aware of class because we had no money and we were surrounded by rich people. At one time King Hussain of Jordan visited, and the place was overrun by police. Sophie worked for a year as a graphic designer in London and hated going on the tube and having to conform each day. We both decided we hated London so we came to live here in Peak District where my Dad was living. This was in 1985. One other brother was living at home too. We lived with them for a year until we moved into our own little house in the same town.

I looked for any jobs and she looked for jobs in graphic design, but then she realised she didn't want to do that. She hated the whole competitive nature of it and it would have meant travelling to Manchester, so she decided to look for work with children and got a job as a classroom assistant at a special school. So we were a dual-income family for a while. We were 'dinkies' – dual income no kids – for about three years.

On moving up here I applied for a scholarship at Keele University to carry on my lone fatherhood research for an MA. I didn't get it but I registered there for an MA in 1986 and got started on interviewing men who were lone fathers. I still have fifteen interviews on tape, much the same life history stuff as you're doing. It was almost identical to this.

I got a job as a oral-history researcher for a museum in Cheshire. I was desperate to get some money. I was interviewing old people about their work experiences in the silk industry. At the same time I was doing my own research, interviewing lone fathers, making contact with Gingerbread groups in Stoke and Stockport and Manchester and getting snowball contacts through them. I went to as many Gingerbread groups as I could. I got deeply into looking at lone fatherhood, marrying ideas on masculinity to the experience of lone fathers. I still think the way to do it is through life histories. It's the only way to get across people's real experiences.

When I came back here I went to a Workers Education Association [WEA] course on anti-sexism and became involved in a group called Manchester Men Against Sexism. I didn't like going, it was constantly in my head that it was a white middle-class comfortable group who were satisfying some need I didn't need to satisfy at a theoretical level I'd been through over and over again. It was just talking about life and I wanted to live it. I always come back to my priorities – which are not words.

I don't need a men's group as support for my ideals or personality. My background has already given me that and I have that kind of support from the relationships in my family. I grew up in a men's group! I can talk freely to Sophie about these issues. I understand the need for men to analyse their situation in men's groups but I've no need for it.

If I'm in a group of men discussing important issues I feel the oneness they feel as a group. I get deeply into the discourse, I can offer things I need to offer and learn from other men, but on the WEA course one of the things was to get men used to touching. I didn't see any need for me to do that. I'd had contact with my father and brothers and still do. People still see me kiss my Dad in the street or before I go out to play football. That's not strange to me at all.

I helped facilitate a session of the Men Against Sexism group at Manchester Town Hall. It was on men hearing but not listening, particularly not listening to women but I didn't want to get any deeper involved than that. I was aware at the time, and I still believe, that certain men dominate these situations and they're not entirely egalitarian or what they seem on the surface. They use them for their own ends. Maybe it's still about power and it's difficult for men to kick off the shackles of power.

I've no desire for power whatsoever, though I use it every day in my job. The power that means that women are treated badly is totally unacceptable. The power that means that children are treated badly is totally unacceptable. The power that means that black people are treated as second-class citizens is abhorrent. I don't want to wield power in my own family situation but I don't want to have power wielded against me either. I hate the situation at work where somebody above you says what goes, and I hate it when people think you've got power over them and expect you to take control. I don't feel any desire or need to do that. I've no desire for money either. My only desire is to live happily and for the members of my family to have peaceful, healthy, happy, long lives.

It was at that time I decided to work with young children. It may have come about through Sophie working at a special school, seeing what it was like. They were slightly older children with special needs. I applied to do teacher training at primary-school level and then, observing an infant class, I decided to do infants. I was sold on the idea from then on.

I did a one-year course in 1987 and then got a job immediately in Manchester teaching middle infants, 5 and 6 year olds. I was there four terms. Being an infant teacher in an environment where all the other teachers and most adults the children came into contact with were female, and many of the experiences the children had of men were not the best, or they had no experience – children from one-parent families – I was very visible as the only man to the children and all the women teachers.

At the same time as being difficult I got a kind of ego enhancement from being the only man in a female environment, from being somebody who cut across the grain, who did something that was not traditional. I get personal satisfaction out of that and knowing that children are seeing a role model that's not what they'd expect to see, or which they would not normally see, whether they expected it or not. It's extremely important that children see a softer side to men, a more rounded side. Not a power-oriented side. That fits everything for me.

My first school was in an enormous white working-class council estate in south Manchester. The indicators of social deprivation are as high there as anywhere, one-parent families, unemployment, poverty, crime. Children were from deprived and disturbed backgrounds. It was good experience for me and for the children. In 1990 I started at a primary school in Derbyshire, teaching 7 and 8 year olds – my present job, but I'm looking to get back to infants in this county, for the personal satisfaction I get from it.

I don't want to go to another county because an important reason I teach is to spend more time with my own children during the holidays and you can only do that if you're working in the county where your children go to school, because holidays vary. Then there's the travelling time. These are important issues to me. If I'm home at five o'clock as opposed to half past six that's important, it's an hour and a half of 'quality time' as Americans call it, especially when your children are young and go to bed at half past six. If you're not there when they go to bed you've missed it!

It's still unusual for a man to be an infant teacher and they're thin on the ground in primary schools. The only other one I know is my eldest brother. It's understandable why they're thin on the ground. It's to do with what men expect and what the profession expects people to be like in education. They still see young children as the preserve of women. It holds down the status of primary teachers because it's seen as women's work and it perpetuates the idea that only women look after young children.

There's nothing I do as a teacher that says it should be a woman or a man. I find it satisfying work. The most gratifying thing is contact with children. Sometimes there's such a nice atmosphere, and one of them says something nice that they mean. They are not throw-away comments, they mean things. They say 'I like you' and 'You're my best teacher' and that kind of thing. It gives you a buzz. Things I don't like about teaching have nothing to do with the children, they're all to do with dealing with other adults, expectations from the administrative side and demands you get from head teachers and maybe parents, but not the children. I love it.

I might feel differently if I was a teacher of older children because different things come into play, the clash between the independence of teenagers and the authority figures that teachers have to be sometimes. As a person who deals with young children I have to strike a balance between being a carer, a big brother, an uncle, and with children of one-parent families maybe a father figure, and also an authority figure who's in charge, that gives children security as well. It's like being a parent but in a more structured situation.

I get on fine with my female colleagues. They're no more and no less than professional relationships. I have no antagonism towards any of them and no deep friendships either. I haven't come across hostility in the job I'm in at the moment. In my other school there might have been older women teachers who were set in their ways in an all-women's situation; also more radical elements who wanted change but whose ideas were undermining their personal careers. They continually say that in traditional women's jobs men get rapid promotion. I can understand they resent that but it's an undue pressure on somebody that doesn't want that anyway. I'm not ambitious. It takes you into stressful situations I want to avoid. It's stressful enough having to bring on each individual child to their best potential. I live a happy existence at the moment.

I'm not committed to the breadwinner role. I've chosen work that's satisfying and fits in with my outlook, but I'd rather be at home if economics allowed. I've no desire to be a breadwinner but I don't think I'm selling out my ideals of anti-sexism by being one. What I'm doing is allowing my wife to do what she wants to do. I'm happy for somebody who wants to be at home with the children and to love them, and is doing a fantastic job of it, to do that. I'm happy to support that. On Sunday nights I feel I don't want to go, but when I get there it's all right.

After I'd finished my course and started teaching I started doing one session a week at a youth club. I wanted something to complement what I was doing at school. I'd done some football with a youth team and got to know some young people in the town. They're teenagers, girls and boys, it's a refreshing change. I wanted to get more involved in the local community here. It was also a way of supplementing our income.

I also thought it would give me a chance to spread my anti-sexist ideas. I still think that. I don't ram it down people's throats, I only refer to it as it arises. I do things by example. People see I care for my young children, they know I do things around the house, and I argue about it in the youth club. There are opportunities for formal sessions with videos and discussions but I usually show them by example, cooking and cleaning. Young men expect you to sit back and let women do it. It's only in a small way but when issues of sexism or gender come up I let them know what I think and I don't find difficulty doing it either. I do two nights a week now, I do another session at a village youth club about three miles up the road.

I always get called on to do what's called 'boys' work' in youth work. There's been a response to feminism in that efforts are now made to do 'girls' work', which means trying to encourage girls to take part in non-traditional activities in youth clubs and efforts are also made to prevent boys dominating the space and taking up time with their demands in youth clubs. In line with that an effort is being made to influence boys in ways that help the work aimed at giving the girls a better chance. That is the sort of work with boys that I get called on to do.

Children at school, young people I work with in youth clubs and people that I mix with in football and cricket, and about the town, may or may not know the kind of lifestyle I lead and the ideas that I have. Some think I'm a traditional type, sporty, a teacher with a wife and two kids. Others see I don't dawdle at school or go for drinks after football and I take the kiddies to the shops and do things around the house, but people expect me to be a traditional sort of chap. I come across those expectations all the time and people still raise their eyebrows when they see me going to the toddler group. People only get little hints, I don't put a banner up in the garden and I don't wear teeshirts emblazoned with slogans. Your ideas have to come out with the way you deal with people. They're little influences, that's the way I do things. I don't want people to be antagonistic towards me for the ideals that I hold. That's ridiculous.

I never finished the MA. I decided my family and career were higher priorities. The highest priority is my family and their happiness and that can only be fulfilled by me having a job. I'm not sure my job's a major priority but the need to earn a living cuts across sharing a more equitable life in terms of childrearing. My wife could have pursued a career if she'd wanted to, but I'm happy she didn't because she's happy she didn't. She could have earned more than I'm doing if she'd stayed in graphic design, but it would have been up and down, given the economic situation.

I'm not currently involved in organised anti-sexist men's activities. I'm more involved in an anti-sexist lifestyle and in work that allows me to fulfil the ideals I hold. I'm not dominating anybody and I'm not in a power-broking male-dominated work environment. I'm in things that require me to think about the way I deal with people, not be selfish, and cast off the shackles of masculinity and lay myself open.

I think about masculinity nearly all the time. It's permeated my life and my lifestyle for as long as I can remember from my earliest childhood, knowing I lived in an all-male family without any female input but not able to make sense of that, through all the stages of theoretical development, the need to look at masculinity as an issue in response to feminist ideas and the way it affected me, to the point where I am at the moment when my whole existence is dominated by issues of masculinity.

I structure my lifestyle not to fall into the trap of – patriarchy for want of a better word – and all its trappings, so that I don't dominate the woman that I love, even though I may do in subtle ways without knowing it. I'm trying to assess everything I do, every time I say something to Sophie I think 'Should I have said that? Was that being macho?' I think like that all the time. This morning off the cuff I said something sharply to her and I thought, 'I shouldn't have said that.' Mostly I apologise for it. I'm trying to counter it all the time, in my work too.

Also it's an issue when I play sport. I don't necessarily counter macho behaviour because it's difficult in an all-male environment and I enjoy more of the experience than I dislike, otherwise I wouldn't do it, but I think about it all the time. Every time I hear somebody say something or see tattoos on a man's arm I understand what's going on. It's an issue that's important to me. I also put it into a global perspective when I see men going to war. Masculinity has been bad for a lot of people, otherwise I wouldn't want to change it. I'd be happy going to work, coming home and putting my feet up.

There are lots of things I'd like to see come about in society. I'd like to see equality in pay, equal access to employment, all kinds of things. From men's point of view I'd like to see universal paternity leave, which I didn't get when my children were born and it was extremely upsetting for me. I went through the official channels and through the union. I was aware some union agreements allowed for two weeks paternity leave, but teachers had no agreement. I was granted three days compassionate leave when my first daughter was born while I was working in Manchester and the same in Derbyshire when we had the second, three days is what you get!

To have no agreed situation across the country is barbaric and you look to continental countries, especially Scandinavia, who have it. There should be a way of working more flexibly where you can take years in and years off to enjoy your children fully. These are important things. There aren't going to be major changes in childrearing unless those kinds of things come about. The only way they're coming about is through male unemployment and female part-time low-paid service industries developing and that's not a good way because when men do get jobs they go back to what they've been doing in the past. That's not a desirable change.

There are two sorts of female company. It's easy in situations with people I work with, but I'm not very comfortable in situations that are sexually oriented, where women might think I'm available. My relationship is strong and I don't want to lose it. In the same way I'm comfortable in some male situations and not in others that are aggressive. I get involved in them in football – but I wouldn't be happy getting on a Leeds United football supporters' coach!

We share the jobs in the house. The same as when I was a boy, we never write things down. If I see a job, I do it. There's no labels, her job or my job, although there are things she does automatically that I'm just no good at, and things I do that she's not good at, some of which by the nature of it tend to be things you're used to doing as a man or she's used to doing as a woman – but they don't have labels attached to them. I'm happy to do things she usually does and she'd do the things I do I'm sure.

It may sound egotistical but I honestly do strive to be happy. I've no career ambitions, no need to fulfil anything in terms of money. What we've got now is all I want. We need a new car because the other's gone, not because we want a more flashy one. I've got modest tastes. I want the best for the people I live with more than for myself, especially now I've got children. I don't think I'm totally altruistic, but with my family I am.

TERRY

I'm 37. I was born in Birmingham but we moved to Staffordshire when I was 9. We moved out of high-rise flats in Birmingham because my parents wanted a house with a garden. There were four of us then, myself and three sisters. I was the eldest. I had another sister when I was 15.

All the areas I lived in had a strong working-class character, high-rise flats, maisonettes, then a council estate. I had a very working-class upbringing. My parents were not big drinkers and didn't smoke. They always had a huge pride that we were all turned out spick and span. My parents bought a house in a village near Stafford. I left there when I moved in with Tina in Stafford. So I've lived most of my life in Staffordshire. I feel now North Staffs is my real home. I've set my roots down here, I'm not a one for venturing off.

My Dad worked in engineering, he left school at 14 and got a job wherever he could, he's always been a handyman, but never did a formal apprenticeship. He was a conscientious worker, bright but a wanderer as far as jobs were concerned. He'd learn a job quickly, then look around for something else. In Birmingham there was plenty of jobs so he could do that. When I was a kid he got made redundant and drove a lorry for a while, but he wasn't long before he was back in engineering factories again.

My mother also worked. Dad's jobs were never highly paid and they always had great ambitions for the family – providing for them. They both came from poor backgrounds and wanted a better life for their children. My mother had a particularly bad life when she was young. My Dad was from a family with eight children and his father died when he was quite young. My parents strived continuously to provide for the children, so they couldn't rely on my Dad's wages only. Mum had lots of temporary twilight jobs, where she could get them, mainly factory work.

I used to go home from primary school and to a neighbour's to fetch the young ones, sit them in front of the telly, get them a drink and wait till Mum came in. I took responsibility for my sisters but it didn't ever feel a burden. I didn't feel I shouldn't be doing this and wish I was out playing. I had to do it so I got on and did it. My Mum often worked for a few weeks, got tired and didn't do it for a month or so, and then went back to another temporary job. She always tried to fit work around the family.

I definitely had an early experience of a working woman. It wasn't a strange idea. My mother is a strong-minded person. Though she was in a typical woman's role she was strong in the way of working-class women who are protective towards the family. I always felt my Mum was comfortable with her role. I know some women aren't. My Mum always dealt out the punishment, probably about once a week she'd go off like a bottle of pop.

Dad was the quiet person in the family, rarely raised his voice. He's not a man of many words but he does think and feel quite deeply. He was away working a lot when I was younger. Some jobs took him away. He felt he had to work hard and put a lot of his energies into doing that. He'd bring the money in, that was his job. He was great to have around. He was good fun and would put time aside for the children. I remember often going out for day trips. I have happy memories of my father when I was a child. He didn't read with me and play football with me or take me fishing. I was a lad who got on and did things but he encouraged me. He taught me to ride my bike. When I was 13 or 14 we did a lot together, built an aviary together and filled it full of budgerigars. DIY stuff. He was very practical.

When Mum was working on shifts he prepared the meal and washed up and hoovered around, but he'd never iron, except his own shirts. He polished his own shoes. I got a rollicking once when I polished everybody's shoes and he said to me 'Don't polish mine, I'll do my own.' It related back to his army days. He was used to polishing his own shoes and his children doing them for him didn't feel right. He did National Service about 1950, just missed going to the Korean War.

He was a nurturing and caring father but sometimes he was difficult to talk to because he always felt he ought to know things when he didn't. His way of coping was to not listen properly or change the subject. He didn't like to show his ignorance. I found out later he couldn't write properly, because when he was little he didn't go to school much. He bunked off with his brother. His writing skills were poor, that's why he never had a formal apprenticeship and that's why he never sat down and did homework with us. He didn't feel comfortable with it.

I take after my Dad. As I've got older and had children I see strong similarities. I also take after Mum. I don't think it's possible to say whether I take more after one than the other. I modelled myself on my Dad, especially in practical skills, I went into engineering as soon as I left school. I wanted to be a bricklayer but my Dad discouraged me. He didn't think I'd get proper training. He wanted me to get a proper apprenticeship. Some other aspects of my Dad I've not really followed. I consciously chose not to, such as the way I've related to my children. I wanted to have more contact with my children as a father, more physical contact, and wanted to be around with them and nurture them and care for them more than my Dad did. He felt his role was earning the money. He was committed to the breadwinner role. It came from his background and his generation. He'd lost his father and for him it was the most important thing. They'd scrimped and begged and borrowed to have meals on the table and he was determined that was not going to happen in his family. He was strong in that and he took a pride in it. He was made redundant again recently and that really kicked him in the guts.

When I think back to starting school I made friends easier with girls than boys, largely to do with having sisters. I was more familar with them. One girl I remember distinctly when I was 6. She was in my class and had an accident, a slab fell on her leg. I helped get her out and rushed home to get her Mum. I remember her more than anyone else at the time. She had a friend in my class. I won a dancing competition with her. We were partners. But there were boys in flats down the road who I played with a lot.

Having younger sisters influenced me. I wanted a brother when I was about 6 or 7, but when I was 12 or 13 I stopped wanting a brother because it was nice being the only lad. My eldest sister three years younger than me was always classed as a tomboy and we were close and still are. We played together a lot.

My younger sisters I don't know so well. I was 15 when the youngest was born. I had a lot to do with her when she was a baby. I hated it when my Mum was pregnant and I was 15. It was embarrasing, it meant they still did it! Everybody knew! But when she was born I looked after her, changed nappies and fed her and enjoyed it. Another thing about having sisters, though I'd never admit it to my mates, my Mum did a lot of sewing and knitting and I could knit. I used to make things for my sisters, for their dolls and stuff like that.

With my Dad away a lot and with all those sisters it must have been a very feminine atmosphere but I wasn't aware of it. I never thought I was missing anything. I used to go out a lot from the age of 11. On Saturdays I'd take a drink and some lunch and disappear all day. There were lots of boys to play with.

It was a mixed infant school I started at and I went though three different junior schools because of our moves, all were mixed. I don't remember playing with girls at school. It was boys I played with in the playground, marbles and football and things like that. I didn't like the physicalness of it, fights and that. I could get upset easily and I found it difficult to hide, so I learned to avoid those situations.

I was always small and thin for my age and felt ugly, and because I was a stranger going into new schools I always felt it was difficult for me, but I didn't get picked on much. I'm good at reading people quickly and finding out who the kids were that would cause problems. I quickly got in with the in-crowd. It was difficult in that crowd but it was the way to survive and I learned that early on. I did the things they wanted me to do, even if I didn't feel comfortable with them. It meant I had to avoid girls at school. It was a problem in my senior school when my sister came to the school. We were very close but I had to ignore her at school.

I didn't pass the exam at 11. The school where I took it, I was only there one term. I liked that school. I wonder, if I'd had a bit longer there maybe I'd have passed. When I went to secondary-modern school they put me in the A stream but I found it too hard. It was changing to comprehensive. That was a mixed school too apart from the playgrounds. I always felt it was ridiculous even when I was quite young. We sat together chatting in classrooms and, come playtime, we were separated but I suspect it was good for the girls. They could play the games they wanted without any stupid nonsense from the boys.

At 11 or 12 girls and boys tended to separate in class. We all took maths, English and science together but separated for things like woodwork and metalwork and the girls had home economics. We didn't do that. I might have been better at needlework than woodwork, but I enjoyed the woodwork and metalwork. Technical drawing was another that was male only, though nowadays we're finding quite a lot of draughtswomen. I come across them more and more. I was good at the practical things but didn't do much good in maths and English, geography and things like that. I fell behind and went into lower streams. Of course we had games separate from the girls. I wasn't a footballer. I used to knock around at home and love it, but at school I wasn't mad keen on it. We didn't play rugby, thank God. I enjoyed tennis but we didn't play with the girls.

In the first and second year we didn't notice the girls, I didn't anyway. Then in the third and fourth years they became a different breed altogether. They became somebody that you noticed and perhaps you didn't understand why you were noticing them. I didn't have a real girl friend until the fourth year when I was 15, but my first strong recognition of a girl was when I had newspaper rounds from the age of 11, morning and evening. She was on the round too. She was a gawky looking girl but she took a shine to me. She had a small round and used to finish quickly and then help me. I found her interesting and I probably would have had more to do with her but I couldn't cope with the teasing from other boys. Her way to get to know me was to befriend my sister who told her when I went out and where I went. I wanted to have a girl friend but I didn't know why. I didn't want anybody else to know. It wasn't a thing I wanted to brag about.

There was another girl who took a shine to me who wrote me a love letter. She was new to the school and attractive but too racy for me! We went down to the local railway station and had a couple of hours snogging. It was the first time anybody had done that, and she had proper breasts! I couldn't believe it. Then she wrote me this bloody letter and handed it across from one side of the class to the other and it got intercepted by the deputy head. He opened it and read it out. She and her friends thought it great fun. She wasn't embarrassed but it absolutely crucified me.

There was another girl who lived near me. Once when her parents went away she had a party. That was the first time I made a concerted effort to get off with somebody. We had a passionate two weeks. We couldn't stop talking to each other and sending each other notes. We could signal to each other with lights from our bedrooms. It was intense but didn't last long. I felt shy about making that move but the excitement made me overcome it. I was still at school then.

Leaving at 15 I didn't take any school exams. I left in 1971 and tried to become a gas fitter. I sat the exam but didn't pass and that was a terrible blow. I really wanted to do that. The next apprenticeship to come up was at a colliery down the road from us – apprenticeships for mechanics down the pit. I had a medical, passed an exam, and they took me on as an apprentice Class One fitter.

I started work at 15 but you can't go underground till you're 16 so I had to wait for my next birthday. It was difficult because some lads I'd gone there with, their birthdays came around quicker and the sooner you were working down the pit the more manly you was. I worked around the fitting shops and it was good time spent for me. I learned skills that I wouldn't have learned down the pit. I worked with a blacksmith for a while and learned blacksmithing skills which I'd never have learned otherwise.

The apprenticeship was nearly five years. I was at the pit in the 1972 miners' strike. The union had a long-standing agreement that apprentices would carry on their training during any dispute so we sailed through the picket lines. It was all right on days at college but at the pit it was a problem, nobody was there. The officials found us things to do.

The strike affected me because it was the first time I became aware I had strong political differences from my parents. They were conservative with a little 'c.' I was the only one in my whole family that ever worked in the pits. A lot of my friends came from mining backgrounds so it wasn't a problem when they got home, probably their fathers were on strike, but when I got home they were running the miners down. I sympathised with the miners, they were my workmates, and at that age they take over from your parents. You never have to try hard with your parents. They'll always love you if you've got good parents but you don't always know if your workmates will like you, so you need to stay with the peer group.

My apprenticeship years made me grow up. I was working with *men*, you know. It was important for me. It gave me courage and I learned a lot about myself. I learned some of my strengths and weaknesses. I learned about not taking life so seriously and to laugh at myself more. Down the pit there's tremendous comradeship, a lot of what we called 'piss-taking', winding people up and having a laugh. It was such an awful place to be and the way to make it work was to have good comradeship, work well together and have a good laugh to raise people's spirits up.

The first time I went for a shower, these men were there showering and I was only 15. I was like a boy. They were swearing and soap was flying about and it was scaring. The first few months I wasn't comfortable. I used to hang back so I could shower later or I'd choose a cubicle where I could have privacy. I was still quite immature, not shaving properly and things like that. Some of the lads at 16 had full pubic hair and a seven o'clock shadow. They seemed to be men much quicker than I was. It didn't last long, maybe six months at most and I was like everybody else, but I always felt shyer, a bit reserved.

It was an absolutely all-male environment. The only women around were in the canteen. Even the cleaners in the baths were all men. After I got used to it, it was OK. I gravitated to the older men. I liked their stories and their conversation. They hadn't got the hot-headedness, that had gone. I felt much more comfortable with them.

The group I avoided were the ones you could never talk seriously to because they never showed they'd got a serious thought in their minds. The older men didn't have that. You could sit and talk to them. It was interesting to hear what they'd got to say. They didn't demand much from you in terms of physicalness. They didn't want to rough you up. So I tended to sit with them and listen to them talking. They talked about politics and what life had been like in the past, what was on the telly last night and what was in the garden, all sorts of things. It matured me tremendously.

The first years of my apprenticeship were a month at college or training centre and a month at the pit, sometimes two months. So I was in and out. I enjoyed the work but I found it difficult physically. I enjoyed college a lot. Again it was all-male. It was a miners' technical college, built with miners' union funds but it had changed to a college of further education. They also taught a beautician's course there, hairdressers and so on. I was going there almost two years before I realised they were there. We didn't see them. The timetable was arranged so the girls doing that course arrived after the boys arrived for the mining courses. Meal times were separate, canteen facilities were rearranged. They felt it would be unfair to the girls, that was what we were told.

I started to want a motorbike and got one when I was 17 and got into going out with my mates and meeting girls at dances and discos. I was into the greaser age, causing skirmishes with skinheads, waiting outside their clubs and revving our motorbikes really loud and roaring off. We didn't get into any serious fights. It was all showing off. I was always aware of where to stop. I had mates that were into big scraps but I always found a plausible reason for not going and still keep my 'street cred'.

I left school with a friend who went to the pit too. We were together a lot and at college a rumour was going round that we were homosexual. I didn't even know what it meant. Someone had to spell it out to me. Smithy was a big bloke and he told everybody that if they went on saying that he'd kill them. So it stopped. I'd never come across the idea of homosexuality and I was 17 then. I always wanted girls. I knew about sex and about excitement and masturbation, and I knew what got me excited wasn't boys.

My apprenticeship finished about 1975 when I was 20. I could have carried on studying to Higher National Certificate in mine engineering. I did another year of day release at college then packed it in. I didn't have the inclination. I spent a year working with somebody more experienced but during the year I had to take responsibilities myself and I was designated an area underground to cover, called a 'heading'. My job was to look after all the machinery in that area, maintenance, repairs and breakdowns. Then I was given a much wider area to look after, working shifts. I did that for another four years down the pit near where I lived with my parents. It was a new modern pit, one of the first in Europe to achieve a million tons of coal in a year and expected to last a hundred years – it's closed down now.

I'd had a string of girl friends at school and then nobody for a bit and then I met one called Doreen and went with her for eighteen months. She was absolutely stunning. Me mates used to say 'You'll never hold on to her', and I didn't. Her father was an absolute monster. He'd come home from work and nobody had to be sitting in his seat. His cup of tea had to be ready, otherwise there'd be words. He'd take another cup into the front room where he'd watch the telly. Nobody could go in and watch it.

He'd have his dinner brought to him and he'd eat it and that was taken away and he was brought his pudding and that was taken away and he'd have another cup of tea. The same every night and if it wasn't it was absolutely awful. Then come eight o'clock, he'd go and shave and at twenty past he'd be off to the pub and he'd come back at half past ten, not drunk but certainly well away.

I bled for her mother, she was a lovely woman to be stuck with such a bloody monster. I'd love to have had him down the pit. We'd have made his life a misery! There were things like that down the pit. If somebody was hurting somebody they would sort that person out. I really wanted to beat him up. I liked her Mum and her Mum liked me. He never gave her much money. She never had any decent clothes on her. We chatted and I helped with bits and pieces. When me and Doreen were experimenting with sex her Mum used to turn a blind eye to it. Doreen was beautiful and immature in some ways but always striving to break out of what she was in. I arrived one day and her Mum was in tears and told me Doreen had gone off with a man.

Then I met Tina when I was 23. I met her at a disco. A friend of mine was going out with her friend and he said, 'Come along and make a foursome.' We met at a rock disco club. I was into motorbikes then, a greaser. At first I thought she was strange, not like women I'd known. She wasn't a girly girl. We didn't see each other for a couple of months and then we met again and started writing to each other when she finished college and went back to Lancashire. We saw each other at weekends. Then we had one really passionate weekend and we knew we wanted to stay with each other. It was 1976, a scorching hot summer and I remember riding up and down to Lancashire on my motorbike in all that heat.

Next year she found a flat in Stafford and moved in with her friend Sheila. I saw them most nights when I was on day shift and weekends, the three of us went out a lot together. We were always together but I wanted it to be just me and Tina. She was nervous to start with but then it seemed right. I wanted us to buy a house. I felt it was sensible rather than renting so we scraped together a deposit and bought a house in Stafford. I was still working down the pit. Tina got a job as a psychiatric nurse and trained for that while we were living together in Stafford.

She was strong-minded and different. She didn't dress with the crowd, almost to make a statement about herself, 'This is me.' It attracted me to her because she was different. I liked the fact that she was independent but also willing to be helped. There were women around at that time who were strong in feminism and were anti-men or didn't want men around. It was the early stages of Tina's development in feminism but she was working things out differently to other women.

Her ideas were formulated when we started to live together and she met other women in the town. Her friend Sheila was a big influence. She and Tina were close and they searched out radical things to look at and boundaries go through, feminism was one of them. She brought back her new ideas to me and we looked at them within our relationship. I endorsed her ideas but the practical ways of doing it were difficult sometimes. I changed because of what she was wanting to experience but it's fair to say that having been brought up with four sisters and a Mum that's very strong, I always had a great respect for women. I just hadn't thought it out. Mum used to fix things, drilling holes and whatever. If she wanted a job done, she didn't wait for my Dad to come home, she'd do it herself.

There's an old saying down the pit, 'Once a pitman always a pitman.' That first started me thinking about what I wanted to do, because I didn't come from a family of people working in the pits. It's bloody hard work but it's good comradeship, but I thought 'Do I want to be here for ever? Is this what life is all about?' I used to change at work next to a bloke called Joe who was in his sixties. One day I arrived at the pit and he was changing to go down and I was talking to him and I could see myself being like Joe in many years to come, body scarred with working down the pit and having only seen the pit as a working environment. He still interested me but I felt there was more I needed in life. He said 'What else is there to do?' and that's how I'd felt. At that point I decided I would look for another job. My Dad pointed out other places where I could use the skills I'd learned.

An important thing was that I'd met Tina and our relationship was like no other relationship I'd had with a woman. She had completely different ways of thinking. My consciousness raising came after meeting her because she was more politically aware than I was. She'd lived away from home and that matured her quickly. I'd never lived away from home. She'd been a student of beauty therapy at college but that was certainly not a hotbed of feminism! She was with women learning to be hairdressers and beauticians. She'd looked around for courses to get away from home. Her idea was to do cosmetic surgery, dealing with scars and things, rather than the beautician side. She was at the end of her course when I met her.

When Tina and I started to live together I was unhappy working at the pit. I began to have ideas sympathetic to feminism, so I found my politics difficult to reconcile with the men I worked with. Tina brought me a new understanding of men–women relationships and it felt right. There were bits I found difficult but the ideology of it I felt was right, so I didn't have as much in common with the blokes I worked with. I took myself out of conversations when men were being blatantly sexist. I can now cope with that much better because I'm much clearer about it but at that time I was going through a radical change in my view of the world, becoming much more aware of racism, sexism, class. A lot of things were going on in my mind and working in that environment felt uncomfortable and difficult.

There was a lot of sexism and racism and hierarchical attitudes down the pit but lots of good fun and banter. I hadn't the strength to argue what I felt so I became aloof, in the background more. The worst moments were when they looked at pornographic magazines. I felt I ought not to look at them and ought not to say the things that were being said about women's bodies. You have to be strong to handle that in a male environment. You have to be clear why you're saying things and careful not to put yourself on the spot. Relationships are tentative down the pit. They'd do anything for you but they'd ostracise you quickly if they felt you didn't fit. So it became difficult. I wanted to look at the magazines and join in but felt guilty because I felt I shouldn't. I was confused.

I was aware before I met Tina of feeling I wouldn't be down the pit for ever but it wore off. It was a secure job and I knew what I was doing, but in the end I decided to get out. I got a job with a fork-lift truck company. I went for the interview and didn't know anything about it but I got on well with the bloke. A lot of questions he asked I didn't know the answers to because it was to do with electro-mechanical things and I was more hydraulics mechanical. I didn't have the electrical knowledge, but he said 'Don't worry about it. We put you on an intensive training course. You'll pick it up.'

So I was a service engineer and I got my own van, tooled out, and I had the West Midlands to cover repairing fork-lift trucks. From working in a small area underground to having all this freedom and my own van with a radio to radio-in – I felt as high as a kite. I could get out of the pit and have a wage to carry on paying the mortgage. It was fantastic.

Tina was very involved in feminist groups then, she spent a lot of time working out her politics. When I was away on my course for the new job she was thinking about the relationship more radically and in more detail than I was. It was a learning process together, learning about each other. I was very insecure and I dare say Tina was as well.

There were other women on the scene that I felt hostile towards. I now know why I felt that but I didn't at the time. I felt guilty for feeling so angry with them. I now know it was to do with class. I searched in myself to come to terms with demands being put on me to re-evaluate how I saw women. I felt tremendous pressure on me to search out from under every stone any prejudices I had and look at them and decide a new way of living. For a time it felt too difficult. Tina was also putting a lot of pressure on herself. When we look back on it, it wasn't a happy time. Other people were having happier times being what society expected of them.

What started to make me think about class in a different way was realising I was oppressed by those women. Middle class women could oppress me. Then I realised you couldn't just look at gender. Once I'd started to do that I looked at the way working-class people oppressed blacks. I looked at the way blacks oppressed Asians. I looked at oppression in a different way and that diluted some of my feelings and thoughts about sexism.

We were pushing ourselves to see what different ways we could react to each other. I wanted to live with Tina. That's all I ever wanted but it seemed that sometimes she was wondering whether a male–female relationship was what she wanted. It needed a lot more energy devoted to feminism before she knew what she wanted. I lived for quite a while wondering whether she'd chuck the cards in. I had to work hard at keeping up.

Then at the women's group another woman said to her 'My partner goes to a men's group' and Tina said to me 'Why don't you go?' For a while I resisted it, it seemed totally alien to me, sitting talking about feelings. I thought, 'You must be joking.' I didn't want anything to do with it but she said 'I think you'll get a lot out of it.' I'd always been one to have a go, so after a while I went along to it.

I came away from my first meeting thinking I'd never go again. It was all professionals there. I thought, all these people stringing together big long sentences with long words – and they all knew each other. Three worked together and two who didn't work together knew the others as friends. They all seemed to be old buddies and they were a different class group to me. I thought, 'I'll never be able to speak to these people. I can't speak to a lawyer and a town planner and a deputy bank manager. I certainly can't tell them how I feel.' I'd never mixed with anyone like that. I didn't go to the next meeting but there was something there I felt worth exploring so I went to a few and got to know them a bit more and didn't feel as alien to them and I was able to get what I wanted out of it.

One of them helped break those barriers because he was particularly aware of class. He was gay as well which also made a difference. He was the first man I'd ever knowingly come into contact with who was gay. What interested me about the men's group were the things they were saying. I was doing something I'd never done before and I liked that, even though I found it difficult. I often felt guilty because they seemed so much further on than I was – better thought out. I always came away thinking 'I wish I was feeling like that.'

I went for quite a long time and it seemed to get bigger, then some stopped coming and others joined so I started to change from being a new member to an older member. I went to men's conferences but I found those difficult as well. Again it was sitting in groups of people who were not my class. They were generally more educated, I found the words they used difficult to grasp and their stance difficult to understand, theorising about things. I used to score because I said things which were so obviously grassroots stuff that it stopped them in their tracks. They got into groups and talked about sexism in a theoristic way. I said, 'This is what male domination is all about, feeling you're in control.' It was giving them a forum to do that.

At that time Tina and I were really stretching ourselves, looking at our own relationship, which way we were going to go. I wanted to start a family and she was tossing around with the idea but it didn't feel right. Then she met women in the women's group who had children and we decided we would. It was a turning point. We were living together, we weren't married. We'd decided we didn't need that. By the time she finished her nursing course she was pregnant with our first daughter. She did all her exams and then went on maternity leave. Our baby was born in 1980. Tina had problems at the time, she wanted to be a mother but felt she mustn't desert the cause, the women's group was very important to her. We'd looked at it – if I was at work and she was at home with a baby. She'd said 'I'll have children but I'm not doing it the way everybody else does it. I'm only prepared to have children if we work together at it.'

That was great for me because I was more experienced with babies than she was. I'd had baby sisters. Tina had never changed a nappy and I had. I'd got up to crying babies at night and given them bottles. So I clicked into it quickly and felt a leading role in doing it. I could say 'This is how you do it.' Then because I was out at work and she was at home and because of the pressures that she felt, of not conforming to the usual mother–wife role, we decided we'd do something radical. We talked to other people who were feeling they wanted to put their politics into practice and we decided to buy a big house together and set up a sort of commune. I don't like the word, but we'd buy a house together and live together and all have separate rooms. A collective we called it.

There were five adults and four children. We had four smaller houses to sell and we bought one big one with seven huge bedrooms. The removal firm moved five houses in a day. I'll never forget it. They started at half past seven and finished emptying the fourth house at ten past nine. Then they took it all up and finished unloading by half past two – and there were only two of them! It was tremendous.

It was only a few months after we had the baby that we moved. It wasn't logical for Tina to go back to work and also I'd packed in my job. I'd started it on a high but it became a drag. I packed it in when we moved because it was part and parcel of the experiment for me, to spend a lot more time with my daughter as a father, not just on a teatime-till-bedtime basis and at weekends, but to be much more important to her. I was only out of work for one week. I got a part-time job working for a wholefood shop, a workers co-operative on a corner of a side street. I was a volunteer for a week but they wanted a new member working three days a week so I thought, that will fit in nicely. I could still claim the dole for the other two days. I had an interview and got the job.

That living arrangement really put our politics to the test! Tina decided she'd have a separate bedroom and that didn't feel comfortable to me, but we did it – and there were other things. Some of the other people had different reasons for wanting to move in together. Jenny, the other woman, wanted to live with Simon but he was wary because he'd had relationships that had ended unhappily. Simon's politics were anarchism. I hadn't understood what that was. I thought it was one step to fascism but having spoken to him and thought about it I still didn't agree but I knew what he meant. He was a interesting person, an archaeologist.

John, the other man, was gay and he was, like us, looking at how we could live differently. It was an experiment and there was a lot at stake, particularly with children involved – but it was so traumatic! I never felt comfortable with it. I knew the day we moved in it was a mistake for me. I needed space and my own door I could shut and lock and having my own bedroom was not enough. I needed to have my moods privately and I couldn't do that in that environment. People see me as a cheerful jokey chap, and I am nine times out of ten, but I do have black times. I have depressions sometimes and I need to have them in privacy. I was just getting used to being a father. My daughter was coming up to 10 months when we moved so it was still new to me. Also Tina was asking different things within the relationship, testing what she wanted to do, her philosophies of life. She was testing feminism, radical feminism in some ways, and she wanted to explore other relationships and that was difficult for me.

My parents couldn't cope with it. They thought I'd gone off my head. There I was with their first grandchild, wanting them to be grandparents but they felt alien to it, even though they liked everybody in the house. John is still around now as a friend and I like the fact that they know him, because their prejudices about gay men have been well and truly stamped out. I've heard my Mum have a go at somebody else because of their attitude towards gay people and that wouldn't have happened if they didn't know John and seen the way he's been.

Eventually Tina and I hit a crisis point where we had to ask ourselves, 'Do we want to carry on together or not?' I wanted a relationship with her. She'd explored and pushed the boundaries and she felt that what she wanted was not that. She didn't want to be on her own striving, searching, never being satisfied. We slowly came back to the roots of our relationship and how we interacted with each other, what was important to us as a couple, and started to feel a release of pressure. We decided we didn't want to push the boundaries any more and we did want to stay together.

The collective was breaking up. Simon and Jenny decided to move out and buy their own house. It was a bombshell when they told us they'd bought another house and the big one had to be sold. John had already moved out by then. He'd felt that living with two heterosexual couples was more than he could cope with. That left Tina and I and the baby in a huge house which was up for sale. That threw us together because we needed each other to survive at that point. Tina was pregnant again. It was difficult because we didn't know where we were going to live. Our cut from selling the house wasn't going to buy a house easily and I was working part time, which was our only income coming in. Tina wasn't working then.

A lovely thing though about our time at that house was that my second daughter was born there and it was beautiful. We decided to have her at home. Our first was born in hospital. Again that was Tina's radical way of thinking. She decided to have a home birth and sought out a doctor who'd let her do it. It was a struggle but she did, and it was tremendous. I was present at both the girls' births. It was an important part of my getting to know them. The first was born in a little cottage hospital and the second was born at home, and the one at home was wonderful because at the first one I was in for the birth and then told 'You go and sit over there.' The one at home wasn't like that, I was much more involved, and at night when everybody had gone I was still there, I didn't have to go back to a quiet house. Our other daughter came in and we all got into bed, all four of us. It was lovely. Later I put the older girl to bed and Tina was absolutely wrecked so I wrapped the new baby up and snuggled her into bed with me. We slept on a mattress on the floor all night, her first night. It felt perfect. It felt the right way to do it.

Tina couldn't get back into nursing at that point. There were no openings and travelling was out of the question with a baby. She didn't get back into nursing for quite a while so she wasn't working. It was worrying. We didn't have much income, about £30 a week. The big house was sold and when the money was divided up we were left with about £3,500 after we'd paid off the mortgage. We'd had the house not quite two years and it had only gained £1,800 which was swallowed up in all the fees. So we moved into a house with a friend.

I worked at the wholefood co-op for seven years altogether. I helped move it to an arcade in the town centre. Then we went into publishing and then another food shop and a bookshop. I went from three days to four days, then I worked evenings. I went full time the last two years I was there but the wages were low. Working there I got involved with people looking at politics in a different way. There were men who'd experienced men's groups and women who were feminists and it was a working environment where we tried to break sexual stereotypes as well. There were jobs men did because they were the skills they'd learned and jobs women did, but when we divided the work we looked at breaking the stereotypes. It was important to us all.

More important than that, I started to look at class and find my roots a lot more. After three years only looking at politics from a middle class feminist perspective in a theoretical way, suddenly I came to looking at my roots and looking at how I acted. I had a love–hate relationship with one man who worked there. He made me think about things that were difficult but I liked him because he made me think about how your actions relate to how you are, and taking responsibility for your actions, to value what you do and to value other people's labour, the idea that wealth is generated from labour, to look at where wealth comes from.

Working in a co-op meant you didn't have a boss to blame, you worked together and tried to make things happen and had to rely on each other to be there. It put my feet back on the ground. I learned not to feel guilty if I had what I would have thought at the time were sexist thoughts. For instance, if I saw an attractive woman and looked at her much longer than I would another, not to feel guilty about that. As long as my attitude of respect for women was strong, as it was because I worked with strong women in the co-op who I very much respected and

I had a partner who I very much respected, guilt could go, tied around sexual feelings as sexist. I was able to separate that out and say, it's OK if I fancy somebody like mad. That's not oppressing them as long as I don't use my maleness to gain something. I started to feel a lot happier in that way.

Tina and I started to feel more comfortable with each other, our relationship seemed better and easier. I had problems at the shop because I was expected to have great loyalty to it and there was a crisis soon after our second daughter was born when Tina fell down the stairs and broke both her wrists and her elbow. The co-op was just moving into a town-centre shop, so everyone was putting a hundred per cent in. I never had a day off while that was going on but I couldn't work in the evening. I felt my allegiance was to the family. Tina was breast-feeding and we had to arrange people to come and help to turn the baby over. It was very difficult.

The pressure on us then was having no money, with a mortgage and little wages coming in. We never got child-minding sorted out but when the girls got a bit older Tina did part-time jobs here and there. She worked as a receptionist for a while, then they made her redundant and she got a clerical job in a hospital.

Finally she saw a job advertised for medical research with the doctor who'd delivered our second daughter. She worked with him for eighteen months and then he encouraged her to get back into nursing. She'd banged against the system when she'd been nursing before. She wasn't keen on hierarchy and the fact that it wasn't patient-orientated but system-orientated. She wasn't liked because she wouldn't keep her mouth shut. He told her nursing needed people like her and wrote her the most fantastically glorious reference. So she applied and got back on the nurse-bank system and soon got a full-time job. She'd been out of nursing for nearly six years.

At that time I decided I couldn't give the co-op any more. It didn't have any more challenges for me. Working co-operatively is great for people who'd never worked like that. It stretches you much more than any other. You have to work closely with other people. You have to understand other people's labour and learn responsibiity for your own actions which put either more or less money in your pocket. I would never have done without it. You couldn't work in a better environment but I'd grown out of it.

So I left in 1988 and joined an organisation that enables me to work with elderly people, which I'd always wanted to do. I'd always had a great empathy for them and felt society gave them a raw deal. I was a good handyman so I thought a good job would be doing repairs and improvements for elderly people. Then this job came up which was a step up from that, they wanted an organiser for repairs like that. So that's what I do now.

I don't think I can say whether I feel more at ease with men or women now. It depends on the men and the women. When I was repairing fork-lift trucks I had to visit workshops where a lot of women worked and they used to shout 'Come on over here lad. Have a grab of this.' They were bloody awful. The toilets were in the corner and it meant crossing the workshop with about twenty women working. Even if I was absolutely bursting I would never have gone past all those women. I'd have been far too embarrassed. I've been to meetings with professional women in this job and it was 'backs to wall' about jobs and protecting their images. I didn't feel comfortable with those either. I've been with men when I felt equally uncomfortable. It's not a matter of sex, it's a matter of personalities. I don't think masculinity means much to me. It's just not important.

A few years ago I got quite involved in the Labour Party and they wanted me to be a candidate for the council but I didn't want to spend the time on it and neglect my family, so I turned that down. I'm fully involved in housework. I do the full range. I don't do much with the washing machine because I've had a few disasters with that, ruining people's clothes, but everything else I do, cooking, cleaning. I've always been fully involved in caring for the children. Tina and I are married now. In the end we decided we didn't need to be different any more and it felt good to make that commitment.

SIMON

I'm 39 and I'm an archaeologist doing post-excavation analysis and part-time teaching. I work a lot at home. I'm about to move to Oxfordshire. I was married at 18 and divorced at 28. I lived with another woman for three years and I've been with Jenny about six or seven years. I've a son from my marriage, now in his twenties. Jenny has two daughters from her marriage. So I'm a father of one and a stepfather of two.

I was born and grew up in Coventry, my father worked in a car factory. My father was a skilled man, a toolmaker and proud of being a skilled man. That was a high status within car factories in Coventry. About fifteen years ago my mother opened a guesthouse and my father took early retirement and went into the guesthouse with my mother. They're both retired now.

When I was little one of my earliest memories is of my Dad coming home off the nightshift. We'd be in the kitchen getting ready for school and he'd come home from work absolutely knackered and go straight to bed. I don't remember him doing much overtime. I saw quite a bit of him. I had a good relationship with my father. I've got fond memories of my father when we were growing up because he was a caring man. He used to do a lot with us and he was always taking us out to places and showing us how to do things – helping us fix our bikes and things.

I never thought he was unconventional. I don't think when you're a child you realise things like that. He was just my Dad and he was normal. Looking back on it, he was unusual. He helped my mother around the house, doing cooking and housework but I never thought anything of it. I thought it was a normal thing to do, but perhaps it was a bit unusual.

He was quite involved. My mother had a nervous breakdown – that's what we were told – when I was 11 or 12. Whether that influenced what my Dad did around the house I don't know. I wouldn't be surprised. He always was, and still is, very caring about my mother and he still does a fair bit around the house. I don't know if he was involved when we were very young, changed nappies and so on. I wouldn't be surprised. It would be in character.

I'm not sure what effect it had on me. My brother is a stereotypical man. He doesn't do anything. He works hard at work but when he gets in he expects his dinner and doesn't do any housework. He takes the typical male role. I've wondered what made my brother and myself so different if we came from the same home and had the same father. Maybe later influences were important. My experience of marriage and his may have been different.

When I first got married I was 18 and my wife was pregnant so we had our son six months after we were married. She was 16. I was an apprentice in a car factory in Coventry – I followed in my father's footsteps, he got me the job. My wife was at home all day but she had an evening job in a shop from about four thirty to about eight o'clock five nights a week. Obviously that left me with the baby from an early age, from as soon as I got in from work until she got home at half past eight. It never struck me as an odd thing to do, to take over looking after the baby. It obviously didn't sharply contrast with what my father was like. That could well be it, I fitted into what I thought was a father's role because my father had done that.

I remember an incident soon after my son was born. I was hanging washing out one evening and the bloke next door came home and made some comment about it. I remember it to this day, standing there hanging out washing, thinking, 'What's wrong with hanging out washing? Why did he say that?' He thought it was a woman's job. He said something like that. It didn't strike me as anything odd to do. I wasn't at all political in those days. I didn't think, it's politically the right thing to do, to hang out the washing. It was a sense of fairness. There was work to be done so we shared it.

That was important to me then, even without a political rationale. I've always had a strong sense of fairness. I've never been involved in party politics. The politics I've been involved in, in recent years, are due to something offending my sense of fairness. I don't know if I got that from my father. I have political arguments now with him. He used to be strongly involved in the union in the factory, a shop steward, he always voted Labour. Recently he started to say and do things that absolutely appalled me and he voted Tory for the first time in his life. We had a heated discussion over that. When I was growing up he was always on the Left. He was from a working-class area of Coventry.

My mother had a complicated background. She was adopted by a working-class family in Coventry though she was born in the south-east. How they came to get my mother I'm not sure but there was a person who lived in Southend we called 'Auntie' and who my Mum used to call 'Auntie' as well. About eight or nine years ago it came out that this woman was my mother's mother. It had been kept secret all those years.

Now I understand my mother's background I can see what a strong effect this had on her attitudes – she's strongly aware of the family unit. She'll go to great lengths to get her family together, my brother and his family and me and mine. She's always trying to maneouvre us into spending the evening together. I'm sure it's a result of what happened to her.

The woman I called grandma – I didn't know her husband because he died when I was young – had a two-up/two-down terraced house in Coventry. I spent time there during school holidays. On both sides my background was working class. My mother was employed too, as a secretary in a factory. She didn't do that for most of my childhood. When I was 6 to 10 my mother ran a baby-clothes shop. Then we moved into a better house. She gave up that job and got one as a secretary when I was about 12. She had a long spell off when she had this nervous breakdown and was in hospital for a time. For most of my secondary-school years I remember her working as a secretary. She used to go off on a moped.

I'm not sure if she was independent, I can't remember her going off doing things on her own other than working, but she had her own income . . . Thinking about it, it was obviously important to her to work. I remember her appearing to enjoy telling people about her job. She was pleased she worked. It gave her an identity other than housewife and it gave me the experience that women can be working women.

Sometimes neither of them was there when we got in from school about four o'clock. We were on our own a couple of hours before they got home. They left us lists of jobs to do before they got in. They involved us in the housework, in preparation for them getting home. I can't remember feeling annoyed about it. We just did it. My father was capable of giving us a good telling off but I can't remember having any severe tellings off for not doing the jobs they'd left us.

I can't remember any friends before we moved. As soon as we moved I started a new school and I made a good friend, the first day. It was a lad who lived down the street we'd moved into. He was my closest friend from that age right through secondary school. He was best man at my wedding and I still know him now. He was the most important friend I had, and there were other peripheral friendships – always boys. I never had girl friends. Secondary school was all boys and my contact with girls was minimal.

Junior school was mixed but I can't remember any girls there. I remember walking home with gangs of boys. There was one girl who lived down our street. We avoided her. When I went to secondary school there was an all-girls' school we passed to get to our school and the girls were figures of fun. We pinched their berets and shouted abuse at them until we got old enough to have pressures put on about having girl friends.

There were some joint events between the two schools, discos for the fifth years. Nothing earlier than that. I can't remember consciously avoiding them. Everything I needed in the way of friendship seemed to come from the boys I knew. There didn't seem any need to know girls.

The games we played were traditional boys' games, football mostly. We used to play football out in the street. We had model cars and what we called 'trolleys', planks with wheels on. I don't remember any definite attitude towards the girls apart from ignoring them. I'm sure we never went out of our way to find girls to be horrible to. We never thought about them. We played amongst ourselves.

I had a brother, no sisters. I had two female cousins but didn't see them all that often. When we saw them we were just polite. Our parents used to push us into the garden or upstairs while they talked. I can't remember feeling openly hostile towards them. I felt awkward. My strongest feeling of being awkward with girls was when I first started trying to date girls in the last year at school when I was 15. I had absolutely no experience of relating to girls in a meaningful way. It was peer-group pressure, other kids were getting girlfriends and it was the thing to do.

Me and my friend Roy used to go down town. We went down on the bus absolutely intent on picking up two girls. We'd both be scared stiff about it, worried but determined. We'd go and sit next to a pair of girls in a pub, we went in pubs then. I felt really awkward, not knowing what to say and absolutely hating it, but feeling I had to do it. I didn't want to. I didn't feel attracted to them at that stage. I don't think I was sexually attracted to girls until . . . it depends if you mean sexually attracted to the idea of a girl, or to a specific girl. The idea came earlier.

We used to have joint masturbating sessions. We didn't do it to each other, we did it ourselves, but we used to do it together and have races! Not just me and Roy, it was a group of us. I remember four or five of us doing it together. Obviously I was sexually aware before trying to pick up girls but it was never centred on a specific girl. It was just becoming aware of our bodies.

It was a painful phase, learning how to relate to girls. I used to have a terrible problem with blushing. I remember absolutely cringing about blushing. I used to blush at the slightest thing and, of course, it was a vicious circle. As soon as I realised I was blushing, I got more embarrased and it got more, and people used to take the piss out of me. My parents commented on it, which I thought was cruel of them. I was painfully shy. I didn't know what to say – I might make a fool of myself, and the thought of blushing when I did say anything . . .

I only had one girl friend before Val who I married. I went out with the other girl about six months. We didn't go very far sexually. Mainly because she didn't want to. I remember I did, but that was peer-group pressure. At that time I was a mod, I had a scooter, and a parka, the whole works, and it was part of the image to have a girl sitting on the back seat in a full length leather coat. That was quite important and the girl I went out with had a full length leather coat, so she fitted in. I can't remember why we finished but then I met Val. She was my first real sexual partner and she became pregnant and we got married. So my experience of girls before I was married was pretty limited.

It's difficult to assess whether my school experience pushed me into masculine activities or what were seen as boys' subjects because it was an all-boys' school. I didn't have anything to compare it with. I remember in my final class at primary school there was a woman teacher but I can't remember any others. At senior school I don't know if they emphasised football and rugby, and science subjects, maths and metal-work and so on. We never did cookery or sewing or anything like that.

My strongest memory of macho behaviour was in games. The games teacher really took it out of any boys who didn't perform well at games. He called us pansies if we didn't get stuck in as he wanted us to. I hated games and especially rugby. I wasn't any good at it. I didn't like the competitive aspect of it. I loved playing football in the street with friends but when it came to playing football properly on a pitch I didn't like it at all – the pressure on us to perform well and win. In rugby I was worried about getting hurt. I used to hang out on the wing by the touchline and hope that the ball never came to me. The games master made fun of ones he thought were a bit sissy. He was a cruel bugger he was!

I can't remember ever being picked on by boys that were more macho. I didn't like games but I wasn't one of the stereotyped weaker type of boy that tends to get picked on. I was a real in-betweener. I wasn't one of those that got picked on and I wasn't one of those that did the picking. I just kept my head down. It wasn't a terribly rough school. There wasn't continual bullying. The time I remember really trying to get in with particular groups was at the end of school when I was a mod. There was a hard core group of mods I was desperate to be in with, and they came across as being very macho, swaggered around with what were really uniforms on. I was always trying to fit in with them, but I was on the fringe.

Their public attitude to girls, what their real feelings were I don't know, but the public attitude was, girls were part of the decoration on your scooter, part of the back seat. Then there was the sexual aspect, it was a time of bragging, boasting about conquests and experiences, and girls were there to be had. They exaggerated their exploits. I'm sure they did. I can't remember ever claiming anything I hadn't done but there again I can't remember ever claiming anything. I was on the fringes of it.

I identified with my father a lot. When we went out to places I always felt comfortable that this man was my father. I was never ashamed of him or embarrassed about being with him. I didn't feel awkward. I suppose that could be interpreted as looking up to him. I didn't know much about his work. It didn't feel a familiar world to me. He didn't talk about it. That was a part of his life I didn't know much about. When I left school I wanted to earn money, that's why I left when I was 16. I went to work as an apprentice in the factory he worked at, simply because he could give me a lift there in the morning. So I must have been quite happy with him being my father or else I wouldn't have gone to work in the same place.

In my spare time I went out with him in my teens. We went to football matches. It's something we did together a long time. We supported Coventry City and went to London together when they got in the Cup Final. I think our relationship changed when I decided it would, rather than when he decided, which was probably when I was about 16. It wasn't part of the image to be seen going around with your Dad. I'm sure the change in our relationship was my decision rather than his. I did go and use him when my scooter broke down. He helped me fix it. He was very good mechanically.

Right through when I had scooters and when I had a car I always did mechanical things with my Dad. He was extremely patient if he was showing you how to do something. He taught both me and my brother to drive and I remember when I got my first car he showed me how to strip down the engine. He completely stripped it down and refitted the whole thing. Of course that was quite a masculine activity. I can't remember him showing me how to do anything that wasn't typically masculine. He never showed me how do ironing. I can't remember him ironing but he did other things around the house. He didn't show me how to cook but I saw him doing it.

When I was growing up work was easy to come by in factories. When I left school at 16 I had the choice of about three aprenticeships to go into. I worked as an apprentice for five years, a full apprenticeship. I ended up as a quality-control engineer, inspecting things to make sure they were right. I didn't mind the social aspect of the apprenticeship. In those days there were hundreds of apprentices. I had some good friends but of course they were all male.

The work was tedious. I didn't like it at all. You spent six months in the training school which was a machine shop, learning how to use a lathe, milling machine and things like that. Then two and a half years going round all the different departments, getting a taste of different machine shops, fitting shops, assembly shops, inspection, and so on. Then you decided what you wanted to be and spent the last two years specialising in what you'd chosen. I chose quality control because it was the easiest and cleanest. You wore a white coat instead of overalls . . . and you sat down! I didn't like machine shops because they were noisy and dirty and horrible.

This was still a male environment, the only women worked in the offices and one of these was my Mum. They occasionally walked through machine shops and fitting shops and there was absolute uproar.

The blokes were shouting and whistling and you could see these women were cringing as they walked through – it was part of the accepted environment. I suppose I took it for granted but I never took part in it. I remember feeling uncomfortable about it. I accepted that it happened and ignored it. It was the same with pornography. There was loads of pornography in the factory and clubs where people would pay two shillings a week and it was pooled to buy magazines, not just *Playboy*, these were brown-envelope things from Scandinavia, real hard-core stuff and everybody in a particular club had half an hour in the toilets with this magazine. I never took part in any of that either. I'm not saying I didn't look at them, but I never felt motivated to join any of these syndicates. I don't remember feeling at the time that it was degrading for the women involved. I wasn't that aware then. I just felt there was something wrong with it. I never felt comfortable with it.

When I finished the apprenticeship there wasn't a job I wanted, so I got another job in a tractor factory as a qualified control inspector. I was 21 so it was when I was married. This was an extremely boring job. I had a lot of spare time in that job. It was extremely well paid for doing virtually bugger-all. I used to sit at a desk for eight hours a day doing hardly anything. I did a lot of reading. It was a very lax place, my immediate superiors didn't bother what I did.

I remember going to the public library and thinking, 'Well I've got to find something of interest', and I was looking along the shelves and I came across this geology book. I took it out and got interested in it and to cut a long story short I ended up doing O level geology by correspondence course. Then I did A level geology that way as well – both during the day while I was at the tractor works. I got very interested in geology and decided I wanted to go to university. Then I got accepted at university to do combined geology and archaeology. So in my mid-twenties I entered Leicester University. In the first year I decided geology was too difficult, archaeology was easier and more interesting.

I went to the tractor factory when I was 21. I'd already been married three years and Tim was about three years old. My ex-wife Val and myself had this fantastic masterplan we dreamed up that involved Val studying for O levels and A levels by correspondence course and eventually going to teachers' training college, then me following on two or three years behind and doing the same thing so that eventually we'd both end up teachers. This plan worked fine to start off with, Val got O levels and A levels and went to the local teachers' training college and qualified as a teacher. She did a four-year course. Meanwhile I was doing exams by correspondence course, mostly during the day when I was at work.

Let me tell you why me and Val wanted to study. I was not very academic at school. I left with four O levels at the earliest I could. I wanted to earn money. That seemed more important then. Val was different. She left school because she was pregnant and we were getting married. She was already in the sixth form, so she'd made the decision to stay on.

She was artistic in an academic sense. She was into the theory of art. Her specialism was pottery, and today she still teaches art and pottery. The teachers' training she did was a four-year B.Ed. course, but her main subject was art. It was a combination of being academic and artistic. She was the driving force behind the idea initially, although once I got into it I was really motivated, fantastically self-motivated. She was an example and then I found a subject that interested me anyway so I followed suit.

When Val qualified we were absolutely over the moon because she got a job in the local comprehensive school just down the road and went off to work at the beginning of the school year. I'd got into the closest university that did archaeology and commuted every day there and it was all going hunky dory. As far as I was aware at the time we were happily married and I thought we had a very fair relationship where we shared lots of things. We shared tasks around the house and I thought we were very close and we spent a lot of time together and with Tim, our son.

Then at Christmas which was the end of my first term at university, I became aware that something was seriously different about Val. It was a terrible Christmas and eventually it came out she was having an affair with a bloke at school and she wanted us to separate and she wanted to go and live with him. I was totally demolished by this. I went and lived in digs near the university for a couple of months while we sorted it out and she stayed in the house in Coventry with Tim. Eventually we decided it would be easier for Tim if he lived with me rather than living with Val and a new bloke. The logic was, it would be easier for Tim to lose a mother than have to lose a father and accept a substitute father figure all in one go. So I got the legal custody of him. I remember the lawyer saying it was the first time he had ever sought legal custody for a father. It was the sort of relationship we had. We didn't think it was an odd thing to do.

It was worked out as the most rational arrangement. It reflected the fact that I'd had as much a part in all aspects of Tim's upbringing as Val had. It was not a thing we decided to do for political reasons. We weren't at all political then. It was sense of fairness, which we both had. Val worked hard and I worked hard so why shouldn't we share all the boring jobs that had to be done and the enjoyable jobs as well? . . . like looking after Tim. I really enjoyed that.

I wanted custody. It was a joint decision. We spent ages discussing it. If Val had wanted custody she'd have fought and got it because the weight of convention was on her side. It was in my favour that she didn't want custody. My idea is that she was so besotted by this bloke she was taken by the idea of starting afresh. The reason she gave was that they were going to live in a small flat and there wouldn't be room for Tim.

Besides, I wanted custody. I did genuinely think it would be best for him. I was close to him and I'd done his nappy changing and so on . . . the thought of feeding and looking after him didn't bother me. I didn't even think about it. The main reason was that this would be the most secure situation for Tim, he wouldn't have to come to terms with living with the new bloke. Once I'd decided it was the most emotionally secure situation for Tim I fought for it.

So our masterplan worked . . . until she went off with someone else. I felt very bitter about that at the time. I felt she hadn't kept her side of the bargain. I felt fantastically let down and hurt. It was terribly disturbing to my studies because after Christmas I went and lived in a one-room bedsitter and was in there until Easter. Coming up to the first-year exams I was in this room and I remember lying in bed at night crying for hours. I had one good friend and he really pulled me through it. He was on the same course and I confided in him. He used to come round and see me at least once a day. We're still good friends.

So in Leicester there was me and Tim and I started my second year at university and had a lot of work to do. I was a conscientious student which a lot of mature students are. I worked hard and I was desperately trying to be socially accepted in my peer group who were all younger than me. So I spent less time with Tim. I didn't notice it at the time but I remember lots of occasions when I put off doing things with Tim because I felt other things were more important, working or going out. Perhaps that sort of regret is fairly common among parents. Looking back you wish you'd done more with your kids.

Tim and I lived on our own for about eighteen months, two years perhaps, before Kitty moved in with us. Looking back I can see that an area I was lacking with Tim was in emotional physical-type closeness. I don't think it was because he was a boy. It was a problem within me. I'd have been the same whether he was a boy or girl. Now I've got two stepdaughters I experience the same problem. It sounds pathetic and it's probably something a lot of men say, but I find it difficult to be physical with kids.

He hasn't commented on it since. I've a great relationship with Tim now. He's in his twenties and for me I'm quite physical with him in that we hug when we meet. He lives in London now. I'm not bothered about touching him now but I'm aware it's an effort to do it. I think about it before I do it, but he responds. I was always convinced it was the right move getting custody. I didn't ever feel I'd not done the right thing. I've no regrets.

One thing bothered me. Tim was 8 when we split up and we tried to tell him what was happening and why. This was in early summer and we were both absolutely flabbergasted by his lack of reaction. He didn't seem upset by it and when we moved he quite matter of factly left Val and came to live with me. Through the summer I probed him gently about how he felt but I didn't push him too hard.

When it all came out was the first morning he started his new school. In the morning he'd shown signs of being a bit bothered about going to his new school and the cat was asleep on his bed. He was up sitting on the side of the bed and the alarm clock went off. For some reason this freaked out the cat and it leaped up in the air and scratched his leg. He absolutely broke down. He cried and sobbed and it started to come out about how he didn't want his Mum to go and he didn't want to start this new school.

It was a low point for me because I needed support and there was nobody there. I didn't know whether to take him to school, and I ended up carrying him to school over my shoulder virtually and he was kicking and fighting. He didn't want to go but I thought it was imperative that I got him there. Perhaps I was trying to prove something to myself. Anyway I eventually got him to school and it was a terrible scene there but the teacher took over and told me to go away. When he got back that evening he was relatively OK but that was when he first showed any emotional reaction to us splitting up and that was three months after he knew about it. He'd been holding it down.

It staggered me he could do that for three months. It suggests he'd already picked up an idea that boys should hold their feelings back, not cry and that kind of thing, not from me but maybe from his mates. It's a thing I found difficult during the rest of his growth, peer-group pressure. He was affected again when we moved here. I feel bad about it when I look back. He had several changes of school. I've been quite rewarded lately because I thought till recently that peer-group influence was more important than mine. My belief has always been that this male–female stereotype business is silly, and that people should be able to do what they want, but Tim has always gone along with his mates. He's been a normal boy I suppose but the last two or three years when he's started voicing his own political views, it's rewarding to see that influences he was exposed to had an effect. He is quite politically aware compared to his mates he went through secondary school with. They come from fairly standard family backgrounds. His views on racism and sexism are much more enlightened than theirs. It didn't just come from me – me and other people.

Nearly all my friends there were on the same course I was on. There were women on the course. We were only a group of twelve and approximately half were male and half female and we were a close group. We did things as a group and went on field trips, because it was a practical sort of course. We went off for weekends. A regret I have is that I was good friends with one of the women and it turned into a sexual relationship. I regret that because it added new dimensions which spoiled it. We ended up living together for a couple of years and it didn't work and ended quite nasty, whereas the eighteen months we were friends before we started sleeping together, it was great. We really got on well. Her name was Kitty. She was the one who opened my eyes to politics. She was a feminist, an important influence. I hadn't thought much about the issue before that.

I hadn't thought about politics at all. I'd never voted and that was significant. It wasn't that I hadn't bothered. I'd decided none of them appealed to me and I had a gut feeling there was something wrong with the system. At university I got interested in the nineteenth-century anarchists and the theory of anarchism as opposed to the party system. Elements of it still appeal to me. I read about theoretical anarchism and it seemed to fit the sense of fair play and justice I'd always had. I remember browsing around bookshops and coming across books, just flicking through them and getting involved. I never joined an anarchist group but it definitely appealed to me.

The appeal of feminism too was just that it seemed fair, and fitted in with what I already felt but I'd never verbalised. Because I'd always felt it, I'd tried to do it in my everyday living practices. Kitty taught me a lot about feminism and I agreed with what she said about it, but I remember situations where as a man I felt threatened. Kitty didn't aim it at me personally, not when I first knew her. When our relationship was going sour that was different but other influences were coming in there. When we first met, when we were friends and first started living together she never directed anti-men feelings at me, but some of her feminist friends did. They used to argue on a very personal level which I obviously found threatening. I remember occasions when I got very unhappy about that. That was the beginning of my political awareness.

This was while Tim was living with me. He was with me when I was living with Kitty. The fact that Tim was there was a lot of the reason why we eventually split up. When I graduated I got a research assistantship in Staffordshire. Our relationship was going wrong. It was a terrible move looking back on it but Kitty decided to move with us. We bought a house in Stafford and after a year Kitty left and got a job down south.

The good thing for me was that Kitty was much more competent in making friends and social contacts than I was. The first thing Kitty did was join a women's group and it was through her contacts that I met people. A lot of the women's group had male partners and it was through meeting them that I joined a men's group in Stafford. She gave me the way in. I already had the beliefs within me, they went back a long way to when I was young, certainly when I was first married I had a lot of the beliefs that I still held when I joined my first men's group when I was about 30.

With Kitty it was my first exposure to feminist ideas. I didn't at that stage think of being involved in men's groups. To be honest I don't think I was even aware they existed then. It wasn't till I moved to Stafford that I'd even heard of them. So it was the move to Stafford and the connections I made there that were the important steps. They didn't seem important at the time. My personal politics had been developing for several years.

I saw joining a men's group as an opportunity to be with other men who would have similar ideas. It worked out like that. I got a hell of a lot from it, the first men's group I was in, fantastic experience. It stretched me, really made me think. We put ourselves on the line a lot, intense pressure. I don't know if this applied to the others, I know it did for some, but I found fantastic pressure on me to think and talk about things I'd never have talked about, personal and emotional things – all within a framework of total trust and friendship. We also did fun things together. It wasn't all heavy conversation.

Some of them were partners of members of the women's group, but not all. One was gay but I think all the others had partners in the women's group. It wasn't a big group, eight or nine of us. I don't know if it was an offshoot of the women's group. I wasn't in at the start. I was just asked if I wanted to join. We were very aware that the women we were living with were feminists and they were in the women's group, and that was colouring our lifestyles fantastically, so we had to react in some way.

We were individually being influenced by feminism or felt pressure from it, but from the start we decided that the men's group was about two things, first how we reacted to women and how we could support the feminist cause, the other part was about us, how we reacted to each other as men and being male. We tried to deal with both.

I found it a really good experience for me. I enjoyed it tremendously. I grew a lot from it. This was a reason why I didn't get so much out of the second group I joined. The first was so good and I had such good memories of it that it made the second seem flat. Partly a feeling of, 'I've been through this before, do I need to go through it again?' The first one was a good experience and the second was almost doomed to not live up to it.

One of the main things the first men's group did for me was give me insights into other men, how they feel and think. I never get to know most men. I've one or two close male friends but the vast majority of men I meet are so superficial, they talk and do the accepted things. That men's group was my first opportunity to get beneath the veneer of what a man should be to what he really is. I found that a fantastic experience.

The group enabled me to get below the surface with men and talk about personal things, sensitive emotions, close relationships. It was a revelation. My personal politics had been practical, they'd influenced my daily life. I'd been doing what were normally non-male things for years. What was nice about the men's group was that it was a different way of doing something practical and fitted into gut feelings I'd had for years about fairness and justice and I'd read theoretical political stuff, theory of how societies can be organised in a fair and just way. That was already there in me and, going to the men's group and seeing men in a different way, it all started to fit together.

Then I met Jenny. We started seeing each other and it developed into a sexual relationship. We started staying at each other's houses. Then a group of us decided to live communally and to do it we had to sell four houses. It was a fantastic feat of logistics. We sold them and bought a big one in another town and lived communally there. There were five adults and Tim and three other children, nine altogether. It only lasted eighteen months and went wrong for a lot of reasons. Then Jenny and me and Tim and Jenny's two kids moved here and the others went their own ways. There were two women, both feminists, and three men from Stafford men's group. A lot of how we organised the house was based on equality and principles we believed in.

The first men's group collapsed when we moved, the rest didn't carry on. I'd got close to one man in the group who we lived with in the big house. It still upsets me to think about him. When the commune split up there was a lot of bad feeling. I've seen him in the street but I've lost touch with him. I haven't spoken to him for years. It still upsets me a lot and I miss him. I don't see any of the others in a meaningful way. That was another problem with the second men's group, one of them was in that and I found it difficult. There's a lot of unfinished business and to be in a group where an underlying principle is honesty, and with a man I couldn't be honest with about things that had happened. I couldn't go through with that.

For me setting up the communal living arrangement was putting anarchism into practice in a small way. The others didn't call themselves anarchists but it was along the same lines. We'd got together and spent a long time talking about it and we decided there should be viable alternative ways of organising domestic life. Part of it was trying to get away from the accepted nuclear family – everybody living in their own house.

We were trying quite revolutionary ideas. The thing most people found difficult to accept, not us but other people, was that we had income sharing. Everything anybody earned or got was put into a central fund and we paid house bills and took money out as we needed it. Some of us were unemployed and others in paid work. People said, 'How can you do that? You're subsidising those two on the dole.' It was something we believed in and wanted to do but it got difficult when things were going wrong.

I felt disappointed and bitter about how it went wrong, fantastic disappointment. People seemed to be waiting for it to go wrong. Our parents thought we were absolutely bananas to try it in the first place and others on the sidelines were waiting for it to go wrong and when it went wrong in eighteen months . . . they could say I told you so.

After that I went into something nearer to a conventional household. It was good for me and Jenny because we'd never lived together before we moved here. We spent eighteen months in the commune and we'd had the relationship about a year in Stafford but lived in separate houses. It was two and a half years before we moved here and I'm glad we did because it's been more stable since. I'm much happier now, I like living with Jenny.

At first we had all the children with us. Tim left home when he was 18. The two girls must have been 6 and 7 when we moved here, which means when we moved to the commune they must have been 4 and 5. Being a father to two daughters opened up a whole new can of worms. I find it difficult, to be honest, being a stepfather. I think about it a lot. It causes me a lot of heartache. It's more difficult being a stepfather than a father because I'm never sure of my relationship and it's difficult knowing the boundaries of how far to go. This is the first time I've talked about it with anyone other than Jenny. It's something that's important to me because I spend a lot of time thinking about it.

Part of the problem is that I'm never sure what they think of me. It's different with your own child because you know there's a bond that's always there, the fact that you're father and child, and whatever you do, however bad a row is, the bond is still there. But being a stepfather that bond isn't there and when we have rows and I tell them off I'm never sure what's going to be left afterwards.

A lot of the problem with my relationship with the girls is within me rather than them. It's important to me to relate well to them. I'm always doing things I regret afterwards and feel bad about it. As I said about Tim, I find it difficult, physical closeness, there's all sorts of complications. Sometimes I feel I can't do things with them because I didn't do them with Tim and I should have done because he's my real child whereas the girls aren't, so if I do these things with them I'll feel guilty because I didn't do them with Tim.

It doesn't make any difference that they're girls. I never give them the impression they should do certain things because they're girls and they're fairly aware of both mine and Jenny's anti-sexist stance. They get irate about sexism at school. Susan likes playing football and the sports teacher wouldn't start a girls' football team and she was particularly annoyed about that. I don't try to get them cooking because cooking is something that girls do, or anything like that.

I want to give them every opportunity as human beings. That's not the problem that bothers me, it's our fundamental relationship. A lot of men go through relationships not thinking and feeling about them and are surprised when they go wrong. I'm aware and concerned about relationships that are important to me. Sometimes I think I'm too aware! I'm sure it's a product of what happened to me in the past. A lot of it was being in the first men's group, it was a big influence. Although there were lots of things before that, it crystallised a lot of ideas I'd had before.

Feminism has influenced me a lot. Indirectly it led to my involvement in the men's group. A lot of the principles the men's group stood for I already believed in. I think if I'd arrived there on my own and heard about the men's group I'd have joined it anyway, whether I was living with a feminist or not. I'm sure I would. It's just that there was a particular group of people thinking along those political lines.

My main leisure pursuit is running. I love it. I go out at least three times a week and go to the club once a week. The biggest benefit is mental not physical satisfaction, and it's not for the social life. I must know twenty-five men. We go off and run together, have showers together and drink in the bar afterwards together, but I find it so irritating that they talk about such predictable things – cars, beer, women and sport. When I think back to other situations when I've been with large groups of men, working in factories, they were the same. It puzzles me whether they're happy talking about those things all the while or whether they're all thinking, 'God, I wish I could talk about something different', as well.

They'd never admit it and nobody knows how to start a conversation. I don't when I'm in the club. As far as most of them are concerned I'm just like them. Perhaps they think I'm a bit odd when I don't take part in the sexist comments that are absolutely rife when we're running along the road and a woman walks past. I don't challenge it because that would be too difficult, but I don't take part in it.

Family life is important to me, family life loosely, the kids are usually out somewhere. Jenny works a lot too. We don't do much as a family. We go away for a weekend now and again together and on holiday in the summer but we're not together every night. We've our own and mutual friends that we see occasionally but I don't do much socially. I work most of the time. It spills over into what would be my leisure time. Jenny's a social worker. When I first met her she worked in the hospital and then she went to Keele University and did a social-work qualification while we were in the commune.

We've got the housework worked out well. I'm happy with the way we organise things. I often cook in the evening. We have a strict system for housework, us and the kids have set jobs. We do housework once a week. The only thing I don't do much is ironing. If I'm really forced to I do it, but I do washing, hanging out clothes, getting them in, cooking, washing up. Ironing is the only thing Jenny does and I don't. Every other job, it's just as likely I'll do it as Jenny. Often it ends up as who happens to have the time when it needs doing. We don't take it in turns intentionally but we take it in turns doing the one big weekly shop, which is a right pain. I can't think of anything else that Jenny does that I don't. I'm sure Jenny is satisfied with it.

One thing I've thought of, as the girls get older, there are things they want Jenny to do with them, like shopping for clothes. I occasionally do it. Not long ago I took them to buy shoes but the older one is interested in fashion and enjoys shopping with Jenny. I don't think she'd enjoy it with me, I don't like shopping. I suppose that's male–female stereotyping.

I've approximated to an ideal sort of situation with Jenny. We try to live up to certain principles within the practical confines our work imposes. We both work long hours and a lot of our lifestyle revolves around work. Jenny works long days and some evenings. Over the last three or four years she's been out three evenings a week, which means I've been in three evenings a week. A lot of my work is home-based. I can work here, which has been convenient but it's meant I've taken over being here when she isn't. I think we've worked it out well but I must admit there are times I get totally pissed off about the hours Jenny works and we've had rows about it. I've felt put upon and doing too much in the house. The sort of thing housewives come up with.

Having experienced a marriage and a successful relationship without marriage, to be absolutely honest I don't think it matters one way or the other. Having been married for ten years and it ended and I felt helpless and had no control over what was going on, and I didn't want it to end, looking back I can't see the point of being married. It didn't make much difference at the time. I feel perfectly secure in my relationship with Jenny and we're not married. What counts is the relationship. At the moment I feel perfectly happy.

Getting married and being married is part of the conventional rules, part of the stereotype. If you go along with those rules then you'll very likely end up doing the usual male–female jobs within marriage. I feel marriage is unfair as well. I know people who aren't married who fall into the stereotypes and people who are married who don't fall into them, so I don't think the fact of being married makes much difference.

I spent a lot of my earlier years in the company of males up to when I finished my apprenticeship, apart from being married by that stage, but if I've a choice of being involved with a group of males or a mixed group I prefer a mixed group. Women add a dimension and a point of view that men don't add or don't usually. I'm perfectly happy being in an all-male group if they're men that I can relate to. In the running club there are four women but they go off and run on their own, so thirty blokes run together but I'm not happy there because I don't relate to them. Again it comes down to the quality of the relationships.

Chapter 5

Gay men

As it happens both the men who tell their life stories in this chapter were brought up as Catholics, though I don't read any significance into that. John is English and was brought up by educated middle-class parents in an affluent London suburb. Anthony is Irish and his father was a road sweeper. Their life experiences also differed sharply in relation to their sexuality, since John did not become fully aware and accepting of his gayness until he was in his early twenties whereas Anthony was aware of being gay from about 4 years old. Both experienced being the only gay man in otherwise completely heterosexual men's groups. Both saw men's anti-sexism as integrally linked with both feminism and gay liberation.

JOHN

I'm 41. My work is training volunteer advice workers. I've been doing that three and a half years. My father was a research chemist. My mother also worked as a chemist before she got married and then as the children went to school she began work again as a teacher and continued until shortly before she died.

We moved around a lot. I was born in Birmingham. We moved to London and then rented a house in Surbiton, Surrey till I was 12. Later they moved to Cheltenham. I've now lived in Staffordshire longer than anywhere else. It feels like home to me now.

My parents were unconventional in gender terms. My mother was a forceful person, a strong woman. I was the eldest of eight. She told me that before she got married she negotiated a deal with my father about her being an autonomous person and deciding what she wanted to do. She wasn't a subservient little housewife. It was traditional in that Dad went out to work and my mother was at home but she wasn't a downtrodden woman, she stood up for herself and expected us to do our bit around the house. She expected the boys to do housework as much as the girls and I don't remember my sisters ever complaining they did more than we did.

I've four brothers and three sisters. A lot fell on me as the eldest and I had to grow up fast. I was expected to do a lot and felt responsible for my younger brothers and sisters. I changed nappies and bathed my brothers and sisters and enjoyed it. It didn't seem strange. It seemed perfectly normal. I didn't know anything different.

I never spoke to my father about this set up so I don't know what he thought. He was a quiet man, didn't say much and was shy. He seemed not to be dominant around the house. I don't remember being terrified of him the way I know some people were of their fathers. He smacked you if you were naughty but my Mum did as well. It wasn't 'Wait till your Dad gets home.'

He commuted a long way – away early in the morning and back late in the evening. When I was young it seemed he wasn't there much because your day as a young person is short compared with adults' and he was away most of that time. I remember him sitting doing calculations to do with work. He liked playing with numbers, he played bridge and was often thinking about how to deal with bridge situations. He didn't like to be disturbed.

He wasn't a nurturing father. He was cold and distant. I was sexually abused by him for a long time so I'm confused between my rejection of him and whether that was him being distant. I actively avoided physical contact with him. I think that was how he was with my brothers and sisters. In my memory of my father, a lot is numbed, I don't remember much and I don't want to poke around. Memories start when I was about 3 or 4. He got into bed with me and messed around with me. It went on till I was 12. When I talk about it I feel uncomfortable and fighting for breath. I coped with it by going quiet and numb and waited till it finished. I didn't tell my Mum.

It had a lasting effect on me. The profoundest effect is that I find it difficult to trust anybody to love me. When one of the two people in your life you expect to trust and love you completely abuses that it's difficult to trust anybody else in a loving relationship. I find it difficult to trust or let anybody else's love in. I do pretty well but it's difficult. Another thing I learned was coping on my own, surviving and not asking for help. It affects me still but I don't go around with a great weight of baggage. I felt close to my mother and distant from my father. Whether that would have been so if I hadn't been abused by my father I don't know. I may have taken on some of my mother's characteristics. I'm pretty firm-minded about what I want and she was strong like that.

I remember thinking about other boys, and my experiences at school. It might have been neat if my Dad had taught me ball skills because that caused me problems. I don't agree with fighting, but it would have been useful if he'd taught me self-defence so I could have dealt with physical attacks and abuse better. I got no instruction or guidance. I didn't feel I could ask him and there wasn't any other man in my life, like an uncle, when I was that age.

I don't remember any difficulty knowing how I was supposed to be as a young lad. Looking at other lads at school it seemed they were how I was supposed to be and I could see I wasn't like that. I don't think I looked for an adult male to get that picture from. We had no TV when I was at home and hardly ever watched it at boarding school. So that wasn't an influence.

We didn't have friends outside the family. I played with my brothers and sisters. My mother was from a middle-class home and had education and I got an impression that messing around with the neighbourhood kids was not the thing to do. People think of Surbiton as affluent but we lived in a rundown working-class neighbourhood, in a three-bedroom terraced house and slept in bunks. I don't think my mother wanted that many children but she was a Catholic and unlike most Catholics she followed the Church's teaching on not using birth control.

I started at a mixed primary school, rundown place with outside toilets. I was there a term because the Catholic primary school was full but there was space for me the next term so I moved there. It was in a middle-class suburb so I was uncomfortable there. I felt completely out of place in that environment and conscious of my worn clothes. I felt poor and different.

That was also a mixed school. We did everything together – music and movement with the radio, and Scottish dancing, boys and girls together, but I thought that was sissy, which is weird because as a child I never felt one of the boys. Rough games and football and rushing around fighting were definitely not me. I didn't want to join in. I was no good at football. I didn't want to be outside anyway. I don't remember doing much playing, hanging around waiting for playtime to end was what I remember.

School work was OK. I got through it. I felt closer to the girls but I didn't have any special friends who were girls. There was more affinity because they weren't rushing around playing football and bashing me over the head, which is what boys seemed to do. Also I was involved in a nurturing way at home. That may have affected me too.

I failed my exam at 11 and went to a Catholic secondary school. It was all boys and absolute hell, I hated it, it was so violent. I got beaten almost every day or threatened and in terror of going home and coming to school. They picked on me and called me a sissy so I got abused and beaten up for that. It was a rude awakening, in a completely other league. I felt isolated. There were one or two others in a similar situation in terms of mob rule – the butt of everything. It would have made sense to get together but that would have been difficult or stupid tactically. I sense it would have made things worse. I don't remember if I got really hurt, it's numb and inaccessible most of that, but I must have done.

The games master particularly picked on me. You were supposed to have skills as a boy, being able to kick or throw or catch. I don't mind kicking a ball around now, I enjoy playing football in a non-competitive way, but then I didn't have those skills and so I got bad mouthed or hit. He was some sort of Olympic contender, he definitely had high expectations and my performances were well below them. He showed me up in front of the other boys and criticised in a nasty way. I don't know if he used the word sissy but it was that sort of thing.

It seemed completely hopeless. I couldn't tell my parents, it was like admitting I was a failure. They'd got other things to worry about. Telling teachers would have made it worse. There were no women teachers, it was all men and they expected you to tough it out. I don't think they'd have done anything about it. I didn't feel love for my Dad, just repulsion. With that and school, life was hell. A phrase that went through my mind a lot was 'I'd be better off dead.' I never got to the point of wanting to kill myself, but I used to wish myself dead a lot. Life was that bad.

I was there a year. Then, I don't know how it happened, whether it was some subconscious device for getting out of the situation, but I'd always been interested in the ritual side of the Catholic Church, incense, candles and vestments, that sort of thing. I'd been an altar boy since I was 8. I think I said to my Mum I'd like to be a priest and it seemed like the next night the parish priest was around asking me about it. I was interviewed at the bishop's palace and offered a place at a junior seminary when I was 12.

So the next September I went there. It was for boys who thought they wanted to become priests, not specifically a training but there were lots of church services and you were supposed to behave well and be priestly in your demeanour, and certainly girls were well out of the question.

It was a boys' boarding school in Sussex, a long and complicated train journey, changing several times. I was away from home in term times and during Easter and Christmas. I came home after that for holidays. It was a huge relief but all of a sudden I was on my own with complete strangers miles away from home and I had to knuckle down and get by on my own. There wasn't the violence but there was loneliness and isolation. I lost touch with my brothers and sisters because I was away.

It was general education apart from the religious emphasis, the usual games, football, cricket, hockey, but the games bit I didn't enjoy. I don't like standing around in shorts getting freezing cold. I don't think we got more games than anywhere else and the people who taught games weren't sadistic like the games master at the secondary school.

I decided soon after I got there I didn't want to be a priest. I'd had an idea that if I wished hard enough and did the right things I'd turn into something saintly, but nothing happened. I faded away from the idea but it didn't make sense to tell anybody, so I pretended it was what I wanted to do. I certainly didn't want to go back to the secondary school! I'd reason to be grateful to the seminary which was why I stuck with it and was wary about doing anything to give the game away and have to go home. By the time I decided to leave I was bigger and could cope with the situation.

I stayed until I was 17. I left because the contradictions got too much. I had a couple of good friends and one decided he was going to go. The late sixties was a time of upheaval in all walks of life, in the Church with the Vatican Council and in society, the music and drugs scene. We knew it was going on. We led an isolated life but we weren't completely isolated. A lot of people in my year were seriously wondering whether this was what they wanted, so I was part of that. It was difficult to tell anybody, the priest and my Mum. It was a disappointment for her. It was difficult to make the decision but I did and I haven't any regrets.

I've a lot of feelings about the Church and its effect on me and it took me years to get straightened out, as I see it. I still think of myself as Catholic in that it's my heritage, like being English. It's ingrained in me but I'm not a practising Catholic, I don't go to church. Most of what the Church teaches I violently disagree with but there are things about it I respect. The Church's culture of nurturing and respect and loving other people is profoundly good. Lots of stuff from the Catholic Church I've thrown out but there are still bits I treasure.

I don't keep in touch with friends from the seminary. I was attracted to one of them. We went out together for cycle rides, listened to music, talked a lot. As we were expected to become priests there was no question of girl friends but gay affairs were completely inappropriate too and I remember one boy who was expelled in disgrace. There was experimentation going on. I heard about it but wasn't part of it, I was too innocent. I wouldn't have dared, and valued my friendships too much to risk it. I knew enough about the boy I was attracted to, to know that if he was interested in anything it was girls. I didn't think of myself as gay. I remember looking things up in the dictionary, coming across words in books and often there wasn't an entry or it would be circular, but you had a sense from the way definitions were written that it was definitely not OK. It was a long time after, when I'd left the seminary and was at university that I realised I was attracted to other men. That was when it became clear.

I went through most of the summer having made the decision and told the seminary I wasn't coming back but not having told my parents. Things seemed to move quickly after I told them because they got me sorted out with a place to do A levels at a technical college about twenty miles away. I commuted by train and did three A levels in a year.

It was a difficult year because I was at home again. I was stretched academically and the tech was a completely different learning environment. This was 1968 and there was a lot going on, it was a time of social change. I was having to think what I wanted to do with my life and where I stood in relation to the Catholic Church and there was the issue of my sexuality. I wasn't dealing with that but it was underneath everything.

The college was a big place. There were hundreds of young people. At the seminary there were perhaps 120 and at the tech there must have been 800, maybe more. It was difficult because I was shy and absolutely incompetent with women. Apart from my sisters I'd hardly ever had to relate to women. My social skills with women were non-existent. I felt I ought to relate to women and if I tried hard and found the right woman whatever feelings I had towards men would disappear, a passing phase. I'd internalised all the religious stuff, that it was a sin, not natural and all that. I didn't have any dates with girls. There were two I was friendly with on the train, we sat in the same carriage and chatted, that was all. Apart from that and being in classes that included women I had no contact with them. I didn't have much contact with men either. I was isolated, enormously shy. There were men I was attracted to but I didn't do anything apart from follow them down the street a bit. Nothing came of it.

I kept out of the way of my Dad most of the time. I was in my bedroom ostensibly studying but probably staring out of the window. I was a voracious reader. One of Hardy's books was a set book so I read all his books to the neglect of almost anything else. I don't know why I did those A levels. One of the lecturers produced university application forms at one of the classes, everybody seemed to be having them so I decided I would. I looked at prospectuses and decided I wanted to be an architect and found I couldn't do it. I didn't have physics or maths, so I chose town planning for which you needed geography. I looked for geography courses without maths or stats and little science.

I got a provisional place at Liverpool and given I was doing three A levels in a year and didn't do much work I was amazed when I got a grade A and two Bs. I'd bunked off from lessons an enormous amount and never read one of the set books at all. The train home went through a beautiful valley under the Downs and I used to get off and walk and go swimming in a brook. In the summer I hardly did any work. My parents were over the moon when I got my results. I thought, 'If you can do no work and do that well, why bother trying in future?' So I went through university determined to have a good time and do the minimum amount of work. I went off to Liverpool to study geography. This was 1969. I got through subsidiary economics by learning things parrot-fashion, which was the way I'd got through Latin at school. I certainly didn't understand what I was doing.

I had a good time and enjoyed it, mainly the social side. I fancied one of my best male friends like hell but never told him because he was rampantly heterosexual. I knew a woman studying psychology who I was close to. He and I both met her at the same time and we both liked her and said to each other she was really nice. I didn't fancy her in a sexual sense but I liked her personality. At the time I was definitely working on the basis of 'Find the right woman and settle down and it will all be all right.' But he got in first and had a relationship with her so that caused jealousy between us. I let him get on with it but there was a vague resentment. I felt if I'd got together with her everything would have been all right. She was the first woman I'd felt attracted to. She was friendly and it was the first time a woman had been interested in me. It felt good. She was a strong woman. She knew what she wanted to do and went and did it. That's what I liked. It reminded me of my Mum.

There was a group of five of us, two women and three men who did a lot together. We went to Wales because the university had a climbing hut in Snowdonia and if the Mountaineering Society weren't using it you could book it. We went to youth hostels at weekends. One summer four of us walked the Pennine Way together. We made lots of meals and went to parties together. We discovered marijuana together and experimented with other things. We'd read that nutmeg or cinnamon in a cake, if you put enough in, gives you a trip, which is true, but it wrecks your stomach! I wouldn't do it again. This was about 1970 and fashionable at the time, people were the exception if they didn't smoke dope. A lot were heavily into booze. I did get drunk but drink was never a major thing in my life. I don't want to sound like a hippy apologist but dope did enhance my appreciation of music and widened my musical taste. I was open to new influences. More difficult music I found interesting and enjoyable. I enjoyed the humour and lightness and companionability that went with dope. It was more social than alcohol which often makes people maudlin. It was much more relaxed.

I was stopped a lot by the police. I looked hippyish, long hair in natural ringlets but I was careful what I carried. Some were caught, but most people were sensible about it. You were careful what you bought and what you were carrying. I tried acid several times too. I don't regret any of it but I wouldn't use any of those things now. I don't smoke tobacco or anything now. I don't take drugs at all and I don't drink but it was an important part of my life and it went on several years after I left university. I tried cocaine sometimes too up to the early eighties. It wasn't just a student phase for me.

I lived near the swimming pool so I did a lot of swimming. I learned to swim at the seminary but it was freezing cold water there and not a lot of fun, but at university it was a huge warm pool. I liked the exercise but was never into competitive swimming. It was a wonderful opportunity to see lots of men's bodies in the pool and the changing room! I was never physically interested in women, curious, but not interested.

This alerted me to having gay tendencies. There was a gay society at Liverpool but I was scared of that side of myself. I saw posters for their meetings but never went. I'd never heard of such a thing. I knew it was where I needed to go but I was scared about being seen going in. Things have changed in the last twenty years but not hugely. It's difficult for young people to make that move and go to a gay soc. There are lesbians and gay men who are known about but never darken the doors of such meetings at all. It's the difficulties people feel they'd face if they were seen acknowledging their sexuality by making that sort of statement.

It would have been difficult for me to be relaxed and easy in my department as a gay man. I'd have had a hard time. It's the overriding presumption that everybody is heterosexual and there's nothing else. It makes you think you're not welcome or the place isn't safe. A lot of that was in my head but there was discrimination. There was abuse and ostracism. In magazines like *Oz* there was beginning to be contact adverts, the beginnings of gay liberation issues. I saw these magazines in Liverpool. They were widely circulated, difficult to read but exciting.

I didn't go to the gay society in my whole time at university. My nearest gay experience was in the changing room at the pool. I was embarrassed when two men I now realise must have been gay made a personal remark about me. I got dressed as quicky as possible and rushed out, but they'd spotted me as potential. I hadn't come to that conclusion myself and I wasn't at a stage when I was prepared to act on my feelings. Near the end of my third year I went to a disco and a woman was attracted to me and pushy about wanting to spend time with me. I thought she was nice and we agreed to meet but we never did. I went back hoping to meet her another time but she wasn't there. It was disappointing. I think that was my last hope of being rescued!

In my last year near finals I came close to a nervous breakdown. I felt intolerable pressure. I walked in the evening through suburban Liverpool out to the countryside. I spent an hour or two sleeping in a barn, got up at about four thirty and carried on walking. I was stopped and questioned by the police in the small hours somewhere in the surroundings of Liverpool. Then I walked back. I remember shouting a lot and letting my feelings go. I was near cracking up. My sexuality was part of it. I couldn't come to terms with how I was feeling. When you're raised Catholic and the particularly strong dose I got through the seminary, it takes time to shake off.

I got through finals and got a place to do a second degree in Liverpool in town planning but couldn't raise the money. They reserved me a place for the following year and my idea was to work and earn enough money to do the degree. I stayed in Liverpool and took a job as a clerk in the Housing Department. I worked with a gay man and it was the first time I'd knowingly come into contact with one. He was friendly and we talked a lot. He didn't seem like an ogre or a horrible person and it was reassuring. I wasn't interested in him sexually and he wasn't interested in me. We just knocked around together at work and went to the pub in the evening.

The idea of saving enough money to do the course was a complete fantasy. I spent my money on dope and having a good time. So I started looking for planning jobs and quickly got one just north of London. It was 1973 heading for local government reorganisation which happened in April 1974. Councils all over the country needed planning people and there was a scheme to train them, so I got a job as a trainee.

It was a lively place to work. There were lots of young people and I got into a crowd who worked there. It was a small town and there was next to nothing to do apart from drink so we went drinking at lunch time. We used to drink two or three pints at lunchtime then roll back to the office and spend the afternoon not doing much serious work and then we'd have a meal and go out drinking in the evening. We spent a lot of time drinking, smoking dope, listening to records into the small hours, singing and making enormously complicated meals. I was still eating meat then and we'd have loads of sauces. We ate wonderfully. I had a really good time.

I met a probation officer who was gay but he wasn't 'out' at work. In a small town you think carefully what you say, it will be gossip all over the neighbourhood. He invited me to a Drag Ball in London and that was the first time I ever went to a place where there was a whole bunch of gay people. It was an enormous annual event and there were hundreds of lesbians and gay men. My excuse was that it was like an anthropological study, I'd go and observe. I was still distancing myself.

That was a big step for me. We stayed with a television make-up artist and that was an eye opener because he was a camp and flamboyant gay man. His house was like another planet, I'd never been anywhere where there was so much money. He assumed my friend and I were sleeping together so we ended up in a double bed and it was the first time I'd ever slept with another man. Sleep wasn't the right word. I couldn't sleep at all, I was so nervous and frightened, but next to nothing happened.

Another thing at that time was more scaring. Two friends and I enrolled for a thing like an encounter group and on the first evening everybody was in a circle. My friends didn't know about my sexuality and the woman facilitating said, 'Tell us who you are and the one thing that you most want to keep completely secret.' It started on the other side and went round and five people before me came out as gay. So I thought, what the hell, so I came out. It was scaring. I didn't want to lose my friends. I worked in the same office and I was anxious how they'd relate to me in future and what would happen at work. I was shitting myself but it was fine, they were relaxed. I found out from them another friend was gay. That was the first time I acknowledged it to myself and to other people. It was a vast relief, I'd recognised it and labelled it and could move on.

I worked there fifteen months and then local government reorganisation came and the whole department split up. I got a job in Manchester and doubled my money in one move. I've never achieved that in a job change since, but I hated it in Manchester. I compared it with Liverpool. There's arch rivalry between the two and I still saw it as the enemy. I found the people cool and distant compared with Liverpudlians.

At Manchester I had my only sexual experience with a woman, which wasn't a lot of fun. I was able to perform but I didn't find it a stimulating experience or attractive. I did what was expected of me and it finally made my mind up, it's not what I want, not how I see having a good time.

I worked for a Conservative authority and I was got there under false pretences. I didn't do what they said I was going to do. It was boring work and I hated the people I worked for. The atmosphere in the office was foul. They didn't work as a team and weren't friendly. I thought, 'I'll stick it for a year but next year I'll not be working here.' Near the end of the year I looked for jobs and it was easy to find work in planning. I had nine applications and four invitations for interviews. Stafford was the first to come up, it seemed an interesting job and they offered me it, so I took it.

So I moved to Stafford and shared a flat. I didn't have any affairs or anything. I joined the film society and got in with a group of people. I met two gay men and we went to a wine bar where there were lesbians and gay men on the quiet. There was nowhere you could go officially. I tried setting up a gay group but that didn't work too well. It's still very closeted in Stafford.

About 1978 I got involved in an anti-sexist men's group. I don't know how it started because I wasn't in at the beginning but I think it was set up by some men in response to what their women partners said to them. The women were in a women's group and said things like, 'Why don't you men get yourselves sorted out and set up a men's group?' So they did. I'm not sure how I got into that, maybe there was an advert in a local paper somewhere. I worked with one member who was married to a woman who was a prime mover in the women's movement in Stafford at the time.

There weren't any other gay men in the men's group. I sympathised with the issue of women's oppression by this time. I went to some men's anti-sexist conferences, one in Bristol in particular. I talked about women's issues with the two gay men I knew. That's probably how I started to think about it and do something about it. The men's group ran jumble sales to raise money for the women's refuge and I was involved in crèches for functions that the women ran. I read magazines. I don't know if *Achilles Heel* or *Anti-sexist Men's Newsletter* were out then but I was definitely reading either those or *Spare Rib*. I read *Spare Rib* every time.

One thing that came out of my involvement in the first men's group I was in was my first experience of co-counselling. The person who started the men's group was into that. He invited me to an introductory evening so I went along because it was too difficult to say I didn't want to. It was probably 1978, about the time the men's group started.

I went to a series of co-counselling classes but I found it difficult because I didn't feel safe. I needed to work on being gay and coming to terms with it more, but the group was mainly heterosexual men and women. The leader made it clear he was open to me being gay but I was unhappy over things he said had been the history of lesbian and gay liberation in the co-counselling community. I profoundly disagreed with its earlier position. So I finished the classes and thought 'I'm not going to do this any more.'

I enjoyed work but the environment became difficult. There were lots of anti-gay jokes all the time. I wasn't 'out' at work. In the union I raised the issue of equal opportunities, not about lesbians and gay men but about women and black people and people with disabilities, and I got completely hammered – and these were union members! I thought, 'If you can't get the union to deal with women's issues, or black people, or people with disabilities then you sure as hell can't expect much sympathy for lesbians and gay men.' I raised the other issues to test the water.

I found the atmosphere at work more and more intolerable. As a gay man, in an environment where it was OK for everybody to joke about 'queers' and everybody to laugh and think it hugely funny, was very distressing. It's like being a black person when all the time people are making racist remarks. So it wore me down and after a time I decided I wouldn't put up with it any more, so I quit. I was then unemployed, but a group of us decided that we'd sell our houses and buy a big place and live together. The two women were both in the Stafford women's group and their partners and I were in the men's group.

I was in Stafford five or six years till 1980. I'd lived on my own. We had to sell four houses in Stafford and buy a big one in another town. There were four children including a baby. One couple had just had a child and the other two were single parents, a man with a young lad and a woman with a couple of young girls. We liked the idea of a commune. It was deliberately communal living. Some of us wanted to spend more time with children. I wanted to in particular. I'd got fed up with doing a paid job and wanted to spend some time raising children. I was not unemployed long before we moved. I quit in August and we moved in September or October. The two were linked. The idea of selling up and moving was the catalyst. I wasn't daring enough to give up my job with a mortgage round my neck.

I've always loved children. The other people in the house were working and earning money and were happy for me to be at home, claiming benefit and looking after the children. So that's what I did. The other reason for me moving there was that I'd be nearer to gay clubs. I thought it would be nice to live on the doorstep rather than sixteen miles away.

We were settling into the house and getting used to living together, but as far as I was concerned it was an absolute disaster. To begin with it was fine, I enjoyed being in the house looking after the children. I wasn't so happy about having twice as much housework. A lot needed doing to the house and we had no money to do it. There were two couples and me in the house and it seemed only a few months until the whole thing blew up. I was piggy in the middle and spent a month counselling everybody in the house but getting no support myself. I ended up collapsing under the strain and left.

The experience hasn't made me completely rule out the idea of living in a commune but if I do I'll certainly go into it more carefully. A trial living-together arrangement would be a good idea. I don't think there's anything wrong with the ideal but we've been socialised to living in small units and we're not used to dealing with the dynamics of living in bigger groups and don't have the skills for handling those situations. It was a learning experience and I'm glad I did it but I'm glad it's over.

I went to live in a room in a house owned by a man I knew through the Gay Centre so for the first time I lived in a house with gay people, a breathing space away from the hot-house atmosphere in the commune. The commune kept going for a while but eventually they decided it was time to call it a day and we agreed to sell the place. I still had a share in it. We basically made a loss on it and it's now an old people's home.

I was still unemployed and on benefit so I had to spend the money from the house or I'd have lost my benefit. So I found a house in Stoke which was cheap. I bought it for cash and did my own conveyancing. I lived there four or five years. I was still there when the Stoke men's group started.

I tried to deal with all this without success and got depressed. I didn't want tranquillisers so the only thing I could think of to help me was to contact the people I'd done co-counselling with in Stafford. They told me of a man in Stoke who had just started counselling and suggested I get in touch with him. We had a few counselling sessions, which was a great help. So I got back into co-counselling.

Then I got the idea of being an advice worker, so I started training. I had a series of paid jobs and I was a volunteer between jobs. I collected statistics and information on local organisations, I was a tribunal representative at social security and medical appeals and a money adviser and

I was manager of a branch bureau while someone else was on maternity leave. Then I started my current job. I recruit and train three groups of people a year. I enjoy it, but it's running out of challenges because I basically do the same thing three times a year.

I'm thinking about working on equal opportunity issues, or HIV/AIDS work either in a local authority or an independent agency. I've been satisfied with my career in advice work because of how personally supported I am. I'm with people where I'm 'out' about my sexuality and they are completely supportive and affirming about it. It's made me decide I'll never work in a place again where I can't be 'out' and where I'm not valued and appreciated for myself. I'm not prepared to hide or pretend. You spend a third of your day in the workplace and I'm not prepared to treat myself – like shit basically – in order to earn a wage.

I've come a long way. I've done a lot of work on my sexuality and I'm well integrated. I moved to Stoke to be more involved with the lesbian and gay community. There was also a gay social centre and I went there most weekends and met quite a few lesbians and gay men. We had regular socials and talks and meetings. I've been involved with the Lesbian and Gay Switchboard off and on for years. I trained and started doing a night's duty on the telephone two or three times month. It's not like Samaritan work because it's not all aimed at people who are feeling depressed or suicidal. You get calls from depressed people but it's advice work as well. I'm involved in the training and we're training people at the moment.

Sometimes it's quiet, sometimes it's very busy, sometimes the calls are demanding, other times they're easy to deal with. It's fulfilling. I like the more difficult calls, being able to see somebody go through from being uncertain about themselves and perhaps depressed or isolated, through to being a well-rounded person and happy in themselves. It's satisfying. Given my own lengthy and unhappy coming to terms with my sexuality anything I can do to make it easier for somebody else is really good.

Growing up gay there aren't many people you can talk to about it. I talked with nobody. Most people even now have to figure it out themselves. If you can get in touch with a gay switchboard there's somebody you can talk to. I had to work my way through all the Catholic stuff. It was confusing and difficult. Now I'm pleased with what I am. My sexuality means I've been faced with having to question things which are assumed to be unassailable. People say gay people are bad, dirty, immoral. I know it's not true about me, and if society says that about one bunch of people, which I know is untrue, then what does society say about other people and how can you trust any of it? It gave me insight into oppression in general.

At the seminary I was disturbed by the Church's attitudes towards Jews. That changed after the second Vatican Council but the Church had negative attitudes towards Jewish people which I felt were completely inappropriate.

I questioned the Church there, and the attitude of society towards black people, the civil rights movement, and what I saw as the Church's failure to take a stand on those issues. I made connections in those areas. So I'm glad about being gay because I don't take things on face value.

Later I connected it with women's oppression. My Mum talked about the situation of women in the Church but it wasn't significant for me then. The position of women in society was more significant later but I came to feel what society said about a lot of people wasn't to be trusted. Not all gay people think like me but it's how it was for me. Some gay men are racists and misogynists, the same as the rest of society, but a lot of lesbians and gay men are forced to face up to things and look at them afresh.

I've continued co-counselling, taught classes and led support groups. A big focus has been dealing with sexuality and sexual abuse. It's helped me come to terms with who I am. I've a clearer idea about what's going on in situations and I can handle them better. It's been useful both personally and in a wider sense.

After a time the lesbian and gay centre shut down. The building was rented and the rent was a lot. All we seemed to do was run fund-raising events to pay the rent – a lot of work and not much fun. So we decided to stop running it. That meant there was nowhere for lesbians and gay men to meet. Then Martin and Lin set up the community bookshop and they had a room upstairs where groups of lesbians and gay men could have meetings. I was on the fringes of that.

About that time two men put a notice in one of the anti-sexist men's magazines, about trying to start a men's group. I saw it and rang one of them and maybe there was a notice in the bookshop. A meeting was arranged there and I went along. That's how I got involved in my second men's group. The first men's group I'd been in I'd enjoyed but I'd moved on quite a bit, so I'm not sure why I went. I was curious and interested to meet other men involved in men's issues.

I took quite a facilitating role in some meetings. I'd picked up skills through co-counselling. There were good men there and we had some good times. I liked the social side, meals together and so on but it wasn't a turning point in my life. I'd gone through a lot of transition in the gay movement and co-counselling by then. I'd done a lot on what it was to be a man and what isn't part of being a man. I was interested to see how this non-counselling men's group would go. I went to help rather than expecting a huge amount out of it. Nowadays I don't do things simply because somebody has asked me or because it will be good for somebody else.

I saw the men's group as part of a wider anti-sexist movement including lesbians and gay men and feminists as well. Some men there saw it as more activist. I'm anxious or fearful of outright political action, partly to do with being gay. I'm wary about putting myself in situations where I may be abused or attacked. I was more relaxed in that men's group than in the earlier one. I'd come to terms with my sexuality, so that was easier. I don't remember consciously thinking the group might help non-gay men understand how life was for gay men but a lot of what I do is about trying to educate people and help them understand. That was probably part of it.

I don't think I would join such a group again. I wouldn't get a lot out of it now. I'm still interested in anti-sexism and in co-counselling but I'd want to have a clearer focus. The group was *laissez-faire*, there wasn't much structure to it. Groups work much better if they're more organised, I don't have patience for chaotic anarchistic meetings. They serve the needs of some people but they work better if they're more structured.

I faded out of the men's group when I got involved in the lesbian and gay campaign against Clause 28 of the Education Bill. Around 1988 Clause 28 was more central to my life than the men's group. There's lots of marginalised or discriminated groups in the country but few that Parliament takes time to discriminate actively against. Parliament doesn't say that schools should not teach that disabled people are as good as anybody else, which is basically what Clause 28 was saying – that schools should not say lesbians and gay men are equal to everybody else. I got involved in regular meetings on that. We discussed strategies to block its passage through Parliament and supported each other during a difficult period. When you've got that sort of pernicious nasty attack on you as a member of a group you need to support each other. At the time it seemed not only that apparent advances in the sixties and seventies were being rolled back but it was the start of a vicious crack down. Gay people felt attacked and threatened.

As a piece of legislation it's full of holes, but it's not what the legislation says but how it works in practice that's critical and the way it works is that people censor themselves. Councils deliberately don't try to do things because they're worried they'll get it in the neck from angry tax payers. They've taken things out of art exhibitions and some have refused to fund any lesbian or gay cultural activities. These are blamed on Clause 28 but that only restricts what schools can do. In practice it has a pernicious effect even though the number of cases going to court are few. It's symbolic and a backward move.

We achieved a lot in the campaign, not in changing the legislation but in mobilising people and politicising lesbians and gay men and others. There hasn't been such unity among lesbians and gay men on an issue for years. It made a huge difference. People got together and links were made with other organisations. Things have changed as a result.

HIV and AIDS, of course, has made a lot of difference too. The whole government health-education response to it has been negative. There's next to no positive advice. The authorities are terrified of seeming to promote homosexuality or advising people on safer sex. I know people who've got HIV and one with AIDS. It feels as if people don't care. It seems people only take notice if it affects heterosexual people. Any number of gay men can die and it makes no difference. The indifference to their fate is shocking. It doesn't surprise me but it doesn't make it less hurtful.

It's part of our work on the Switchboard to advise people about safer sex. I did a training course for befriending people with HIV or AIDS. A group of us were trained locally but it was too early in this city. There weren't many with HIV here then and nobody with AIDS. So there wasn't a demand for it. There's a Body Positive group in the city but as far as I know they aren't interested in having 'buddies'. People with HIV support each other rather than wanting support from people without it. They want to keep their confidentiality. The gay community here is small and people gossip, unfortunately. I've done counselling and advice work on HIV and AIDS and an equal opportunities policy on lesbian and gay issues. I've done HIV/AIDS and sexuality training for university students. I enjoy it, it's important to me and I'm good at it.

Living alone, I do all my own housework. My Mum always expected us to do it as a child. Everybody had to clear up their own mess, wash up and make our beds. I've always done that. I don't enjoy it and I'm bad about cleaning windows and dusting. I iron shirts if I need to but most of the time I don't see the point, I've better things to do with my time.

I'd like to see gender roles evaporate into thin air so people can be their unique individual selves, having relationships and friendships with whoever they want whenever they want. It's difficult to conceive of what things would be like because the socialisation of women and men into their roles is so strong. It is difficult to get a picture of what things would be like if that didn't exist.

Eliminating sexism is crucial and lesbian and gay liberation is part and parcel of it, because the way lesbian and gay oppression is put into people is related to the way sexism is put in. You are told you're a sissy, which is like saying you're not the proper gender. Sexism reinforces lesbian and gay oppression and lesbian and gay oppression reinforces sexism. If you don't act like a 'proper' man or woman you must be one of 'them'. It's mutually supporting, so both have to go.

It's a slow process but things are changing. When you look at what's happened over a long historical period things are immeasurably better than they were. It's often frustrating in the present because you can see what needs to change and how rapid change needs to be for justice and how unwilling the Government is to provide any lead at all and the opposition it shoves in the way most of the time, but I'm optimistic, you have to take a long-term view. Clause 28 is a setback. It's a battle we lost in the war but we are going to win the war. No doubt about that.

Marriage is an institution set up to support sexism. It's a method of controlling things socially. It's there to control women in the interests of men so that men know the children in a relationship are theirs. If people want to get married that's their decision, but as an institution I don't see any need for a piece of paper to say you have decided to make a commitment to each other. You can make commitments which are just as meaningful in ways which don't need the state to regulate.

As an institution marriage oppresses people who choose not to get married. Whether they're mixed couples or lesbian or gay couples they suffer disadvantages like responsibilities for children in relationships – the law is completely different if you're married – rights to succession, tenancies, intestacy laws if you die – a whole range of institutionalised forms of discrimination against people who choose not to be married. As an institution I'm against it in that it's used to bolster sexism, it's oppressive. I wouldn't be so opposed if the rights and responsibilities of marriage were also available to people who choose not to get married. If it wasn't oppressive I'd be neutral about it.

I'm concerned about other forms of oppression too. I'm against racism absolutely. I don't think it's the same for everybody who is lesbian or gay but for many lesbians and gay men, having to deal with the oppression that comes with their life experiences often makes them understand other forms of discrimination. On class, I'm confused about my own class background. My parents could be called middle class, both went to university but with such a big family and my father being not well paid I was raised poor, so from that point of view I feel closer to working-class people. I live in a working-class neighbourhood. I'm very conscious of class and it's what I like about living in Stoke. It's a working-class city. I've lived in places that aren't working class and I don't feel comfortable in them.

I've changed my life a lot over the years. I'm now a vegan, I don't drink alcohol, smoke or take any kind of drugs, and I don't drink tea or coffee. I see an acupuncturist every month. I get regular exercise, though not as much as I'd like, and I'm very much involved in co-counselling. I feel extremely healthy these days.

ANTHONY

I'm 42 and I'm unmarried. I teach art and design history. I was born in Northern Ireland and my father was a labourer, a road sweeper. He'd always been some kind of labourer. He'd been a message boy, a golf caddy, a gardener and then a road sweeper, which is how I remember him.

My mother didn't have paid work after I was born. I was the youngest of a large family and she became almost an invalid. We needed the money but she couldn't work. Before that she'd been a maid in domestic service. My father was 46 when I was born and my mother 41. My mother had two sons and six daughters but only three girls were alive when I was born, the others died in infancy. It was a poor background. We despised the rich. Having come out of the Depression my parents had all those values – don't get into debt, don't buy anything on credit, don't buy things you can't afford. We never bought anything much!

But we ate well and we all had music and elocution lessons. There was only one acceptable elocution teacher we could go to, I suspect because she didn't charge much. My parents believed in feeding us well and giving us a cultural basis. I thought we dressed adequately but when I see photographs of us as children we were in the next thing to rags. I always wanted to be a dress designer as a child, I was always dressing dolls and making dolls and clothes. We were obsessed with clothes. I wonder if it was because we didn't have many. We were encouraged to be interested in colours and textures and that's stood me in good stead because I can identify fabrics closely and it's something I never had to be taught consciously.

My parents were very literate, they were interested in words and had extended vocabularies. My mother was the product of a kind of schooling in Ireland which was based on literacy and valuing words, basically peasant schooling but thorough. My father was a singer, almost a professional. He had a magnificent singing voice and had been offered professional contracts but didn't take them. He was unambitious – underambitious. He wasn't lazy, he had no ambition to succeed. He was conscious that he had no background, no money, nothing. He was underachieving to the point of being walked over generally. He opted to be nice and loved and respected rather than rich, admired and famous, although he was very talented.

We were Catholics and I've recently gone back to being a Catholic. I left Northern Ireland in 1969. I got involved a bit with the Civil Rights Movement when I was a student but I left before the big demonstrations that were violently broken up. It hardened our position as poor people, but my parents were incredibly tolerant. We had an untypical Irish Catholic background in that we were encouraged to have Protestant friends and my parents always helped the neighbours who were generally Protestants. They were well known for helping people out.

We were strict Catholics, always went to mass and we went to Catholic schools. My parents were keen on religious practices but had a scepticism about church authority which would never have been expressed. They had a bitterness and resentment about the Protestant status quo in Northern Ireland but never about individuals. I went to a Catholic boys' grammar school on the Falls Road, Belfast, but we lived in Bangor, County Down, which is regarded as posh. People still think I'm posh because of my Bangor accent, little knowing the hardship we had.

My parents were traditional, my father was the breadwinner and my mother was the homemaker. I didn't know my mother had ever worked until she started telling me stories about what it was like in service in the twenties and thirties. I presumed she felt she was above going out to work. I think this was a working-class thing, this idea about other people being 'common'. We didn't do 'common' things. My mother was identified as one who stayed at home and baked and cooked but because she was not well and had breathing problems and a heart problem she didn't do much cleaning. She couldn't. As you see from my surroundings here, I inherited that! It isn't a prime thing to do. Keeping yourself clean and having domestic skills like cooking were important but cleaning up wasn't. As I got older I inherited some of the cleaning duties of the house from my sisters but it wasn't an amazing task – it was like cleaning the stairs once a year!

My father was not a handyman, hardly mended anything. He was obsessed with the garden, although it was a postage-stamp thing. He never cooked and would not have liked it if meals had not been ready when he came in. It was a traditional masculine attitude. My mother cooked most of the weekend. I went home when I was 21 when my mother was in hospital, and my father and brother both came in expecting me to have food on the table. Because I was at home not working they thought this meant I had to time my entire day making sure the boiled potatoes would be ready when they got home. It was amazing and we had blazing rows about it.

I had three older sisters, one six years older, one eight years older and one fourteen years older. I grew up in a predominantly female household – a feminine atmosphere. I didn't speak to my brother for years. It wasn't disharmonious but we didn't have anything to say to each other. We slept beside each other until I was 19 because we had only two usable bedrooms in the house. It wasn't until I was about 17 or 18 that we actually spoke at all. It developed after my mother died and I came home regularly to visit my father. That brought my father and I, and my brother, much closer.

My brother and I were very different, probably because of my sexuality. I was aware from about the age of 4 that I was sexually interested in men – not boys. It expressed itself as a class thing. A young man across the road was a teddy boy and I thought the important difference wasn't sexual but class. In fact we were both working class, but because he was 'rough' and butch I was very attracted. At an early age I knew I was gay.

This remained unspoken and still remains unspoken between my brother and I. Everyone else speaks to me freely about it except my family. The whole family knew, even my mother. She loved me and got on well with me but she was aware I wasn't developing as they'd have liked. It never got to the stage of causing religious difficulties, it was more that it was not acceptable in society. It got worse when I got older and began to parade it, as an impulse rather than deliberately. I just had to grow my hair long and wear odd clothes.

My father didn't react. It was classic silent disapproval. I remember dressing my hair before I went out to mass. I didn't have a social life but I was obsessed about my hair and clothes by this stage and my mother helped and advised me while my father sat in the corner glaring into the fire. I'd had a lot of abuse and disapproval from my peers and my parents didn't want to add to it so I was relatively comfortable at home. In fact they were similar. My brother is an expressive speaker and uses his hands a lot. The whole family expressed themselves by imitating people, lapsing into accents and taking on other identities. I occasionally pretended to be a woman or an old man in conversation and I still do. My brother is heterosexual but we all had family characteristics that people think are camp.

My father was the same, he would put on voices and as a singer he could sing falsetto soprano, which I can do as well, but I don't think he was in any way gay. In fact he was a ladies' man. He was under 5 feet tall, a diminutive, good-looking man, very fetching, a twinkly blue-eyed blond man. He'd dance and imitate people, he'd lie down in the street as a joke and he was well known. He was the sort of man people might think of as gay. He was a natural mimic. He'd have been a good actor but his strength was as a singer. I took after him quite a lot even though we didn't speak to each other much. He didn't do these things at home. When he came home he was a different person. As a road sweeper the street was his theatre, but at home he was quite different, a melancholic basically. I take after him in some ways but my mother was a stronger influence.

My emotional responses come from my mother. That was to do with feminine virtues. My mother inculcated me with virtues of patience and self-denial. It was neither polite nor seemly nor feminine to sit like that, or to eat the last biscuit, or whatever. So though I wasn't a girl, an apprentice woman, I was brought up to have these virtues. There was a lot of self-denial in our family because we didn't have much. My brother was allowed to be not ladylike whereas I was brought up have these virtues. He was allowed to be a questing person who did different things, learn to drive and swim and go out, more masculine things. Neither of my parents went out, partly because of genuine poverty and my father would have been ashamed to drink the little bit of money we had. We didn't have television or a record player. We sat in, listened to the radio and read newspapers.

I had three big sisters who I absolutely adored and they were more immediately influentual than my mother or my father or my brother. I had a completely feminised fantasy world which was entirely occupied by women. I never thought about God or Jesus as a Catholic but I thought about the Virgin Mary, and I absolutely adored female things, the quintessence of camp of course. I always did well at school and once I came joint top with a very posh boy, and they had two books as prizes, *Heroes of God* and *Heroines of God*. I got given *Heroines of God* unashamedly by the teacher, who said 'I think you're probably going to be more interested in this!' There was a constant recognition of the fact that I was a person who might plump to be a girl at some point.

I may have buried a lot of the disapproval I met but there was some because I learned the limits you can go to, and how to do it creatively of course. Going to a strict Catholic school, though I was basically 'out', I was virginal. I had no thought of doing anything with anybody. It must have been a quality that came across, a person being completely outrageous and suggestive about himself but they didn't feel threatened. I suspect that is something that a lot of gay men develop. It was a talent I got from my father, allaying people's fears. It's like telling people but not telling them. Subsequently I told people because I got tired of play acting. Unfortunately it means that if I'm camp people think 'Oh, he's just another camp gay man', not seeing that this has been an ideological struggle!

My sisters were the most important element in my life. I consciously followed their lead, I was completely like the fourth sister of the family. A lot of the time I actually thought I was a girl. I did the same things as them. I remember them having a row with a girl who lived at the bottom of the road and I immediately took their side and snubbed this girl, the sort of behaviour one associates with schoolgirls, sticking your nose in the air and a sweep down of the eyes. I liked things my sisters introduced me to, gentlish street games, non-competitive games. I'm not saying women aren't ever competitive but I preferred those games to football. I hardly ever played football. I was dragged in once or twice but I never wanted to play team games or race or that kind of thing. I liked imaginative games where you could pretend to be someone else. I hadn't thought of this but perhaps I wanted to be a girl or a woman. I took any opportunity to play those games, they appealed to me, they seemed much more creative than football. I can watch it now and I see it's skilful but it still seems a complete waste of time. I put myself apart from the boys in the street. I played with my sisters but it couldn't have been for long because they were a lot older. Occasionally we put on concerts.

I grew up in a family of intelligent women and highly talented women. Although they inherited the ladylike thing and grew up in a time when if you were a Catholic and a working class woman there was little chance of getting on, in fact they did get on as much as they possibly could do by sheer dint of being brighter than almost anybody else. They should have been professional women, doctors and so on but at that time, in the fifties working class women never did that. So they became secretaries, but they did that with a vengeance! My middle sister won a national competition for shorthand and typing and the Royal Society of Arts Gold Medal. She was a private secetary in the Town Hall, then gave it up to be a nurse in London and won the gold medal for that too. She was a brilliant woman with extraordinary general knowledge. She was widely read for a girl from a provincial town. She had amazing abilities as a mathematician and linguist and her grammar was faultless. She induced awe in me. I really admired her. She was good at everything. She was good looking, had good dress sense and people liked her, she made them feel at ease and was trustworthy.

My youngest sister was a good musician, should have been a professional singer, and was a champion Irish dancer. They were different in appearance and had different abilities, like completely different people. They represented absolutely all the qualities that you could ever want to be and were tremendously important to me. I thought 'My God I've got sisters who are nationally famous.' They'd been on the radio as actresses when they were young. They appeared in pantomime as children. I thought they were wonderful, these women could do anything. They could do all the things that I valued. Perhaps I valued them because they were good at them. They made life interesting for themselves and for other people. Then there was my mother with her gentle and genteel stoic attitude. They were all strong women in their different ways. I thought women were absolutely 'ace' and the *n*th thing in human creation. Men played a marginal part in my life.

I appear to have been more successful than my sisters and I genuinely feel I'm not as talented or as clever as them by any stretch of the imagination. I feel it was a fluke. It didn't happen to my sisters and it should have. It was because they were women. Having a fundamental handicap in being a very 'out' gay man who can be extremely effeminate it was still more acceptable than being a woman! I've had to negotiate a path through life but it still helps being a man. If I'd been a girl my parents would have given me the same chances they gave my sisters but I would not have ended up any better than them. I meet lots of brilliant secretaries and I think it's amazing that the women I work with from that generation have an ability to calculate, to take on complicated computers, and they don't go on about it like the men in the department, they just get on and do it. They're so talented and clever and don't get enough. I don't know how they afford to clothe themselves on the money they get.

To be honest I didn't realise when I was at home that women had a more difficult chance in life. I suppose in that class background there was so little anyway that men and women didn't seem to have a different deal. I'd learned that patience was a feminine virtue but I didn't know what they had to be patient about.

I'm not a great believer in the absent-father syndrome in producing homosexual boys but my father was tired by the time I saw him. He lived and worked for his family. He was worried about influencing us in betting and drinking and smoking. He was from a poor background and he'd seen the worst things that could happen from drink. He took care not to set a bad example. He wasn't demonstrative in his affections. I'm a touching person, I get it from my mother, certainly not from my father.

He thought earning money and giving it all to us was expressing his love and we had to guess that. He was a terrible nag and disciplinarian, particularly to the girls. He would strike them well into their teens. My relationship with my father was troubled because of that. I remember my mother saying to him, 'If you don't show your children you love them they won't love you back.' He couldn't show us he loved us. My mother made a feature of the love in the family and my father didn't. I respected what he was doing and I learned working-class values, giving value for money, and I overwork because of that.

He made a feature of hard work, a penance. He had little to do with the children when they were babies but he liked children and was sentimental about them. He had strong maternal tendencies that he suppressed. He was much easier than my mother to get sympathy from if you were ill. If I wanted a day off school I would deliberately go down a street where I knew he was brushing the road. I never sought him out any other time, I was embarrassed by his job. I'd tell him I wasn't feeling well and he'd say 'Go right back home and tell your mother I sent you.' He was caring and could be tender when you were ill but my mother was less patient because she really was ill and could spot a malingerer a mile off! Unless she was unable to move she had to do cooking and washing all the time.

I started school at 4. My father had already taught me to read and write. It was a small Catholic primary school attached to the church, half for girls and half for boys. The girls were taught by nuns and the boys by priests. There were no barriers but we were not allowed into the girls' playground. It was absolutely not done. I'm afraid I broke the rules.

The girl who lived two doors way from us was a Catholic and she went to the convent school. She was my dearest friend. She was virtually the same age as me and I'd met her before we started school. It was important for me and though we weren't of equal development I was aware of the fact that she was being a bit hived off because she was a girl, not being taught the same things. Although we spent every waking hour of our lives together when we weren't with our families or at school we were different in development. She was good at playing imaginative games and had a good sense of humour. She was absolutely my main friend.

There was a boy the same age as me but there were religious problems. His family were strict 'social' Protestants. Although we were allowed to play together there was a sense in which this wasn't desirable. They thought they were a cut above us, they had purchasing power. He was supposedly my best friend for a while but he wasn't. He didn't like imaginative games. He wasn't good at football but he felt he had to back the football people because it gave him some identity. He could join boys' clubs, which I couldn't as a Catholic. So from being a gentle soul he became resentful and began to say things like 'People think you're a girl' or comment on my gym shorts. So I ended up with my girl friend who I thought was absolutely wonderful. We were perfectly in accord. We'd formed the friendship before we could walk or talk.

We were obsessed with the Beatles and she encouraged me to run away to see them but we were found out. The consensus view was that she was a bad influence. I was forbidden to see her, which was difficult when she lived two yards away. We were at different schools. I was at the grammar school and she was at secondary-modern school. About that time I wrote her an awful love letter and her mother found it and showed it to my mother, so I was forbidden to see her. My mother thought I was going to be 'caught' at an early age by this girl who was not so clever. We were about 15 by then and I've not seen her since my twenties.

Because my sisters were good at mathematics and things like that I thought it was all right to be good at them, though I did subsequently identify them as male subjects and mentally refused to do them. They came to seem dull and uncreative. So I stopped doing maths after learning basic arithmetic at about 11. I've still no idea what equations are for, even though I went to a grammar school. That had a lot to do with identifying male and female subjects.

My brother took a different route. He went to the local technical college instead of grammar school. He was good at maths and physics and his night time reading seemed to be logarithms! He did an appretice-ship as an aeronautical engineer. He wasn't suited to it but he was forced into the masculine thing. He was bright but the side of him that had been encouraged at home, writing, drawing and music, all got lost and he became roughish. He was allowed to be a 'boy' person and his getting a 'trade' was approved of. I thought all these things were completely masculine and I didn't want anything to do with them. I consciously rejected masculinity. It was also tied up with the way the maths teachers looked. I couldn't believe how maths and science teachers could be so dreary looking and wear such awful clothes, whereas the other teachers were perfectly acceptable. I was obsessively attracted to the arts side.

My sexual tendencies didn't meet with open opposition at school. None of us ever had sex. All sex was taboo, of whatever kind. There were better things to get on with, fasting and abstaining, not just from sex but from food and other things. It was a Catholic culture. I pretended I was influencing the other boys but the teachers completely ignored it.

After I left school I went to art school in Belfast. I was 18. That was the first time I had the chance of being myself and also of meeting a lot of girls of my age. Although I'd been brought up by fairly strong women they were in other ways quite traditional. So it was interesting to go somewhere which was fairly way-out, like art school, and like a lot of provincial art schools it was almost deliberately way-out. The students were provocatively bohemian but a bit dated, it was beatniky at a time when other art schools were much more cool, not even hippy. It was 1968.

It was interesting for me to observe the women. I felt I knew and understood women but these were quite different from my expectations. They were so self-consciously bohemian, and middle class as well, and I also had problems because I began to be attractive for the opposite sex. I was also attracted to them out of fascination, almost like an anthropologist looking at the behaviour of young women in art schools, their clothes and their way of talking and relating. It would be an exaggeration to say I got pestered but I did have several girls pursuing me and I didn't know what to do about it. I didn't find them sexually attractive but I found them interesting.

I had some awful incidents being pursued by girls and not knowing what they wanted. Even if I'd wanted to sleep with any of them it wasn't really possible in Belfast because everyone lived with their parents. I could see these girls had sexuality and they were operating some kind of choice. Although I was a flambuoyant pushy person I was a bit shocked when girls obviously had sexual needs and desires of their own because I'd thought dressing up in short skirts was all a kind of game. I didn't think it was a natural selection process. It was to do with personality not procreation and sexual attraction. My sisters may not have been chaste virgins by that stage but there was a kind of working-class propriety about their life, but these girls were raunchy and poised about their sexuality. I was fascinated but a bit threatened and I kept it at a distance. I had a girl friend who was very boyish and in command of herself. I made sexual advances because I thought that's what you did. Not because I really wanted to, it was ritualistic, but I soon got slapped down.

I thought a lot about being gay but – I suppose I'm coming across as very cerebral about sex – there may have been lots of other gay men there but only a few were interested enough to do anything about it and make it apparent. People thought I was absolutely outrageous compared to most people but I had no sexual experiences at all. I was pursued by a man I didn't find at all attractive. He became my best friend and we did lots of things together. He was bisexual and he was also fascinated by women and described himself as a lesbian. He was immensely well read at 18 and a good artist. People just presumed he was my boy friend and were quite open about it. In fact we were completely innocent – at least I was. He'd had quite a lot of sexual experience with both sexes but it was a complete surprise to me when he declared himself at a party. He was well off and always giving me presents. I suppose it was courting but I didn't realise. I'd presumed I'd be courted by some middle-aged man and there'd be polite courtship under which there'd be smouldering passion, but it never happened. I was pursued by dreary boys, and dreary girls I'm afraid, so I left the course as chaste as when I began.

There wasn't any feminist activity there then. I first came across it after my year at Belfast when I'd moved to London, where I also led a completely chaste life in a kind of commune. I did a degree course at an art college in north London that was considered terribly daring and racy, it's why I wanted to go there. I thought I'd be courted and wooed and made the object of somebody's desires but it didn't happen there either because I was too frightened of it, but I had lots of women friends because I'd got more comfortable with women the previous year. I lived in a communal house. Some of the girls were having relationships with some of the men rather freely and they all became a kind of surrogate family.

When I first went to London my working-class background was a sort of secret shame because though art students could be from working-class backgrounds they were all English so they they didn't seem like proper working-class people to me! They were also quite boorish whereas I was used to quite a refined working-class outlook.

One reason my life was chaste was because I had a religious conversion experience on the way to England, on the high seas! It was on the ferry from Belfast to Liverpool, which took all night so they could sell as much Guinness and whiskey as possible on the boat. I was trying to flee my Irish Catholic working-class background but I met a man who I thought at first was sexually interested in me but instead he talked to me about Jesus! When I got off the boat I was a born-again Christian but I decided I must not reject my past. I wasn't going to be a born-again Evangelical Protestant, so I went to mass and communion every week and I went into the art studio with Thomas à Kempis and the *Discipline of Saint Bernard* under my arm and I took it terribly seriously. I gave away most of my grant to the poor and I only drank water and bathed in cold water. It was all completely batty! It lasted a few months but it was an important experience because it meant I knew I couldn't run away from my background.

In the second year of my course I met several academic feminists at the college. Two of them were my tutors and one of them had a terrible crush on me which she made apparent, but nothing improper happened. She organised a course on women and art. It was 1970 or 1971 so it was very early in the feminist movement. I did the course because it was mixed, although there weren't many men on it, and I met people like Kate Millett who came to visit. So I got used to the discourse. Of course up to the time when I met a lot of women I felt I was a woman and then I realised I wasn't. In some ways I was more stereotypically feminine than they were! They were much more diverse in their behaviour, whereas mine was as if I was translating something. It was quite a shock because the early feminists in that circle were very intellectual, didn't wear make-up and were austere, almost Quaker-like. To use a pejorative word they were blue-stockings and they were overridingly middle class. Posh, I thought.

I suppose I was always 'passing as white' but I was affected by my working-class background. It was just like recently when I went for a job interview and I felt 'I won't get this job because these people are very posh.' I thought 'But they won't know I'm not posh', then I thought 'They will because they don't know me and they know all the posh people, so I can't be posh.' The classness of my tutors was used consciously to try and break up the gender status quo. I suspect they felt that as middle-class women they could do that and they were within traditions of academic disciplines and scholarship that allowed them to use certain kinds of discourse, so it wasn't that radical.

The class thing at the time was instructive because I was used to strong women who could bake and sew and manage a house, which are really good skills but I was too close to them to see that they were skills, so it was interesting for me to go away to a world where women were in charge of departments or courses. At Belfast there weren't any women teachers at all. So it was interesting meeting women who were writing courses, holding seminars and inviting guest speakers. They seemed undaunted and none of them were lesbians.

So this was a whole new genre and I threw myself heart and soul into it, and although I don't know how much I understood of feminism then, it seemed a simple political movement which has now become much more complex. There was no sense of being 'politically correct' about it then, it was much more open-ended. It was good to have to read the texts. That was something that stood me in good stead at least five years later when I got involved in the men's movement. I'd actually read the pioneer feminist texts and met some of the women who'd written them, in seminar situations.

What was more important to me personally at the time, but which was of course political because one of the great tenets was 'The personal is political', was living in the commune, and they weren't 'right-on' at all. The girls quickly began to wait on the men hand and foot, very traditional in some ways but other things were untraditional, typical of artistic circles and very free and easy. We lived what was in the air at the time. At university later there was a shift to trying to live out an ideological position. They were less joyous times because one was always living in fear of being reported to the head feminist or the head anti-sexist man. In fact I'm afraid at one time I probably was the head anti-sexist!

I had a year back in Ireland after finishing art school. That was even more chaste than usual in the bosom of my family. I worked as a labourer. I was a gardener in a forest park near Belfast. At some stage about then I did some labouring in London as well. I did grass cutting for the local council. In Ireland it was a work-relief scheme and my father took an acute interest in it because he'd worked in one of those in the thirties. We were digging in teams of men and I got on perfectly well with them.

I'm always surprised that as a gay man who'd always been a gay child and had been the object of fun and sniggers, that I ever developed confidence to go out amongst people at all, but they were fine. Sometimes I'd be in gangs of about six men working in the woods, lopping trees or turfing. It was fun and I really enjoyed it. The men seemed coarse but vigorous and full of life. There's a kind of good manners in situations like that. God knows what they said about me behind my back, but I found working people much more broadminded than middle-class liberals said they would be. The way they're represented in the press is much cruder than the actual individual or small group dynamics. I was always accepted and, I think, liked, even to some extent admired. Though I wasn't 'out' as a gay man I never pretended to be heterosexual and they just let me be.

I was going through one of my self-denying phases. I thought if I didn't get out of there I'd be walled up as a virgin queen! So I went back to England to do a teacher training course and much more saying yes to life. I joined the Campaign for Homosexual Equality [CHE]. It was about 1973–4. I left the commune and moved into a room of my own – but it was another chaste year! I decided not to be a school teacher but to go to university and also I decided to try and form a sexual relationship. Instead of playing a flirt with both men and women I would try to meet other gay men. So I joined the local branch of CHE. It was my first taste of personal politicising.

There was a link between this and feminism. Like a lot of people, I joined CHE not because I wanted to be political but because I wanted to meet this handsome grey-haired man who was going to court me. At the first meeting I thought I'd met him but he was going home to whoever it was he lived with, so he politely said 'No thank you.' Looking back on it I'm surprised I got quickly involved in the political debate. I suspect it was because I realised those years were also going to be chaste and I might as well do something for other people and defer the day when I would actually get into bed with someone. I got involved with the newsletter and through that I met people who were very 'right-on', a bit dismissive of CHE, they'd been involved with the Gay Liberation Front which was much more radical. They invited me to demonstrations. So I went on marches and things.

One of them was also interested in the trade-union movement and fighting for gay rights in the workplace, so he'd made contacts with lesbian groups. There weren't many lesbians in our CHE branch so it was all kind of academic that we were fighting for lesbian rights too, but through them I got involved with bits of the feminist discourse I'd been involved with earlier. They suddenly came back and fell into place. Subsequently when I got involved with feminist groups at university it didn't seem odd. The whole discourse was the same, about sexuality and gender and oppression and also I quickly got involved in things about race and so on. So I'd got the whole anti-oppression package by the time I was about 26 or 27. That lasted for quite a long time. I moved in what I'd describe as politically 'right-on' circles and they extended into other groups.

For most of the 1970s I wasn't aware of a separatist feminist movement. It seemed there was no reason that as a man one couldn't be a feminist. I felt it was a campaign and a discourse that everyone could join in. Being a Catholic was a problem and I did push it to one side and I went on many big pro-abortion demonstrations. Now I don't think it's the simple question that I thought it was then but in my job I'm always supportive to women students who need counselling about it.

After I'd finished the teacher-training course I got a place as a postgraduate at Keele University in Staffordshire. I just headed off north not knowing where the place was or anything and that's where I've stayed. That must have been about 1975. I came because of the course. By the time I left London I'd met a nice man and was having a straight down the line relationship with him, faithful, loving and caring. When I came here I still maintained friendships with the gay activist scene in London and I sold gay magazines at Keele. After a while I made contacts and we started a gay group which was quite successful. It was a student–staff social group not a pressure group. We also started the Gay Switchboard which is still running and I trained personnel for that.

The following year people joined the gay group who were more radical and we became a very radical group, rather foolhardily radical. I think we did a lot of harm, not welcoming enough to gay people who were not radical and I know people left because of that. One reason why I got disaffected with that and joined the men's group was that I was absolutely fed up with consciousness raising, which was such a feature of the feminist movement and borrowed from them by the gay movement. There comes a time when you're artificially going through raising consciousness for new members and it's impossible to maintain that artificiality.

Personally my life also became difficult. I started a relationship with somebody in the group while I still had my relationship with my lover in London and it was a mistake because I always maintained monogamy was the ideal for me, but I'd got into the political agenda of free love and had argued so much about sexual liberation I think I was testing it myself. But it wasn't for me, it was a disaster and I had a breakdown.

The youngish man I had an affair with at university left me and I was depressed for a long time and that affected my feelings about rights. The person who was most impressed by my stand about rights and openness had claimed his rights and did it very ruthlessly. I felt betrayed, in a way ideologically. I still maintained that the way forward was through personal political movements but I felt let down personally and not supported by the gay group.

That was one reason I got involved in the men's group. They didn't have those expectations. I felt more like a man than a gay man at that stage and they were very supportive. I did become the token gay man in the group and that was difficult. I came across these men through feminists because we'd always mutually joined each other's groups. Men could be feminists and the feminists, because the debate was the same, joined the gay group. They just came along and talked about sexual politics. A lot of feminists then were going through attempts at discovering whether they were lesbians who'd blotted out their true nature. It might have been useful if we'd also all gone through whether we were heterosexual and had suppressed that. The men in the men's group were husbands or lovers or ex-lovers or would-be lovers of women in the women's group. So I kind of got forwarded like a parcel to them. That was about 1978.

My friendship with several of the women I met at that time has persisted and I see them a lot whereas the men in the men's group I don't see often now. There's a fondness still there for those men but for the women I feel a genuine friendship and actual contact. When I see them we rattle on about our lives but when I see the men we talk about the past. It's not a living thing but the men's group was good, very heartfelt and genuine.

I learned how to do massage. The massage class was led by a woman from the women's group who came and gave us a demonstration, and we had touching games and trust games which were all good. We cooked for each other and didn't go out drinking. I was still a Gay Switchboard activist and that was a barrier for the men's group because my experiences were so different. I was happier with the women's group not because I thought I was a surrogate woman by that stage but because I could understand women's experiences more. I'd come into men's groups directly through feminism. I'd inherited the idea of men as enemies which I'd got from years of contact with either radical feminists or just women who'd come to distrust men, and from knowing how men oppress women and how heterosexual men oppress gay men. That formed part of my reaction at that time.

I liked a lot of those men genuinely and felt fond of them but against my better judgement I became emotionally involved with one of them but it was just an experiment for him. A lot of lesbians felt that about a stage women's groups were going through then. The token lesbian was practised upon by several disenchanted feminist housewives and then dumped.

Personal growth and active anti-sexist things like running crèches were both on the agenda and given equal weight in the men's group. It was very middle class, very English and very Protestant and coming from the gay group, even though I preferred monogamy, I was surprised at how monogamous the men's group were. There was a feeling that they had to be faithful to the women they had relationships with. Some of the people I'd mixed with in the gay movement were having nine sexual encounters a day with different men and felt it was politically necessary, but in the men's group there was no real sexual exploration. Coming to a middle-class provincial men's group was nice and secure but it was almost a new form of respectability. Perhaps this was radical, an alternative to sexually predatory masculinity – the crèches they ran and the childcare – and the monogamy might have been part of that, but it seemed to me part of the class bias of the men's group.

Later I had a lodger who was in the men's group with me. He was heterosexual and a lot of our friendship was based around sitting talking about oppression and urging each other on to yet greater acts of non-oppression! The men's group did a lot of touching and crying. I suppose I'm a bit cynical about it now. It's like having gone through a conversion experience and coming out the other side but I don't think you're ever quite the same. You're always aware of the debates and I've never debunked those debates and wouldn't want to. What I would debunk is the cant that surrounded a lot of it.

I wasn't only involved in 'right-on' circles. For five years from 1978 I worked as a telephonist with about seventy women and I was the only man, and of course they weren't feminists, they didn't give a damn! I'm not saying that was good but their perspective on things was interesting. They were mainly working-class women of a wide range of ages and had interesting experiences to relate. They were being ripped off by their employer because they weren't getting equal pay. I was getting the same as them but we were all lowly paid because telephonists generally weren't men.

I really liked and admired these women and the way they got on with things, it was fascinating. They were women who had to go out to work because their husbands' wages weren't enough to keep the family on. I honestly don't think most of them wanted to work. They had to work through necessity but they weren't paid much, and we had miserable holidays – about three weeks for the whole year and during those three weeks often they had to decorate the house. In their lunch breaks they had to go out and do the shopping. I'm not saying it was good but their expectations and their real joy with things and their diversity of personality was very interesting. I was beginning to find the 'right-on' thing quite suffocating because there didn't seem to be room for individual expression.

I finished my Masters degree and did well in it and as a consequence I won a scholarship and started a Ph.D., but then my relationship broke up. So for two years I did nothing, very expensively. The big disappointment was that I'd let my tutor down and I didn't have anything to show for it. I limped on and finished it eventually but the reason I stayed in this area was to maintain some contact with the university and use the library. I took the blandest job I could do. So I had the whole package, I was Irish and Catholic and gay and working class and I was working in a women's job and one which, for men, was associated either with being disabled or homosexual! I did it because I knew the job wasn't going to be demanding. I also became the trade-union representative there!

Also after a gap I had a relationship with a local man, a pottery worker. It was a stormy and passionate relationship for about two years.

I became identified with the local area and with working-class people. I suppose it was only my accent and the fact that the house was chock-a-block with books that distinguished me from any of them. I went out drinking with them, I went to local things, all my friends were local apart from the men's group and the women's group. So my experiences of things were different from most of the men's group or the women's group.

The local man I was going out with at the time thought they were the living end. He was bitter and resentful about it. My friends were always popping in and out of each other's houses and he would just be putting his feet up to relax and the door would knock and there'd be some distraught person from the women's group wanting to talk to me and he'd sit through that and then there'd be somebody from the men's group with a basket of elderberries or something. He found it all too fictional.

It was important to me that I was part of the local community but I felt in a battlefield between on one side, the women I worked with who were dreadfully oppressed but who were really positive and elated about their lives and a man who did hard factory work and lived with his parents and brothers and sisters and was picked on and oppressed at work; and on the other side, people who wanted to express themselves personally and who were basically middle-class people who I liked and was fond of. I was caught between two worlds. In fact one of the most radical of the feminists threatened to hit my boy friend over the head with a bottle and push the broken glass into his face – unbelievably horrific and violent to someone who himself wasn't at all violent, but he obviously represented a kind of male attitude to her. Some of the middle-class people in both the men's and the women's groups were incredibly manipulative and selfish. So it all became personalised for me. I was a living truce-line.

Some of us in the men's group would get together and talk about music or poetry as if men couldn't do it normally without seeming feeble, whereas in gay circles culture was always on the agenda. It was an interesting contrast. There was also a conservationist thing, which interested me coincidentally but which was much more live among the heterosexual members of the men's group. In fact it may have been a thing that brought them together. Some of them knew each other through a food co-operative that had developed in the early seventies initially around a workers' co-operative wholefood shop which had been set up by some women who were part of the women's group and their menfolk.

Several years later these men formed the nucleus of the men's group.

Issues of food and conservation were important. We spent a lot of time talking about the effects of washing-up liquid! I think several were members of Friends of the Earth and we were all, to a man, vegetarian. There was a certain thrift which appealed to me because I was in straitened circumstances anyway. It was nice for it to be a virtue again. We all lived close to each other in rather cheap rented accommodation. None of us owned our own houses.

What happened to the men in the group was that our burgeoning middle-classness burgeoned rather too much and we all became professional people. I've now been in academic teaching for the last nine years. We were at an age where those pressures had to be either embraced or rejected completely. We could still play about into our thirties and then all of a sudden other possibilities arose, and of course the eighties were yuppy. We weren't yuppy by definition, but we got more respectable. What happened to me is perhaps what happened to a lot of them. I became more reclusive, more defined by my job and I've chosen the narrow bed of celibacy. For all my campaigning what I was seeking was not going to come through campaigning. I'm not seeking a relationship now and haven't done for years. I'm alone in that men's group in being like that. They were monogamous then and they are now and I respect that. They weren't fighting for sexual liberation and I was, but somehow they have the relationships and I haven't, which is an irony. It was a formative thing for me, the men's group, a phase in my development, not one I reject, though I do get a bit sneery about it from time to time, but only in conversation, not to myself.

Anti-sexist ideals are still important to me. There are certain ideas I have clung to. Being a positive role model is important. I am a gay man, I teach as a gay man and it's absolutely important that my employers know I'm a gay man. I'm completely out. I don't think it's a virtue but I want people to say 'There's a gay man doing a job as a gay man.' It's a social-justice thing. It's really bad that gay people are still discriminated against. I also think it's important to have heterosexual male friends who I feel positive about and who feel positive about me in the full knowlege that I'm a gay man. It still happens and I feel really good about it. We can have a sort of purified friendship. It happened in the men's group, a couple of them I felt really fond of without any suggestion of a sexual relationship. Just a nice friendship.

Anti-sexism also still affects how I relate to women. I try to encourage young women in education and positively discriminate if I think there's negative discrimination. With my nieces and god-daughters, I try to do good role-modelling. I want to make them feel confident in themselves and not take them for granted and yet be myself and let them be themselves. The whole debate about gender and sexuality and role models is still important to me. I don't think there's a day when I don't think about them.

Every time I see a reference to that Robert Bly book I think, 'Under no circumstances will I read that.' It seems to be a new orthodoxy that underlines masculinity. It doesn't seem challenging at all. I really dislike masculinity and the power thing and I despise it. On the other hand I don't think there's any point in 'outing' people. It's a personal conversion thing and having experienced it I know the hardest thing is to hold on to it. You shouldn't try to hold on to the initial thrill because then it becomes corrupt. I got tired of consciousness raising, pretending to be a born-again gay man over and over again for other people's benefit. You take what you can from these movements but I can't keep embroidering the banners every year. There was a time for those movements for me and I hope there is still a time for them for younger men today but they must carve out their own way.

Chapter 6

Househusband

Some interviewees had not been members of anti-sexist men's groups and did not necessarily perceive their lifestyles as politically significant but were performing roles and assuming identities which were unconventional from a traditional masculine standpoint. When interviewed they also expressed sympathy with feminist ideas. Vince, who tells his story in this chapter, was a primary childcarer and houseperson in a role-reversal situation. He may perhaps be a good example of such men, who find feminism acceptable if it is not being 'hammered down your throat', as he says.

VINCE

I'm 43. I'm a musician but after discussion with Sue I decided to be a househusband and she'd be the breadwinner. It's my third year now. I took over looking after my son when he was 9 months old and he's 3 now. Sue looked after him before that and I was working. Now I've a daughter 2 months old.

It was so Sue could carry on with her career and have children. I thought I'd have time to get more into music at the same time as bringing kids up. It was convenient in that we both in theory can get what we want out of it. I worked for fourteen years as a coalman, self-employed, and I didn't want to carry on in that. It was a bloody hard job, although I liked the independence of it. I never intended to do it as long as that.

The reason I did it was that in my first marriage my brother-in-law was a coalman and he asked me to help him part time. I hated it but I hadn't much money and me and the drummer in the band thought we'd give it a go. We thought we'd do it for a year and we could buy new kit and stuff. That's how I got into it and it lasted fourteen years. We were delivering concessionary fuel to miners but we did other work as well. We took some rounds over, delivering to domestic households.

I was born in Ashbourne, Derbyshire. My father was a toolsetter at Rolls Royce in Derby before I was born. He was a corn salesman later. We used to go to market with him on Wednesdays. I don't remember him working at the factory. We lived in a village near Ashbourne till I was 8. I've a twin brother and a brother five years older. My Dad used to go by motorbike to Derby which was quite a way. He was a Methodist lay preacher as well, a fanatic. When we were kids he carted us off to churches and we'd be up in the pulpit while he was laying down the thunder. When we moved from Derbyshire to Staffordshire there was a Methodist church across the road which he got heavily involved with and my mother played the organ. He changed when I was 16. He took up golf, so he swapped one fanaticism for another! He was a much better person after that!

My mother was an infant teacher. She's always taught and still lives in the village. She continued teaching right through. She had some time off when we were small but we went to school when we were about 3 and we were in her class, a little village school. So I had an early experience of a working woman with her own career.

In the main I had a happy childhood. The early part was much better than the years from 9 onwards. When we moved my Dad became more Hitlerian. It was double standards really. He'd be either blowing thunder or quite sensitive and he used to apologise in later life. He'd say 'I'm sorry I was hard on you when you were kids.' Some of it was OK but some was repressive. He was strict at times, biblical, trust in the Lord, that sort of stuff. He was a perfectionist. In some ways he was closer than my mother. She didn't show her feelings. He could also be sensitive but when my Dad was angry he was angry! I remember times on holiday camping. He was quite a family man but the fanaticism, the religion, spoiled it. I got on well with him in the earlier years but not later. Me and my twin brother both played guitars and he hated that. Once he threatened to phone the police because we were playing in a pub. We played in churches and at pie suppers in huts and things like that but there comes a point when you have to play somewhere else. He was overcautious about that. He encouraged us both to drive, he was helpful there.

I remember my mother as a tough character. My parents were in most ways pretty conventional but my Mum liked her independence. That's why she went on teaching. She probably earned more than my Dad. She wasn't a cowed housewife. She hadn't got loads of friends, she wasn't gregarious at all but she was steady and secure in her job. She liked her work and she never complained about it.

My Dad got on with his work too but he was a complainer. He used to say 'I've got this and that to deal with', belly-aching. He moaned about his health as well. They were conventional in the home when we were younger. It got on my Mum's nerves that he was so fanatical about preaching when she could have done with more help at home and looking after us. He did put his three-pennorth in, but he didn't see it as his responsibility. They both had funny histories because her father died when she was 7 and my Dad's father was an Italian who abandoned them. He never spoke about it but reading between the lines his Dad disappeared when he was 4 or 5. It had a big stigma between the wars. I'm sure it had a big effect on him.

I see myself in both parents reasonably equally. I didn't model myself on my father. I rebelled against him because he was so authoritarian. He wanted us to be preachers, doctors or lawyers, things that were totally wrong for us. I don't think he had a positive feeling about being a breadwinner, but everything had to be the righteous path. It was his duty to have a job but I remember at one point when I was about 12 and he must have been having some sort of midlife crisis because he wanted to sell up and go and live in France, a sort of escape. I'm sure the job was getting a bit weighty for him. He had a fascination for France. They went touring there a lot after we left home.

My infant school was mixed. I remember quite a bit about it. I don't remember them treating girls and boys differently. We were mixed in together, in the playground too, and we played together, 'O'Grady says' and 'doctors and nurses' and stuff like that. Me and my twin brother were close and I remember two girls we played with in the playground. It was sexual experimenting, we were saying 'You show us your bits and we'll show you ours' but we chickened out and ran off when it came to our turn. We did the usual boys' things, climbing trees and getting into scrapes. I remember my brother having blood washed off his head in the school kitchen and also, I'm not sure if it was a separate incident, when I was hurt. Generally, life at the school was pretty good.

When we moved I still went to the school where my mother taught but by this time I was in another class. They seemed to know a lot more at that school. It was like stepping out of a backwater. I felt like a country hick coming to the town. It was more working class but it was still balanced between girls and boys. The headmaster was competitive in sports. I can't remember us playing football. We raced Dinky toys in the playground and the girls were involved in that. I can't remember them standing in a bunch outside it, being ostracised.

We used to play with the girls, everybody played together. It's possibly something to do with being in a rural area. I don't think they emphasised different subjects for girls and boys, maybe in the later schools, but there wasn't a sharp difference at the junior schools. I had a girl friend at the village school. I remember putting flowers in her hair.

We failed our exam at 11, which my parents weren't pleased about. They sent us to a private school that was a bit rough-and-ready, not what you'd expect of a private school. That was mixed too, it's been consistent right through my schooling. There wasn't much difference in the treatment of girls there either but they didn't mix so much in the playground. I suppose the sexual thing was coming in more then. I had more male friends there. I remember fancying girls in the class but not having much to do with them except one who talked to anybody and had no snobbishness or aloofness.

We were a couple of years there. Then they moved us to another private school which was terrific. We had to take an exam to get into that one. A lot of the kids from the first school were moved there. Quite a few parents weren't impressed with the other. The teachers were of both sexes at all these schools. I had a couple of good friends at secondary school. One was a girl. We used to travel by train and all sat together, we didn't avoid each other. I remember her diving under a coat with my twin brother and investigating him, on the train! I had more friends at the second school. I remember girls having parties and being invited, and having crushes on every girl in the class.

At that school I was top of the class most of the time or in the top three. I was good at maths and English subjects. My friends paid me to do their homework at one point. I played football and enjoyed it, and hanging on the bars and all that stuff but I wasn't the best in the class at sport. I found cricket too fierce, that hard ball coming crashing towards you.

I can't remember being picked on at school. I recall a big lad picking on another lad and I stepped in and got a bloody nose. I learned a lesson there, don't always barge in. There was more bullying at that school than the other one. It was the only school I went to where there was bullying. It wasn't a tight-run ship. They could get away with it. If there was ever any trouble my twin brother would keep shouting, even though he was being hit he'd carry on. I took the other route which was to shut up, say nothing and let it pass off, but then you're repressed and allowing it to happen.

My brothers had girl friends but I didn't have enough confidence to step out and ask a girl for a date. That weighed heavily on me. I had a problem in my teens, it all went wrong for me then. I didn't feel I could approach girls. I felt terribly shy, I was afraid of being rejected. It took me a long time to work it out but that's what it was. I thought about it a lot. I played in a band and I met some right characters and I started to feel a bit under the spotlight because I thought they were thinking 'Why hasn't he got any girl friends?' I felt a bit of pressure. They were working-class lads from the Potteries. One of them, the drummer, who was later my partner in the coal business, he only had to look at a girl and he was there. None of this messing about, none of this mind stuff. He couldn't understand it about me. He said at one point 'I used to think what was up with you.' Maybe he thought I was homosexual. He obviously thought I'd got a problem. Which I had, I was shy, and afraid of rejection.

I got involved in the band when I was 15. We played Beatles and Rolling Stones tunes. It was that era. I was in a Methodist youth club and a bloke came to the club and brought his guitar, and that was it, we were hooked. My brother who was the more forceful character of the two of us, took up the guitar and I went on to bass guitar which nobody else wanted to play. We played at the youth club and churches. We had headlines in the local papers like 'Guitars twanged in so-and-so chapel'.

After I left school at 16 I went to a college of building. I was heavily into the band by then. I remember the physics teacher saying, 'Look, you pack in the band or pack in physics.' So I said I'd pack in the band but I carried on, there was nothing he could do about it. I was being the 'Yes man' again to keep the peace. Building was my Dad's idea. I didn't have any strong preferences, I wasn't academic at all. I did well at my last school but I'd got no yen to be a boffin. I wanted to be a musician. I didn't have any other career in mind. Once I'd started playing an instrument that was it. We've had a couple of records out – near misses!

I studied surveying and technical drawing at the college of building but I wasn't thinking of going into that. I was sent there and did what I was told. Then my Dad fixed me up with a job in the drawing office of a heating and ventilating firm, my first job. I was about 18. I did that till I got the sack! A young lad was clocking me on in the mornings and I used to roll up in the band's van at about ten. I've always been a night owl for as long as I can remember. I should be a professional musician because those hours suit me. I can go to bed at three in the morning and get up at ten and it's fine. I was playing with the band all that time and staying up till the early hours as musicians do. That was my main interest. I was making more money at music than at the job. If I got three or four gigs a week it was as much as my wages. I played a lot, mostly in pubs.

I only lasted nine months at the first job. I wasn't bothered. It was colouring in lines around technical drawings. I didn't dare tell my parents I'd lost the job as I was still living at home, so I got a job at a service station. I had a good friend I met at college, I befriended him. He was a halfcast and looked lonely. He turned out to be a good friend. I got the second job because he mentioned it. I got responsibility quick and it was fatal because they gave me the job of opening up in the morning. Once that happened I didn't last long because of the thing about getting there. I was supposed to be there at seven thirty and if I got there at say quarter past eight there'd be a string of vans down the road waiting for fuel. I'd have to rush in and switch all the pumps on. That lasted about five months. I was about 19 then and active with the band. I went to work in the band's van.

I had a part-time job at a plant nursery and went there by push-bike. I worked there with the drummer. I don't remember why I didn't have a vehicle then. I remember buying my first car for £15 and on the day I arrived at the nursery in it I got the sack. I had a series of jobs but the band was the constant thing. When we were 20 we went to play in a hotel in Switzerland for a month. We bought an old van for £80 and off we went, as green as anything. We met another band out there from London and this Cockney said to us 'I thought we were green but you're even greener!' We must have looked a right shower. We were being ripped off.

It was there I had my first girl friend, in Zurich. It was a red-light pub. She was a lady of the night, you know. I had holes in my shoes and she wanted to buy me a pair of shoes and she used to buy us food. My brother who was in the same band, he was engaged, and he felt out of it because he was in love with his girl friend and everybody used to disappear during the day and he'd be left doing nothing. He must have felt lonely because we'd all got girl friends and disappeared. They wanted the band to stay on and I pleaded with my brother but we all left in the end. After we came back from Switzerland the band folded because my brother hadn't been happy there and his girl friend was possessive and didn't like him playing. She came to the gigs to keep an eye on him. Then I a job on an ice-cream van down south and then moved back up here.

I lived at home till my Dad kicked us out. He got fed up with us when we were about 20. He hated the idea of us lying in bed. I've always been nocturnal so I'd roll in about four a.m. then at eight or nine o'clock my father would be shouting us up. After that I moved to the keyboard player's house and slept on his floor for a while. There was a gathering of us there. Then I met the girl next door and moved in with her parents for a while, then we got a flat and got married.

After a while most of the band got together again. I got back with the drummer and members of different bands I'd played with before. I got a job at a toy company packing toys till the band went to Germany for a month. Afterwards I got a letter from the toy company asking if I wanted the job back. That was handy, so I did a few more months there. The band had a kind of fairy godmother. There was this woman who owned garages and was into music and the drummer was her boy friend. She had a house and we all lived there for a time and she supported us while we were writing stuff and she paid for a studio for us. We played at clubs in Liverpool and London. We did quite a bit of travelling. For a time we backed a black band. We did some touring with them playing soul music.

The band were ambitious at that time. We had a couple of singles out, but I was still doing day jobs to survive, so I was semi-pro. I had a big run-in with the Social Security at one point because I signed on. It was a pittance but it was better than nothing. Somebody had obviously shopped me, saying he's in a band. So I got investigated by this heavy from up north. It was frightening. I'd have said anything to get out it. He gave me the third degree but fortunately the drummer in the band at that time kept immaculate records. He came along with his file and that was the last I heard of it. I didn't get prosecuted so I carried on as normal. It did me a favour because it proved most of the earnings went on the van and equipment. I never made much out of it.

We branched out into other things, soul and blues. I did one residency for six years on Sunday nights. I finished that about eighteen months ago. I was playing with other bands as well, always on bass guitar. I've always seen myself as a musician, the other jobs were purely for survival. The bands were mostly men, there was a woman in the band later on. She was a singer. We got on the BBC playlists which is what you aimed for. I can remember sitting in the coal lorry listening to our band on the radio, but we got blocked somehow in the competition between record companies. We were with a new company and the others wanted to stop it. That was what stopped us getting to the big time.

I was never encouraged to but I certainly wanted to have relationships with women. I was attracted to them but the shyness got in the way. I never came out of it. My Dad used to say things like, 'You don't want to get married. Don't bother with women.' I was 24 when I got married. With my first wife I had a council flat. We were married for ten years. I was the breadwinner then. She had a part-time job, not well paid. She was reasonably interested in the music. She came along sometimes, but she had depressions and I didn't recognise it and probably wasn't as supportive as I could have been. I helped with the housework. I'd got no qualms about going round with the hoover or doing the windows but general housework I didn't do a lot. Washing up was my worst area, I wasn't keen on that.

We didn't have any children. I'd have liked children. I was excited when she said she was pregnant. I remember telling the band at the recording studio and I was looking forward to it. It was a disappointment when she had a miscarriage. We did a lot of work on the house together, put floors and windows in ourselves. She was quite handy, she put a false ceiling in the roof on her own. I've enjoyed most of the physical things I've done, like when I worked as a coalman. Even now I like practical things, laying floors or putting windows in. I've always enjoyed that sort of thing. Last night I met a woman who was doing a loft conversion and she asked me how to get the wood up into the loft because it's too big. I gave her some tips. I admired her for having a go. I thought it was great she did that.

My first marriage was depressing really. I was quite long suffering but eventually I snapped and thought, 'I've had enough of this.' I was the one that instigated the split. It was like a rebirth time for me. I packed up smoking then as well. A friend of mine said 'I think it's your renaissance' but it was a difficult phase. It was hard to stick to. People said 'You'll regret it.' I haven't, but it was difficult for eighteen months. I don't think I should have been married really, I should have stuck to music and not got involved in the coal business. There was pressure on me to get a job when I got married.

She wanted to move out of the city and I didn't. She didn't drive. I offered to give her lessons but she'd didn't do that. She had to be at work by nine and I'm hopeless at getting up early. The reason I liked the coal job was that I was self employed and I could please myself what time I got there within reason. I might work ten hours in a day but not start till eleven. It was up to me. That meant a lot to me. I had pressure to get her to work and then she'd have to hang around at her sister's late at night waiting for me to pick her up to take her home. That created a lot of tension. If we'd lived closer she could have got home herself.

When we went on the tours abroad each was a month's residency in a hotel. We did long hours, seven hours a night. One in Norway was the best one, it was wonderful. Musically we were a lot better when we came back because that's what you want, seven hours a night. It's wonderful to get you playing better, but it didn't help us get into the big time. There must be thousands of people like me. I remember saying if I hadn't had some success by the time I was 30 I'd pack it in but it's got stronger. I enjoy it, so I'm not really bothered.

The touring with the band was before I had the coal round, but I never stopped playing. We did things anywhere in this country, locally mainly. I had lots of late nights. That didn't help married life either but I was only ever away full time for three months in five years. The first time, in Switzerand, I didn't know her, but I was married the other times when we went to Germany and to Norway.

I got divorced because I thought we were doing each other no good. I couldn't believe how easy it was once I'd done it. I was glad at that time I'd got a job. If I'd lost my job as well it would have been rough. I'd got friends coming round and we recorded stuff, that all helped. I had a couple of women friends in between the marriages, but it didn't work out. I didn't consciously think 'I need a relationship with a woman', but when I met Sue I found myself phoning her up. I was surprised about that. She responded and we got on well. I met her at a pub where I played a long residency. She came to listen, she's always been a keen music fan. After about a year I sold my house and moved into hers.

I'm better suited to Sue. We're a better match. She's pretty career oriented, a busy person. She's got lots of interests. I don't know if things will stay like this. If I was offered a tour I'd probably take it and put the children in a nursery. Then I'd go back to looking after them again. I'm in the lap of the gods. It gives me more time than I've ever had to work on my music. It took me a while to adjust to not earning any money. I could sometimes earn a couple of hundred a week, but it didn't take me long not to worry about that. I wasn't always thinking 'I used to have lots of money.' This arrangement evolved after discussion with Sue. We wrote down the pluses and minuses and looked at it to see if we could afford to do it. When you get down to it, it's governed by monetary things.

Why this situation works is because Sue wanted to carry on with her career and I could look after the kids and find more time to write music and study. It's been of great benefit to me. I believe in sex equality, not competition – I can help you in this area and you can help me in that area, equilibrium but not competitive.

It's possible I've been influenced by feminism. Sue is quite a feminist. She's involved with women's groups and co-counselling groups, things like that. It's all part of her job. She goes on lots of courses and mind-expanding things. It appeals to me. Feminist influence might get my hair up on end if it wasn't delivered properly. I'd think 'Somebody is standing on a soapbox shouting.' If it's not being hammered down your throat it's more acceptable. I could be stubborn if I felt it was being hammered into me. I'm interested in what Sue is involved in but otherwise I'm not interested in politics. If people are downtrodden I can see why they get together, like the Suffragette Movement.

I'd played in bands with the same people for a long time but about the time I got divorced I met a lot of new people. I'm in a blues band now. I play only about once a fortnight at the moment. I didn't cut it down, it's just gone a bit slack. It's a temporary lull. It goes like that. I've been on a jazz course the last three years at evening classes. I thought it was time I learned some theory. I had three bands going about three years ago, jazz, blues and country. I've got a feel for those three.

Two days a week my son goes to a crèche so I get a good day to do some music. I pick him up for dinner and then take him back till about quarter past four. I've done that for four or five months. He enjoys mixing with the other kids. Last year when he was smaller he slept in the afternoons. I had an alarm system so I could do practical things. As soon as I heard him crying I'd go and look after him. Other times he had a playpen. I fed him and changed his nappies. That was no problem, it's something you get used to. I know some mothers who're alone with young children feel isolated but I've other activities. Every day is different. If I've a few gigs coming in I enjoy them more.

I enjoy domestic work. I don't do much dusting. Sue's not bothered about that either. I wash clothes. None of us is very fond of ironing so it's a case of ironing what you need before you go out. I iron her things too. When she was in hospital I ironed loads of stuff. It probably takes me longer but I do it. I do all the cooking. I've learned a lot more about that. I was an egg, chips and peas man before. Washing up is part of my job now, I don't enjoy it but I don't mind. It has to be done.

I wouldn't be rattled by the idea that what I'm doing isn't seen as masculine. I don't feel feminine. In pop music a masculine image is important as a stage thing but when you move into other areas of music it doesn't seem so important. Generally I feel more at ease in the company of men because of my shyness. It's the sexuality thing that's a sort of threat. Lately I find it easier in the company of women. I don't worry about it so much. A while ago they had a charity thing here for the women's group and I was the only man here. I didn't feel bothered by it.

I don't feel any awkwardness at the crèche. I don't think the young mothers there feel any either. In my role now I've got more in common with women. Although I don't talk much about kids there's a common denominator. There aren't many men picking up young children from the crèche but I've seen a couple of others there. My friend, a piano player, he picks his little lad up. It's because he's at home in the day and can do.

My view of marriage is that people should be able to choose what suits them. I like the idea of firms having flexi-time. It's easy to say people can rearrange marriage but experiencing it is different, emotions come into play. Marriage says to somebody that you want to be with them. To think that nobody needs to be married and you can pick somebody up here and put them down there would mess most people up. It would certainly mess me up.

I don't think I've come across people expressing hostile attitudes because I've become a househusband. A lot of my friends are musicians and they accept things like that. They are unconventional anyway, so it doesn't seem strange to them. I think my mother is a bit negative but, as I said, she doesn't show her feelings much. I haven't met any outright opposition from her or from my brothers.

Conclusion to Part II

In Part II I have tried as far as possible to present the eight life stories in the men's own words but inevitably they are edited versions of the original interviews. As Porter and Weeks say in the Preface to their book of gay men's life histories, 'All life stories are reconstructions, attempts to make sense of a complex reality, to provide a narrative structure for oneself as well as for others' and like them, as editor on behalf of my interviewees, I have 'inevitably been selective, and therefore have in turn helped shape the material' but also I believe 'the individuals whose lives are presented here, offer insights into both their own lives and the milieu in which they lived' (Porter and Weeks 1991: 2).

The editing involved condensation for reasons of space, a small amount of chronological reordering so that experiences appear in their proper time sequence and the removal of repetitions and conversational clichés, but I have tried to remain truthful to the original interviews.

The division of these interviews into categories for chapters was admittedly somewhat arbitrary and many other combinations of these and other interviews from the whole sample could have been used. For this reason I present here a series of alternative categories by which other comparisons of these eight life histories could be made:

under 35: Steve, Tim, Terry;
over 35: Alan, Simon, John, Anthony, Vince;
married: Alan, Tim, Terry, Vince;
living with woman partner; Simon;
no woman partner: John, Anthony;
actively involved in childcare: Alan, Tim, Simon, Terry, Vince;
currently in paid work: Alan, Tim, Simon, Terry, John, Anthony;
not currently in paid work: Steve, Vince;
not identified with father: Steve, Alan, John, Anthony, Vince;

identified with nurturing father: Simon, Terry, Tim;
strong mothers: Steve, Alan, Terry, John, Vince;
influenced by siblings: Tim, Terry, John, Anthony;
influenced by childhood friendships: Anthony;
had adverse macho experiences in school: Steve, Simon, John, Vince;
had positive experience of mixed schools: Tim, Terry, Vince;
experienced higher education: Steve, Tim, Simon, John, Anthony;
important experiences in employment: Tim, Terry, John, Anthony;
influenced by feminism: Steve, Tim, Simon, Terry, John, Anthony;
strongly influenced by woman partner: Steve, Alan, Simon, Terry, Vince;
has woman partner, does housework: Steve, Alan, Tim, Simon, Terry, Vince;
in touch with feelings: Steve, Tim, Simon, Terry, John, Anthony;
favours reformed egalitarian marriage: Alan, Tim, Terry, Vince;
favours unmarried partnership with woman: Steve, Simon;
has experienced such partnership: Steve, Simon, Tim, Terry;
has been a primary childcarer/houseperson: Vince, Simon, John;
involved in shared care-giving: Tim, Terry, Simon, Alan;
has experienced being a lone father: Simon;
has experienced communal household living: Terry, Simon, John, Anthony;
committed to breadwinner role: Alan.

Part III

Theoretical and practical issues

Chapter 7

Summary and Conclusions

I have sought to make an original contribution both to existing sociological knowledge and to sexual politics by means of a research-based study of anti-sexist men. Such men have not previously been the subject of qualitative sociological investigation of this kind in Britain and there has been little in the United States or other English-speaking countries. Though my interviewees were all British their stories reveal themes in men's experience which may be common to pro-feminist men elsewhere.

Connell was justified in saying that,

> study of the historical dynamic of gender relations is still in its early days. . . . To make sense of these projects requires a history of the formation of groups and categories, and of the types of personalities, motives and capacities drawn upon in sexual politics.
>
> (Connell 1987: 149–50)

Feminists have made a major contribution to published information on men by revealing much that was previously concealed about the behaviour of the dominant gender type, male chauvinists, whose characteristics correspond to what Connell called 'hegemonic masculinity'. Gay scholarship has also built up a body of published knowledge about gay men. But so far books by and on anti-sexist men have consisted almost entirely of theoretical/philosophical and methodological discussions. There has been little empirical work to illuminate the subjective experiences and understandings of anti-sexist men in their attempts to respond sympathetically to changes among women. This book is a step towards filling that gap. Space restrictions meant that the number of life histories had to be limited. I hope to add further to this literature in due course.

In this concluding chapter I do three things:

1 summarise the main themes and findings of the book;
2 discuss their implications for some existing theoretical work;
3 discuss the findings in relation to women's liberation and to gender oppression in general, with particular reference to problems involved in anti-sexist men's contributing to struggles against gender oppression.

SUMMARY OF THEMES AND FINDINGS

Since about 1970, women have achieved advances in many aspects of life in most Western developed societies and long-established ideas of masculinity have been called into question. This study aimed to further a sociological understanding of one type of male response to this situation by studying anti-sexist men's life experiences; and also to contribute politically by encouraging and promoting a wider understanding of men who are non-macho, mostly non-gay, and opposed to sexist oppression.

As stated in the Introduction, I see gender as socially constructed, not determined by biological sex. Feminine and masculine roles and identities can be redefined and lived differently. To support this view I presented life histories of men with anti-sexist outlooks, who were attempting to live non-sexist lives. These were based on qualitative interviews with a small sample of such men. My research aims were exploratory analytical description and a contribution to grounded theory construction.

In the interviews I aimed to trace three aspects of life experience related to the development of anti-sexist attitudes among men: (a) early life history; (b) experience of adult gender relations; and (c) current activities and lifestyles. In a qualitative analysis of all the life histories, including those not included in the present book, I examined common themes in the men's lives.

It is not possible from the type and size of sample in my study to draw any firm conclusions on the composition of the British anti-sexist men's movement comparable to the data given on the United States by Shiffman (1987: 295), but the characteristics of my sample are of interest to note even though I do not claim wider representativeness.

Shiffman wrote that, 'An early paper written during the movement's gestation period depicts the men's movement as the white middle class progeny of the women's and lesbian/gay liberation movements' (Snodgrass 1975). Gross, Smith and Wallston reported 'The typical participant in the men's movement is a youngish, college educated, middle class, straight, white male' (Gross, Smith and Wallston 1983:

75–9). Shiffman's findings from a study at a California Men's Gathering in 1984 contradicted the notion that participants were young, but over 90 per cent were white, nearly half were gay and nearly 20 per cent bisexual. Participants were well educated but their incomes were substantially lower than the national average, 42 per cent could be identified as professional, 26 per cent as working class (Shiffman 1987: 301–3). There were special reasons which may have explained Shiffman's finding on high gay/bisexual participation.

My sample of thirty men were aged between 21 and 54, most between 30 and 45. Half saw themselves as working class: thirteen were from manual home backgrounds, thirteen from non-manual and four from ambiguous backgrounds; when interviewed twenty-three were in non-manual occupations, three in manual ones and four were not employed. No evidence was collected on current income levels but from impressionistic evidence few could be described as highly paid. Less than a third were professionals and a minority had experienced higher education. All were white as no ethnic-minority men were members of the men's groups studied. Twenty-six of the men defined themselves as heterosexual, two as gay and two as bisexual. Three-quarters were married or in stable relationships with women and eight were divorced. Only four had never lived with a woman. Two-thirds were fathers and four had been lone fathers. Two still were when interviewed.

My main finding was that more than three-quarters of the men had experienced a combination of two interacting and reinforcing influences in their lives: early life experiences which departed from conventional gender expectations; and adult experience of feminist influence, usually in a close relationship with an active feminist. Twenty-four of the thirty men had experienced the first, twenty-seven the second, and twenty-three had experienced both. Twenty of the twenty-six non-gay interviewees had had close relationships with at least one feminist woman.

Features of their early life experience conducive to developing an anti-sexist outlook varied widely but the most frequent and relevant influences were non-identification with traditional fathers or identification with nurturing fathers; experience of strong mothers, usually involved in paid work; parents who did not conform to conventional domestic roles; the influence of sisters or brothers; and childhood friendships with girls, or with both sexes in situations where gender was not emphasised.

All but four reported that their fathers were not significant role models for them and all the four who did identify with their fathers had nurturing fathers; fourteen said they identified more with their mothers and sixteen reported either a mixed parental identification or said they did not identify with either parent.

Most of the men who said their parents were non-traditional had mothers who were in regular paid employment at some stage during their childhood – a significant point for the coming generation since this has now become virtually the norm. In the context of unconventional parental gender roles it was mothers rather than fathers who more often had a decisive influence since few men had nurturing fathers but half said they had strong mothers.

Brothers and sisters were sometimes important influences, as examples to follow or to reject, or as younger children to care for. Nearly half the men said they had had childhood friendships which were unconventional in traditional gender terms. School experiences had an important influence for some. They either enjoyed being with girls in mixed schools or had adverse experiences of macho behaviour by other boys or male teachers. Several interviewees described employment or higher-education experiences that had a gender influence on them, including living away from home.

Feminism was the most striking adult influence for most of the men. All but one of those who joined anti-sexist men's groups said their earlier unconventional gender experiences had been reinforced and developed by feminist influence, and significantly, in most cases, in the form of a close relationship with a particular woman with a feminist outlook.

It is highly significant that all the heterosexual men said they had been influenced by feminism, and of these, all but six said the influence had come from one or more specific women with whom they had had close relationships. One bisexual man was also influenced by a feminist partner. The two gay men also acknowledged less personal feminist influence. These, and the six heterosexual men who did not attribute their views to one particular woman, referred to the influence of several women friends; involvement in organisations in which feminists actively participated; exposure to feminist literature; and the men's own prior commitment to egalitarian values which they then applied to gender relations.

Various influences were mentioned for joining an anti-sexist men's group, usually several in combination, but one frequently mentioned was getting involved in discussions with men whose partners were active in a local women's group. Some joined a men's group to try to deal with their emotional problems over their partners' involvement in feminism. Other frequently mentioned influences were alternative bookshops and anti-sexist magazines. Since the influence of individual feminists was so widespread an experience of men who joined anti-sexist men's groups it is perhaps not surprising that only a small minority of men's group members were gay.

Men's initial experiences in anti-sexist men's groups often involved wariness about all-male groups, followed by relief on finding that the other men involved did not fit the macho stereotype. Sometimes this relief took some time coming because of other differences, such as class, which were felt alienating. This was notably true for working-class men. No doubt there would also have been a strongly inhibiting influence for black men. The subsequent experience of being in men's groups involved coming across new ideas and feelings, mutual support in rejecting macho attitudes; and a different and preferred awareness of self. Groups fluctuated in membership and levels of activity, and diverged over whether to emphasise outward-looking anti-sexist activity or personal development. Some men got involved in the wider men's movement, subscribing to anti-sexist magazines and attending national or regional conferences.

Half the sample had negative or mixed attitudes to the breadwinner role. Several were housepersons and active fathers, not currently in paid employment, but for some men, continuing commitment to bread-winning was compatible with thorough pursuit of a non-sexist lifestyle. The younger men hoped to share mixed breadwinner/homemaker roles with their women partners.

Most men interviewed said they took an active part in housework, in most cases as a matter of principle and established habit. Previous surveys on household divisions of labour provoke reservations about this but it should be remembered that those surveys were based on samples which included a substantial majority of conventional sexist men, while these men were deliberately chosen as anti-sexist in outlook.

Most of the men did not regard masculinity as important to them but one very aware interviewee felt masculinity dominated his whole existence and he organised his life around a constant effort to counter its influence. Half the sample favoured reformed egalitarian marriage as the ideal relationship with a woman. The other half favoured equal partnerships without marriage. Fatherhood was an important commitment for all the men with children, whether living with partners or not.

It is notable that many of the interviewees were aware of sensitive and vulnerable feelings, believed it was good to be in touch with these, and that this helped them have better relationships with women and children as well as with other men.

These findings strictly speaking relate only to the thirty men studied, but if we assume they give clues about the lives of other anti-sexist men then they provide encouragement for feminists who are not radically anti-men, and women in general who want intimate relationships with men on equal terms. Evidence from these interviews suggests that feminist ideas have had a marked effect on at least some men, and that individual feminists can have a personal political influence in relationships with individual men.

At the same time the findings also suggest that fertile ground is needed for feminist influence. Boys need to have early life experiences which prepare them to relate to women on more equal terms. It would be naive to think that traditional men will respond in this way. Some important early experiences are suggested by this study but much more research is needed on early experiences that might encourage this kind of responsiveness.

IMPLICATIONS OF THE RESEARCH FOR SOME EXISTING THEORETICAL WORK

Much existing discussion of masculinity is based on limited empirical evidence, often personal and anecdotal to the writer and not derived from detailed empirical studies of men's experiences and feelings. A phase of theoretical discussion is useful since facts never speak for themselves but can only answer questions asked of them, but I believe the stage has been reached when the most urgent need is for fieldwork research, theoretically informed and related, but strongly empirical. For this reason my main aim has been to make available theoretically relevent empirical data and it has not been my purpose to engage in elaborate theorising. Nevertheless it is appropriate here to discuss aspects of my findings which bear on recent theoretical writings.

We must start with the humble assumption that we do not yet know much about the range of male identities, influenced in a variety of ways by gendering experiences, or about the distinctive ways that men, as gendered beings, live their lives. As Brod argues,

> What is familiar is often not really known, precisely because it is so seemingly familiar . . . men's public lives . . . represent a retreat from their personal lives. . . . Public events and achievements, not personal feelings and experiences are what count . . . denying the subjectivity of the experience . . . [is] crucial to the pretensions to objectivity of the male construction of experience.
>
> (Brod 1987: 2–3)

We, of course, know plenty about men as workers, managers, soldiers, leaders, artists, scientists, etc., but our knowledge of men *as men* is still scanty. Feminist scholarship has contributed most of what we do know, but the main contribution has been to knowledge of macho or male chauvinist men; gay scholarship over the same period has increased our knowledge of gay men. There is almost nothing about the range of non-macho non-gay men who, like myself, feel they do not fit existing generalisations.

As Brod says, 'overgeneralisation from male to generic human experience . . . precludes the study of . . . specific male experience'(Brod 1987: 2). He adds, 'While women have been obscured from our vision by being too much in the background, men have been obscured by being too much in the foreground' (ibid: 40–1). In other words, men's public selves have been visible while their private selves have been almost invisible.

An area of agreement has emerged among North American, British and Australian writers in recent years that we no longer talk about masculinity but about 'masculinities'. Titles of recent publications, or sections in them, reflect this. For instance among American books, Part I of Kimmel and Messner (1992) is called 'Perspectives on Masculinities' and in Brod's book, *The Making of Masculinities*, he states, 'The most general definition of men's studies is that it is the study of masculinities and male experience as specific and varying social-historical-cultural formations. Such studies situate masculinities as objects of study on a par with femininities' (Brod 1987: 2).

Among British books, one collection (Hearn and Morgan 1990) is entitled *Men, Masculinities and Social Theory*; Lynne Segal's *Slow Motion* (1990) is subtitled *Changing Masculinities, Changing Men*; the historical collection by Roper and Tosh (1991) is subtitled *Masculinities in Britain since 1800*; and Arthur Brittan writes, 'My position is that we cannot talk of masculinity, only masculinities'(1989: 1). From Australia, Russell (1983), provided empirical support for the point, and Connell also wrote 'Multiple femininities and masculinities are . . . a central fact about gender and the way its structures are lived' (Connell 1987: 63–4).

This book contributes to our knowledge of this multiplicity by providing qualitative evidence on the social construction of types of male identity which are neither hegemonic nor usually gay, but my own concern is to study specific male experiences, not necessarily 'masculinities'. After all, feminist studies of women's lives are not conceptualised in terms of 'femininities'. There is a concern to avoid the restrictions of femininity, singular and plural.

I accept the theoretical value of exploring varieties of masculinities and femininities to discover how power operates in the gender field. As Brod says, 'men's studies must take care not to ignore or obscure the questions of power raised by feminism' (Brod 1987: 8) but in general I am doubtful of the practical value of these terms. As I see it, the ultimate goal is not merely to study forms of masculinity and femininity but rather to understand the possibilities for a commonly shared humanity not defined in terms of gender. As Gayle Rubin says 'Far from being an expression of natural differences, exclusive gender identity is the suppression of natural similarities' (Rubin 1975: 179–80). The same can be said of less exclusive gender identities.

My view about much recent writing on masculinity is that often I cannot relate it to my own views or experience. An example was my reaction to the book *The Sexuality of Men* (Metcalf and Humphries 1985). The chapters by heterosexual men were as alien to me as those by gay men. There was much discussion of domination and control rather than shared physical enjoyment and it made me wonder how many other men feel as I do, that sexuality and domination are not inherently connected. In the context of hegemonic masculinity male sexuality seems to be socially constructed in terms of domination, but for me sex is about shared pleasure not about dominating. Am I peculiar as a man in feeling that way? Or are there other unresearched non-predatory heterosexual men who feel as I do?

This is an example of where general statements about heterosexual men based on limited empirical evidence of the variations among them may be misleading. Theory in this field requires a clear conceptualisation of the fact that it is not only feminists and gay-liberation activitists who oppose hegemonic masculinity and that this is not the only type of heterosexual identity. The non-macho non-gay identity needs to be distinguished.

American gay writer Gregory Herek has noted, 'Men cannot change without clear alternative ways of living. Formulating such alternatives must constitute an agenda for all who hope to improve our society' (Herek 1987: 80). I agree with Brod's view that 'gay studies serves as a model to correct the unfortunate tendency in men's studies to assume too much commonality among men'(Brod 1987: 61).

But gay studies also, may wrongly assume too great a commonality among heterosexual men. Herek's term 'heterosexual masculinity' to describe the dominant identity implies that all heterosexual men conform to it and so it is a more limited analytical term than Connell's 'hegemonic masculinity'. It overlooks the non-gay non-macho anti-sexist men who were the main focus of my research.

I have drawn much inspiration from Australian sociologist Robert Connell and I fully acknowledge my debt to him. My research strongly supports his point that, 'There are costs for men in their social advantages, sometimes serious ones . . . some groups of men . . . can recognise injustice when they see it and are far from comfortable with the position they have inherited' (Connell 1987: xi).

My life histories provide qualitative information on how some British anti-sexist men experienced and perceived the key dimensions outlined by Connell: the division of labour; the structure of power; and the structure of emotional attachments (ibid: 91–116). My findings support his views on factors which might detach heterosexual men from defending patriarchy:

> (1) . . . beneficiaries of an oppressive system can come to see its oppressiveness, especially the way it poisons areas of life they share;
> (2) . . . men are often committed in important ways to women . . . and may desire better lives for them . . .
> (3) . . . men are not all the same or all united, and many do suffer some injury from the present system;
> (4) Change in gender relations is happening anyway. . . . A good many heterosexual men recognise that they cannot cling to the past and want some new directions; and
> (5) . . . men are not excluded from the basic human capacity to share experiences, feelings and hopes.
>
> (ibid: xiii)

But it is not enough for some men to become aware of the masculine role's limitations. A link has to be made between that and a decision to become politically active in support of feminism. The most significant link illustrated by the experience of most men in my study is the importance of direct personal political influence by individual feminist women.

Another link is that hegemonic masculinity, manifested in patriarchy, can be detrimental to males and this can form the basis of solidarity with others oppressed by it. The etymological meaning of patriarchy is 'rule by fathers' implying that older men dominate younger men as well as men dominate women. Some of my male interviewees had suffered from patriarchy in the generational sense and linked this oppression to women's oppression. I argue that this two-dimensional view of patriarchy is an asset rather than a liability – precisely because it may enable alliances to be made between feminists, gays and anti-sexist men against what can be perceived as a common enemy.

This means rejecting one feminist view which seeks to restrict the term 'patriarchy' solely to gender relations and to exclude the generational aspect. The determination of some feminist writers (e.g. Walby 1990) to remove that dimension from the term seems misplaced when 'male domination' is a perfectly adequate term to describe the system which oppresses women. It is essential in my view to recognise that patriarchy is in fact two-sided. If we are to understand men's anti-sexism as well as feminism it is necessary to retain the generational as well as the gender aspect.

A widespread assumption about the social/psychological acquisition of masculinity is that it requires identification of boys with their fathers. As Brittan says 'it is taken for granted that male children do need to identify with the parent of the same sex, and that if they fail to do so, they will have both gender and personality problems'(Brittan 1989: 33). Eardley writes

> In Freud's account of a boy's sexual development emotional rejection of the mother is an essential stage in the proper resolution of the Oedipal Conflict through which heterosexuality is developed . . . failure to reject may result in fixation at a stage of homosexual inclination.
>
> (Metcalf and Humphries 1985: 103)

And American writer Joseph Pleck says of Freudian 'sex role' theorists, 'To these theorists, the idea that the male child might identify with the mother, leading to cross-sex identification, would have seemed quite novel' (Pleck 1987: 30).

It is my contention that if identification with traditional fathers is the social norm there is no reason to regard this as either necessary or desirable. It is the norm only because male domination is the norm. Some such identification is one of the main mechanisms by which hegemonic masculinity and male chauvinism are reproduced over generations and therefore helps maintain male domination and patriarchy. This study has shown that it is sociologically possible to avoid this process, and this could enable the development of a different norm more conducive to sex equality. I agree fully with Eardley when he continues,

> rejection of the mother by the son under the social pressures which draw him towards the external world of the father . . . has . . . been given too little consideration. We do not have to see this process as universal or transhistorical. . . . It is the consequence of socially defined gender expectations and it is in turn the structure through

> which expectations are reproduced. The rejection of the mother and the relationship of nurturance which binds mother and son together is in itself a violent and dehumanising process because it involves an internal rejection and suppression of the son's own potential qualities of nurturing, in favour of the coercive . . . attributes held out to him as his reward. . . . Part of this process is the devaluing of the gender to whom those rejected qualities are assigned.
>
> (Eardley 1985: 103–4)

If, as Freudians believe, identification with the father shapes the 'normal' boy's character structure then it is clear this is a major process by which male domination is preserved. Until most fathers are non-macho nurturing fathers this 'normal' process will continue to reproduce the 'norm' of male violence and misogyny. Even non-traditional fathers today struggle against an invasive cultural background of male chauvinism from boys' peer groups and mass media, not to mention patriarchal institutions. Childrearing does not take place in a social vacuum. Sons of nurturing fathers, or boys who do not identify with traditional fathers, may still pick up conventional sexist attitudes from other sources. In fact there can be over-compensation.

An alternative model of identification which has received much attention in recent years is that of Nancy Chodorow who, as Lynne Segal says, 'pointed to the overriding significance of exclusive mothering by women in the creation of male dominance and polarised "masculine" and "feminine" identities. . . . Paternal absence from childcare means that masculinity is always defined negatively as that which is not feminine' (Segal 1990: 47). 'A boy represses those qualities he takes to be feminine inside himself and rejects and devalues women and whatever he considers feminine in the social world' (Chodorow 1978: 181). A problem with this view is that, as Brittan says, 'it is also taken for granted that women are somehow to blame for their own oppression' (Brittan 1989: 33), and it 'gives men an opportunity to deny their responsibility for oppression' (ibid: 195).

Chodorow's approach, which is similar that of Dorothy Dinnerstein (1987), convinces me more than the traditional Freudian view but I agree with Segal when she comments, 'Despite the insights of this approach into men's fears of intimacy . . . it cannot . . . carry the weight of explaining male domination' (Segal 1990: 81). As she says, 'Chodorow's explanation of gender differences relies upon . . . a mother's . . . performing her maternal functions according to the conventional script.' Real families often do not correspond to this, 'without . . .

threatening patriarchy or, as yet, undermining conventional patterns of masculinity and femininity'. She rightly argues that 'for mothering to create in Chodorow's words "the psychology and ideology of male dominance" we need to presuppose a society where femininity is already devalued and masculinity already more highly valued' (ibid: 82).

Clearly for male domination to end there need to be far-reaching changes in social structure, not merely changes in childrearing practices, but these must still be part of the process. If, as I assert, gender is socially constructed these identification processes not only *can* change but *must* be changed if male domination is to end. My study suggests that men who do not identify with traditional fathers or who do identify with non-traditional fathers are more likely to have sympathetic attitudes towards women and to feminist ideals. A major reason why father identification continues to be seen as necessary is the assumption that without it a boy will grow up homosexual. Whatever one's views about this attitude, my research demonstrates that lack of father identification does not necessarily produce this result. I myself am a case in point.

IMPLICATIONS FOR SEXUAL POLITICS

Feminist scholars have been understandably wary of the emergence of 'men's studies', if only because the field of gender has to some extent made possible 'jobs for the girls'. Men interested in gender are, not unreasonably, suspected of wanting to muscle-in on scarce teaching posts and research funds. I was conscious of this throughout this research and for this reason, despite being urged to do so by a female head of department, I refrained from applying for research funding which might have gone to women researchers.

Contrary to what some feminists have argued, it is not true that all men hate women. Some dislike or fear their own sex (this is the literal meaning of the word 'homophobia': the prejudice against gay men usually referred to as homophobia is more accurately called heterosexism).

In future, boys growing up may be more likely to come into contact with at least some men like my interviewees who consciously and sometimes openly reject traditional male-chauvinist assumptions. Though few in number, such men can provide valuable alternative role models for future generations of boys if they become more open and confident of their views and lifestyles. They can demonstrate that men can free themselves from feeling constantly obliged to act out the masculine stereotype and instead can relax into expressing all human feelings and enjoying the full range of human characteristics. They can show that gayness is not the only alternative to being macho. In any case some gay men are very macho.

Also anti-sexist men can contribute by making it more widely known among men in general that sex equality can mean important gains as well as losses for men, and that the gains will be principally in the form of beneficial effects on the quality of their relationships with women, with children and with other men, an effect which can flow from an improved ability to express sensitive and vulnerable feelings.

This realisation stems from the personal-growth element in men's group experience which has led many men into various therapeutic activities – co-counselling, assertiveness training, meditation, massage, bioenergetics, and so on. These have been invaluable in helping them get in touch with their more sensitive feelings and opening themselves up, but all too often this has led to a narcissistic concern with 'men's liberation' while forgetting men's responsibility in the struggle against other forms of gender oppression. The personal-growth oriented stream is necessary and valuable but should never be allowed to divert attention from practical activities supportive of women, opposing other oppressions or making the existence of men's anti-sexism more widely known.

Robert Bly's men's movement seems to me to be a dangerous example of the inward-looking tendency. It has already become a new therapeutic cult recruiting from the ranks of anti-sexist men. Bly has no sociological understanding of gender and how it varies. He makes the spurious assumption that there is an eternal innate 'masculinity' which modern men have lost touch with and which is expressed in ancient myths. He reveals his biological reductionism when he states, 'Geneticists have discovered . . . the genetic difference in DNA between men and women amounts to just over 3 per cent', and in the next paragraph, 'it is important to emphasise the 3 per cent that makes a person masculine' (Bly 1990: 234).

It needs stating emphatically that this genetic difference does *not* make a man *masculine*, it makes him *male*. Bly's failure to understand the crucial distinction between gender and sex is the fatal flaw in his argument. He claims that young men need an older male 'mentor' to help them contact the 'Wild Man' (innate masculinity?) he imagines is deep inside them. He laments the decline of fathers' influence today so that boys are not introduced to the male world by the men most suitable to do so. (But it is precisely this male world which oppresses women!)

He thinks young men must break from their mothers. (To ensure they will reject half their human heritage and absorb patriarchal misinformation?) He ignores the fundamental feminist point that relations between the sexes are power relations (men oppress women). He makes no call for his followers to ally themselves with women in the fight against male domination.

Men do not need a new exclusively male organisation, rather we need a mixed-sex anti-sexist movement, but since there are good reasons for women to organise independently it must be men's groups that open their meetings to women without expecting a reciprocal response from women's groups. Men's anti-sexism has a long way to go before feminists trust its members as allies. Bly's movement will not inspire trust, more likely a justifiable suspicion of patriarchy raising its ugly head in yet another guise. At best his movement might help broaden the range of emotions expressed by some men trapped in conventional masculinity but to my mind this is done much better within co-counselling. Bly misinterprets man's situation and could distract anti-sexist men's energies from the struggle against gender oppression.

The men's movement has a great problem over its credibility not only in the eyes of the mass media and most other men but also of women, and particularly feminists. Men's anti-sexism involves a contradicton in that it is a political movement for giving up power – or at least 50 per cent of it. The movement is small and unlikely to impress feminists as a useful ally. There is a great deal of entirely understandable feminist scepticism, even complete dismissal of any possibility that men can change or that they can ever be trusted as allies.

As Connell wrote, 'There are currents in feminist thought which do not welcome men's involvement, and there is a fine line to tread between intruding on women's business and sharing the work on common problems' (1987: xii). He also comments relevantly,

> Many, perhaps most . . . campaigns waged by feminists and gay activists have involved acting in alliance with people outside their ranks. . . . Movement rhetoric usually ignores this, stressing opposition from the rest of the world and attributing all gains to women's or gays' own determination and strength. The political reasons for talking this way are obvious enough: but the habit . . . often creates the impression that alliance or support is not wanted.
>
> (ibid: 283)

Perhaps Carrigan, Connell and Lee were being too optimistic when they wrote, 'There are potentials for a more liberating politics . . . in the form of coalitions among feminists, gay men and progressive heterosexual men that have real chances of making gains on specific issues' (Carrigan, Connell and Lee 1987: 100).

Nevertheless there have been some among the ranks of feminists who have been prepared to take men's anti-sexism seriously. For instance, bell hooks, a black American feminist, writes,

> Men who actively struggle against sexism have a place in feminist movement. They are our comrades. . . . Those women's liberationists who see no value in this participation must rethink and reexamine the process by which revolutionary struggle is advanced. Individual men tend to become involved in feminist movement because of the pain generated in relationships with women. Until men share equal responsibility for struggling to end sexism, feminist movement will reflect the very sexist contradictions we wish to eradicate. . . . In particular, men have a tremendous contribution to make . . . in the area of exposing, confronting, opposing and transforming the sexism of their male peers.
>
> (hooks 1992: 570–1)

Also Betty Friedan writes,

> Women can't solve the problem alone by taking everything on themselves, by trying to be 'superwomen'. And women don't have the power to change the structure of the workplace by themselves. But while more and more men decide that they want some self-fulfilment beyond their jobs and some of the life-grounding that women always have had in the family – as much as women now need and want some voice and active power in the world – there will be a new combined force for carrying out the second stage of liberation for us all. . . . The dialogue has gone on too long in terms of women alone. Let men join women in the center of the second stage.
>
> (Friedan 1988: 579)

Similarly the Australian feminist Lynne Segal, speaking of anti-sexist men, has written, 'Their efforts have often received faint praise from feminists sceptical of the potential for individual men to overturn a gender identity so bound up with the customary assertion of power and privilege' (Segal 1990: 280), and, commenting on the actions of such men, 'These were all activities which, in my view, were often important in providing personal support for individual women. They were also important in sustaining a wider radical milieu which helped women's liberation to flourish throughout the 1970s' (ibid: 285). She continued,

> many women who helped build women's liberation in its earliest days were mothers, seeking escape from the loneliness and

> uncertainties, the feelings of guilt and inadequacy accompanying isolated mothering. Often they were able to put their energies into women's liberation . . . only because the men in their lives accepted new responsibilities of sharing childcare, helping to run playgroups and community nurseries, and supporting them more generally.
>
> (ibid: 285)

And again,

> What the pro-feminist men's movement literature and practice make clear is that, once aware of it, at least some men are very unhappy with the idea that they are caught up in a system which is exploitative of and oppressive of women and gays, and certain other men. They do want change. . . . It is important most of all, simply in the evidence it provides that men *can* change.
>
> (ibid: 290)

Nevertheless, members of anti-sexist men's groups must face the fact that they cannot realistically expect to be accepted collectively as allies of the women's movement for years to come. They must prove their sincerity over at least a further generation before that begins to be possible. Anti-sexist men, whether in men's groups or not, must steel themselves for the long haul. To influence other men by their principles and gain the respect of feminists they must persist doggedly in being allies even though not accepted as such. Instead they must expect to be subjected to ridicule not only by conventional men but also by women. They must nevertheless go on refusing to be women's enemies regardless of how much distrust they encounter. The long term is the only realistic view.

The movement's future is problematic if only because men who become less macho tend to become more domesticated and so less able to be involved with influencing others *en masse*. There is therefore a problem of continuity in the men's movement. Being in a men's group tends to be a phase in the lives of anti-sexist men, important but temporary. Having gained encouragement and validation for being a different kind of man they tend to move on to other activities rather than further men's groups – domestic roles, work situations or mixed-sex liberatory activities where anti-sexist principles are put into practice. It may be that the men who stay long in the men's movement are power seekers who have missed the real point of men's anti-sexism – to give up power-seeking and learn to share.

To avoid their domination and being taken over by therapists, the men's movement needs a constant supply of new blood, learning by practical anti-sexist activity before moving on to other fields and handing over to a new influx of activists. Coherence over time will be difficult unless clear principles and long-term strategy are established and handed on.

Whatever the outcome for anti-sexist men's groups, the prospect for individual anti-sexist men is more promising. Feminists collectively may not trust anti-sexist men collectively but there is a much better chance of individual women being prepared to trust and accept individual anti-sexist men as genuine and sincere friends and allies. But there are no grounds for complacency. Alertness to unaware or unintended sexism must be always present. If men learn not to dominate in intimate situations, they are much more likely to avoid it in other areas of life.

Most of my interviewees have now, like myself, moved on to practising anti-sexist ideals in other fields and are no longer active in men's groups. This record of their experiences and their views on life may at least help men now active in men's groups to avoid some of our mistakes and be forewarned of some of the disappointments they may meet.

Appendix

In British schools now, girls outperform boys on average at all levels. Further and higher education and many types of professional training are seeing increasing participation and success by women, not confined to traditional female subjects. More young women are entering full time higher education, nearly 48 per cent of the total by 1989–90, with similar trends among part-time students. In further education non-advanced courses women were a clear majority by 1989.

By 1989 women were nearly 46 per cent of candidates gaining first degrees and they more than tripled their 1970 share of higher degrees to 40.5 per cent. Women have moved increasingly into vocationally related studies as well as continuing a strong presence in traditional female subjects. In examinations for some professional qualifications women have achieved spectacular increases in recent years and in some cases now form a majority of successful candidates, for example among solicitors, veterinary surgeons, chartered secretaries and administrators, and journalists.

In paid employment, both full time and part time, women were nearly half the UK labour force by 1990 and in the service industries nearly 6 out of 10 employees were women. Even leaving out part-time workers, most of whom are women, by 1990 women formed more than 35 per cent of full-time employees compared with 30 per cent in 1975; and over 45 per cent in the expanding service sector. Women of all age groups over 16 showed increasing economic activity while men's decreased. By 1990 almost three-quarters of women between the ages of 20 and 54 were in some form of paid employment. Between 1971 and 1990 a million more women also became union members and by 1990 almost 4 out of 10 unionists were women.

In the professions too, women have advanced. Among hospital doctors and dentists in Britain the proportions of women substantially increased between 1970 and 1990. In the junior ranks they almost reached parity with men and they made clear advances among seniors. In general practice roughly a quarter of doctors and dentists were women by 1990 and among those aged under 30 they were close to parity. Doctors and dentists of all age groups had substantially increased proportions of women. Their share of qualified optometrists more than quadrupled between 1970 and 1990.

There were similar trends among lawyers. By 1990–1 women were almost a quarter of solicitors holding practising certificates, a substantial increase over 1980, and women formed almost a fifth of barristers, nearly double their share in 1980–1. In universities, women formed 20 per cent of academic staff by 1989–90, double their share in 1970, and in other higher- and further-education institutions women's percentage of lecturers had risen to 30 per cent by that year. In the higher civil service, managerial occupations, other higher-status occupations and among the self-employed, women also achieved impressive increases between 1970 and 1990.

Women in Britain are therefore carving out a sharply different and more active space for themselves. In education and paid work they have shown they no longer accept the home-oriented restrictions of the old feminine role. Consequently they are less obliged to enter marriage through lack of alternatives, to stay in unsatisfactory marriages, or risk remarrying. This could be one major reason why in all age groups, especially the younger ones, marriage has become a less common civil status. Larger proportions stay single or become and remain divorced. A significant aspect, compared with earlier times, may be a shift in women's attitudes towards marriage and, more generally, in what they expect of men.

Nearly three-quarters of British divorces are now initiated by wives and the reason most cited by women is 'unreasonable behaviour' by their husbands. The evidence also indicates that it is women far more than men who do not remarry and this trend has risen dramatically since 1971. In addition the proportion of married women separated from their husbands is always greater than those divorced. A trend of increasing separations in each marriage cohort has appeared since 1960.

As a corollary there has been the increasing practice of cohabitation. It seems likely that a significant proportion of cohabiting is influenced by women not wishing to submit themselves to a status which is increasingly recognised, especially by younger women, as onerous and oppressive for women. Women are also taking more control of their sexual and reproductive behaviour. The availability of effective female controllable contraception, legal abortion, increased acceptability of unmarried motherhood and artificial insemination, have all contributed to this. There is also evidence that non-married women of all age groups and civil statuses have become more sexually active.

Finally, women's personal mobility has been improved by their ability to drive. In 1972–3 only 20 per cent of British women had full licences; by 1988–90 almost half had them, and 60 per cent of women aged 20 to 29 had them.

Bibliography

Bertaux, D. (1981) 'From the Life-History Approach to the Transformation of Sociological Practice' in D. Bertaux (ed.) *Biography and Society, The Life History Approach in the Social Sciences*, Beverley Hills: ISA/Sage, 29–46.
Brittan, A. (1989) *Masculinity and Power*, Oxford: Blackwell.
Brittan, A. and Maynard, M. (1984) *Sexism, Racism and Oppression*, Oxford: Blackwell.
Brod, H. (ed.) (1987) *The Making of Masculinities*, Winchester, MA: Allen & Unwin.
Bly, R. (1991) *Iron John*, Rockport, MA: Element Publishers.
Carrigan, T., Connell, R.W. and Lee, J. (1987) 'Toward a New Sociology of Masculinity', in Brod 1987, 63–100.
Chapman, R. (1988) 'The Great Pretender: Variations on the New Man Theme', in Chapman and Rutherford 1988, 225–48.
Chapman, R. and Rutherford, J. (eds) (1988) *Male Order*, London: Lawrence and Wishart.
Chodorow, N. (1978) *The Reproduction of Mothering, Psychoanalysis and the Sociology of Gender*, Berkeley and Los Angeles. University of California Press. See Segal 1990, 47.
Christian, H. (1988) 'Convention and Constraint Among Semi-Professional Jazz Musicians' in A.L. White (ed.) *Lost In Music*, Sociological Review Monograph 34, London: Routledge, 220–40.
Connell, R.W. (1987) *Gender and Power*, Cambridge: Polity Press.
Denzin, N. (1988) *Interpretive Biography*, Newbury Park: Sage.
Department of Employment, UK (1990) *Employment Gazette*, London: HMSO.
Dinnerstein, D. (1987) *The Rocking of the Cradle and the Ruling of the World*, London: Women's Press.
Eardley, T. (1985) 'Violence and Sexuality', in Metcalf and Humphries 1985, 86–109.
Ford, A. (1985) *Men*, London: Weidenfeld & Nicholson.
Friedan, B. (1988) 'Their Turn: How Men Are Changing', in Kimmel and Messner 1992, 572–9.
Gerson, K. (1987) 'What Do Women Want From Men? Men's Influence on Women's Work and Family Choices' in Kimmel 1987, 115–30.
Glaser, B.G. and Strauss, A. (1967) *The Discovery of Grounded Theory*, Chicago: Aldine.

Gramsci, A. (1981) *The Prison Notebooks*, London: Lawrence and Wishart.

Gross, A.E., Smith, R. and Wallston, B.S. (1983) 'The Men's Movement: Personal Versus Political', in J. Freeman (ed.) *Social Movements of the Sixties and Seventies*, New York: Longman, 75–6. See Shiffman 1987, 299.

Hearn, J. (1987) *The Gender of Oppression*, Brighton: Wheatsheaf.

—— (1992) *Men In The Public Eye*, London: Routledge.

Hearn, J. and Morgan, D. (eds) (1990) *Men, Masculinities and Social Theory*, London: Unwin Hyman.

Herek, G. (1987) 'On Heterosexual Masculinity: Some Psychical Consequences of the Social Construction of Gender and Sexuality', in Kimmel 1987, 68–82.

hooks, b. (1992) 'Men: Comrades in Struggle', reprinted from hooks, *Feminist Theory: From Margin to Center*, Boston, MA: South End Press, in Kimmel and Messner 1992, 561–71.

Jackson, D. (1990) *Unmasking Masculinity*, London: Unwin Hyman.

Kaufman, M. (ed.) (1987) *Beyond Patriarchy*, Toronto: Oxford University Press.

Kimmel, M.S. (ed.) (1987) *Changing Men*, Beverley Hills: Sage.

—— (1991) *Against the Tide, Pro-Feminist Men in America 1776–1990*, New York: Beacon.

Kimmel, M.S. and Messner, M.A. (eds) (1992) *Men's Lives*, New York: Macmillan.

Metcalf, A. and Humphries, M. (eds) (1985) *The Sexuality of Men*. London: Pluto.

Morgan, D. (1992) *Discovering Men*, London: Routledge.

Morris, L. (1990) *The Workings of the Household*, Cambridge: Polity Press.

Oakley, A. (1981) 'Interviewing Women: A Contradiction in Terms', in Roberts 1981, 41–58.

Office of Public Censuses and Surveys, UK (1992) *Social Trends*, No. 22, London: HMSO.

Pleck, J. (1981) *The Myth of Masculinity*, Cambridge, MA: MIT Press.

—— (1987) 'The Theory of Male Sex-role Identity: Its Rise and Fall, 1936 to the Present', in Brod 1987, 21–38.

Plummer, K. (1983) *Documents of Life*, London: Unwin Hyman.

Porter, K. and Weeks, J. (ed.) (1991) *Between the Acts*, London: Routledge.

Roberts, H. (ed.) (1981) *Doing Feminist Research*, London: Routledge.

Roper, M. and Tosh, J. (eds) (1991) *Manful Assertions*, London: Routledge.

Rose, G. (1982) *Deciphering Sociological Research*, London: Macmillan.

Rubin, G. (1975) 'The Traffic in Women', in R. Reiter (ed.) *Toward an Anthropology of Women*, New York: Monthly Review Press, 179–80.

Russell, G. (1983) *The Changing Role of Fathers*, London: University of Queensland Press.

Rutherford, J. (1992) *Men's Silences*, London: Routledge.

Segal, L. (1990) *Slow Motion, Changing Masculinities, Changing Men*, London: Virago.

Seidler, V.J. (1989) *Rediscovering Masculinity*, London: Routledge.

—— (1991) *Recreating Sexual Politics*, London: Routledge.

—— (ed.) (1991) *Achilles Heel Reader*, London: Routledge.

Shiffman, M. (1987) 'The Men's Movement, An Exploratory Empirical Investigation', in Kimmel 1987: 295–314.

Snodgrass, J. (1975) 'The Women's Liberation Movement and the Men', paper presented at the annual meeting of the Pacific Sociological Society, Victoria, BC; reproduced in Shiffman 1987.

Stanley, L. (1990) *Feminist Praxis*, London: Routledge.

Stanley, L. and Morgan, D. (eds) (1993) Editorial Introduction to *Sociology, Special Issue: Auto/Biography in Sociology*, Durham: BSA Publications Ltd, vol. 27, no. 1, 1–4.

Tolson, A. (1977) *The Limits of Masculinity*, London: Tavistock.

Walby, S. (1990) *Theorizing Patriarchy*, Oxford: Blackwell.

Wheelock, J. (1990) *Husbands At Home*, London: Routledge.

Index